My Father's Secrets

A MEMOIR

Marilyn Johansen

HELLGATE PRESS  ASHLAND, OREGON

MY FATHER'S SECRETS

Copyright 2024 Marilyn Johansen. All rights reserved. No part of this publication may be reproduced or used in any form or by any means, graphic, electronic or mechanical, including photocopying, recording, taping, or information and retrieval systems without written permission of the publisher.

Hellgate Press
Ashland, OR 97520
For information: *sales@hellgatepress.com*

ISBN: 978-1-954163-98-0

Cover and interior design: L. Redding

Printed and bound in the United States of America
First edition 10 9 8 7 6 5 4 3 2 1

*For my father
and
all the children in military families
who grew up in this life of
service to their country*

Contents

Introduction	*vii*
Prelude	*ix*
Chapter 1: The World Before I Was Here	1
Chapter 2: My Arrival and the Korean War	41
Chapter 3: Belgian Embassy: March 1955-November 1957	71
Chapter 4: Our New Assignment: Laredo AFB, Texas December 1957 – May 1959	123
Chapter 5: The Sierra Nevada Mountains and Stead, AFB June 1959 – April 1961	133
Chapter 6: Tactical Missile Training: June 1961 – March 1962	155
Chapter 7: Life on Okinawa: 1962 – 1965	171
Chapter 8: Next Assignment: MacDill AFB, Florida	205
Chapter 9: My Father's Retirement: May 31, 1966	215
Chapter 10: I Graduate College	233
Chapter 11: The Day My Life Changed	241
Chapter 12: Wedding Bells	249
Chapter 13: My Father Passes Away	263
Chapter 14: Stalag Luft III Reunions	267
Chapter 15: Appreciation of the U.S Military	273
Chapter 16: My Mother Passes Away and I Reflect on My Life	287
Epilogue	*293*
Acknowledgments	*297*
Resources	*298*

MY FATHER'S SECRETS

Introduction

WORLD EVENTS TURNED Eugene Francis Phillips into a soldier. Three wars turned him into an eternal battler of circumstances and an aviator of extraordinary abilities. The total events of his life were beyond what three people would expect in their time on this Earth. He was challenged repeatedly. His survival bordered on divine intervention and exceptional skills. His name would never be etched into the memorials of three separate wars, but he would contribute as a fierce participant in each one. His reward was not recognition, awards, or medals. His reward was the reinforcement of his love of country, belief in law and order, and his deep faith.

Who else lives these events? Definitively, the members of a soldier's family. As his daughter, I found life in a military family has its lessons and perspectives. While I was witness to many great, historical events of our time, I also experienced the absence of what many consider family normality. Three schools in one year, the first day of school in a foreign land, unable to speak a word of French, and the inability to make lasting friendships all came with the territory!

Every life is a story. We come to this Earth and the things we see, endure, and overcome, define us. Our decisions and experiences make us. I share my story so you may see what I saw around me.

My story is steeped in history. I love history, not because I studied it but because my life is wrapped in it. Everyone I knew and every place I would live is defined by our military assignment. Each of those assignments was meaningful to world events. The people I knew and loved were faced with immeasurable choices during their lives. My story is also steeped in a world view of modern military defense.

MY FATHER'S SECRETS

I am a second generation American. My parents are the children of European immigrants. These relatives left their homeland and came to the U.S. because of changing conditions in the places they grew up. These changing conditions were influenced by wars and governments.

Wars and changing governments continue in our world. There are many perspectives on wars and why they exist. Having grown up inside of the military culture, I am sharing my perspective.

Prelude

IT WAS EARLY MORNING AT the end of August, when a young Eugene Francis Phillips stepped out of a taxicab at the end of the driveway of the farm where he had been raised in Plymouth, Ohio. He was handsome and well-built with dark brown wavy hair. He wore his summer Army uniform and was carrying a packed military-issued duffle bag. His youngest brothers Clyde and Henry were walking toward the barn to milk the cows when they spotted him. They looked at each other with excitement. They ran back to the house to prepare their family, especially their mother, for the wonderful news that Gene, as he was called, was home.

The farmhouse had a blue two-star flag in the window, one for Second Lt. Gene and one for Private First Class Jim. Gene had left for war in January of 1942, already well-trained thanks to a civilian pilot training school. He was a different man than the one who left. He was returning from the European theater of World War Two (WWII). His younger brother Jim, an infantryman, followed Gene into the Army a year later.

As he entered the farmhouse his mother was in tears seeing her oldest child physically whole and looking good. It was also the first time she had seen him in uniform. When he left for war, things were rushed, and he was not allowed to take a leave to return home before his deployment. During the time he was away, she had received several telegrams from the U.S. War Department. The first said that he was missing in action; the second, several months later, said that he was identified as a prisoner-of-war in Germany; and the third that he was on his way home.

MY FATHER'S SECRETS

The family hugged and greeted him with a warm welcome. Not everyone was there at that time. His brother Jim was still in Europe under the command of General George S. Patton. Jim was with recovery teams in Europe. His mother, Elizabeth, sister Irene, Clyde, and Henry were there though, full of questions, and were all ears for the stories Gene had to tell. During the war, his brother Thom married his girlfriend, Eleanor. They were living with her family. The good news was shared with them and they came over for dinner that night. His father, Ed, was out at the time but came home a bit later to welcome Gene back from the war. Gene was happy to see his father living back at home again. The house was smiling and the blue stars in the window would certainly shine brightly on this wonderful day for this family.

Gene would tell them about all he thought they could understand about what he had been through during the almost four years he'd been away. He told them about military training in California, Arizona, Oregon, and Washington state. He spent time that day walking around the farm he had worked so hard on all his young life. He reflected on his life; he had come full circle. He was now back to where he had started. He was only twenty-four years old but had endured and seen more than most.

He shared some of the stories of his missions flying out of North Africa, of being shot down and becoming a prisoner-of-war (POW). He told them about the massive escape from the POW camp in March of 1944, and the death march in January earlier that year. Gene spoke of the men who had died during the march and the frostbite many suffered from marching in weather too cold. The horrible living conditions and starvation in Moosburg were part of his conversations. He told them about liberation from the POW camp in Moosburg, Germany and how General Patton had come through the gates of the camp and started the mass movement of 140,000 American and Allied prisoners to camp Lucky Strike (also known as La Havre, France). When General Patton had come through the gates of the overcrowded POW camp, he brought flyers with him. The flyers were asking the men to rejoin the military and continue the fight to push the Russians back into their borders.

After liberation, Gene would spend weeks on a hospital ship recovering from malnutrition and frostbite, mostly on his feet. He told one sad story from the hospital ship. One of the other prisoners, suffering from malnutrition, bought five Hershey chocolate bars in the ship commissary, even though he was told not to eat them. He didn't believe the doctors warning and ate the chocolate bars. This poor fellow died from eating them. After suffering malnutrition, the body needs time to adjust to food again.

He would also share that he had been sent to Atlantic City for the last two weeks before returning to the farm for rest and recuperation. He met a girl there and was going to stay in touch with her. Her name was Lynn Nadel, a shortened version of Helen Nadolski.

Jim would not be home for a while. He stayed in Germany to help build the gallows for the hangings after the trials in Nuremberg, Germany, for war crimes and crimes against humanity.

Gene would start to put his thoughts on paper. His time in the POW camp had given him time to reflect and now, being back home, he wanted to share what he had experienced in a philosophical way.

MY FATHER'S SECRETS

1

The World Before I Was Here

THE "WAR TO END ALL WARS" ended in 1918. However, it was not to be the end. The future remained clouded after Germany surrendered. Harsh reparations were imposed in the Treaty of Versailles. Signed in June 1919, Germany was not allowed to have submarines or an Air Force. It could have an Army of only 100,000 men and a Navy of only six ships. It was not allowed to place any troops in the Rhineland which established as a demilitarized zone to increase the security of France, Belgium, and the Netherlands against future German aggression. This area of Germany was also important for coal, steel, and iron production. Germany had to pay fifty billion gold marks ($12.5 billion) in reparations for damages done. Germany also lost land

    The United States had been drawn into the four years of World War One (WWI) toward the end, but Americans grew tired of it soon. Isolationism became popular. Over 100,000 Americans had become casualties, and the thought of further involvement overseas was unpopular among the American people. The United States even refused to join the League of Nations in 1920, which was the idea of President Woodrow Wilson.

However, as Americans became isolationists, there was a push within the military to become more prepared for any future warfare. At the time, aviation was considered supplemental to the Navy of the United States. Aviation was only promoted for coastal patrols, surveillance, reconnaissance, and battlefield support.

Air power became a complex political battle. A strong proponent of air power was General Billy Mitchell, a military aviator who saw the future. He observed the growing seeds of air power in places such as Japan and Germany and felt strongly as to what direction our country should be taking. He wanted to be able to carry the fight to the enemy through the air. Mitchell was born in 1879 and joined the Army in 1898 during the Spanish American War. He served in Cuba, the Philippines, Alaska and in Europe. He eventually became deputy commander of Army Aviation during WWI, winning many awards.

But he was met with disdain and opposition in the political discussion and even within the U.S. military as the prevailing feeling was that the U.S. Navy was the present and future of fighting battles and wars. Mitchell was very confident in his viewpoint that brought conflict and disgrace upon him. He even pointed fingers at others until finally, he was court-martialed for insubordination. He resigned from the military in 1925. It was probably not until ten years later that everyone finally figured out that Mitchell had been correct!

The 1930s, the decade following The Great Depression, saw fifteen percent of the workforce unemployed. Food lines, unemployment and the years of the Dust Bowl in the Great Plains scarred the times of workers and farmers. However, it was not just the United States in stress, as the financial contagion spread around the world. It hit excessively hard also on the post-war, struggling Germany and its citizens. The desire to punish instead of reconciling after WWI and the expansion of the totalitarian policies of Nazi Germany began to bear fruit. They found agreement with Japan and Italy. This alliance started in 1936 and became known as the Axis Powers. It would strike on September 1, 1939, when Hitler would invade Poland in eighteen days.

In the United States, most citizens were happy to hear President

Roosevelt's declaration that the U.S. would remain neutral over Europe's troubles. Our country remained focused on recovering from the hard days of The Depression. Even after the invasion of Poland, Congressional funds were directed towards domestic issues rather than future military needs. Congress did repeal the Arms Embargo provisions of the Neutrality Laws so that arms and equipment would begin to flow towards France and Britain. But the war was already going poorly. It was only a matter of time before America would become involved. Preparations that would affect my family directly had begun.

The Army Air Corps, under the command of General H.H."Hap" Arnold, was tasked with the job of reinventing and enlarging the flying services. Only about 500 to 750 pilots were being trained but Arnold knew that rate of training was unacceptable. Congress was still reluctant to allocate funds. General Arnold took a bold step in May 1939. He called the owners of eight major civilian flight schools to meet with him in Washington, D.C. At the meeting, he asked them to train the future American military pilots. He promised no pay or compensation for their efforts. Yet they all agreed to help.

While the civilian trainers were hopeful, they found that taking in workers and farmers and teaching them to fly was not the easiest of tasks. By June 1940, France had fallen to Germany and President Roosevelt pushed for a major build up. Congress was still reluctant. Instead, they allocated money to support Britain. Without committing troops, Roosevelt wanted us to become a great arsenal of democracy.

America's capacity to produce hundreds of thousands of tanks, airplanes and ships for its allies was amazing. It also taught us how to better equip our own military, specifically the Navy. Approval was eventually passed by Congress to give the president the power and authority to enhance our military, including the support of the civilian flight schools. The government would now support all those flight operations.

The United States had not been prepared to enter WWI. But with war clouds on the horizon, things were going to change this time. And soon my father would fit into these ranks.

My Father

My father, Eugene Francis Washura, was born in Cleveland, Ohio, on July 7, 1921. He was born with a veil over his head, also known as a caul birth, many have found this type of birth to mean good luck! He was born to his eighteen-year-old mother, Elizabeth, living in a Catholic Charities Home for Unwed Mothers. In those days, young women, girls most of them, were forced to have their babies put up for adoption.

My grandmother, Elizabeth Washura, was the oldest child of European immigrants from Hungary and Slovakia. While in high school, she worked at a local bakery in Cleveland. The story that was told is, she got pregnant by a young man who also worked at the bakery. Apparently, the man who impregnated her left town when he found out about the pregnancy. Attitudes were different back then. Raised in a strict Catholic family, her condition was a disgrace. She was thrown out of her parents' home and sent to the unwed mother's home in Cleveland.

Elizabeth felt alone, isolated, and ashamed during this time. Two of her high school friends, Gene, and Viola, as well as Elizabeth's sister Marie, were her only support. Gene and Viola would eventually marry. They remained friends with my grandmother throughout her life. When Dad was born, he was named after Gene and Viola Franks: Eugene Francis Washura.

My grandmother's sad and shameful situation was about to change. Maggie and Albert Phillips could not have children. One bright morning, Maggie and her husband went to the unwed mothers' home to look for a baby to adopt. They were interested in a baby boy. Maggie met my grandmother that day and liked her very much but showed little interest in my infant father. However, the connection she established with Elizabeth prevailed.

Maggie's brother-in-law, Ed Phillips, had returned from military duty. He had fought in the Argonne Forest in France. The Meuse-Argonne offensive was the largest in United States military history, involving 1.2 million American soldiers. It contributed to the end of the Great War.

Ed had received a "Dear John" letter from his girlfriend, effectively ending their relationship, so he was down in the dumps about the whole issue. However, his sister-in-law, Maggie, knew best! She introduced my grandmother, Elizabeth, to her brother-in-law, Ed Phillips. Ed must have liked my grandmother, as they were soon married, and my father was adopted by Ed. My father's name then became Eugene Francis Phillips.

Ed was a farmer, and he moved the family to Plymouth in Huron County, Ohio. Ed came from a family of farmers, and he loved the earth and his animals. Ed would teach all his children about weather, soil, and plant growth. They would learn about the Farmer's Almanac. Kids raised in Dad's era know about weather just from being outside. These kids learned that change in the weather affected their ability to earn money for the family. My father would become the oldest of six children in this order: Eugene, Jim, Thom, Irene, Clyde, and Henry. There was another boy, Billy who lived to be three years old and died of diphtheria and a girl, who was still born.

Everyone worked on the family farm. The house was not wired to electricity and there was no bathroom in the home. They used kerosene lamps in the evening and an outhouse was the toilet. The kitchen had a pump, which you had to prime, to get water to flow into the sink. A large wash tub would be brought into the kitchen and water would be heated on the stove, poured into that tub, and then each kid would take a bath using the same water. Usually youngest to oldest. There would be a pitcher and basin bowl in the home to just wash your face and hands back in those days.

Dad's life was hard working on a farm, and he shouldered the responsibility of being the oldest child. But he also suffered social snubbing and put downs from many who knew he was illegitimate. Perhaps the social pressures, perhaps the difficult farm life, formed his character.

When he was only seven years old, his father, Ed Phillips had a terrible accident that resulted in a traumatic head injury. This farm had no tractors, so land was worked with a team of horses. Ed was moving his team of horses across the road when a car spooked the horses and Ed was thrown to the ground. After the accident Dad started getting into fights at school and was not promoted. Ed's sister who lived in Cleveland took my dad so he could repeat his second-grade year in school. Ed needed time to get used to life with his injury. Unfortunately, Ed found relief for his pain in drinking. In Cleveland with his aunt, Father's perspective on life changed for the better.

In the school in Cleveland, he stopped getting into fights and started really enjoying learning. One day the teacher was asking each child what they wanted to be when they grew up. My father stood up and announced he wanted to be the first man on the moon. I'll never know all that was going on in his head during his years growing up. It seemed his sights were already set; he was looking toward the sky.

Through necessity, instilled values, and a strong moral compass, father returned to Plymouth with his parents and siblings. He would eventually take the role as head of the household. He worked on the farm, led his siblings, and supported his parents for the years to come. Even though his stepfather Ed was still around, the weight of the responsibility he took on at such an early age was heavy, important to the whole family and life formational. It made him a profoundly serious young man.

While most Americans enjoyed relative prosperity for most of the 1920s, The Great Depression for the American farmer really began after World War I. Much of the Roaring '20s was a continual cycle of debt for the American farmer, stemming from falling farm prices and the need to purchase expensive machinery. My father's family farm had no expensive machinery.

In 1922, The Agricultural Appropriations Act passed on May 11th, creating the U.S. Bureau of Agricultural Economics in the Department of Agriculture. It also consolidated the Office of Farm Management and Farm Economics and the Bureau of Markets and Crop Estimates. Congress passed the Soil Conservation and Domestic Allotment Act on February 29, 1936, giving the government power to pay benefits to farmers who contract to reduce production of wheat and other soil-depleting crops and plant those that replenish the soil. Congress would pass a new Agricultural Adjustment Act, reinforcing soil conservation through acreage allotment in 1938.

During this period, nationwide, farming exports fell thirty to forty percent below the average of the ten depression years that preceded WWII. Grain exports, for example, fell thirty percent in one year between September 1939 and 1940. In the early 1940s there was a shortage of farm workers and replacing these workers was hard to do. The reason? The war had started in Europe on September 1, 1939, when Hitler invaded Poland. Thousands of men took jobs in shipyards and airplane factories thinking they could be exempt from going to war and seek deferment because they had essential operations.

With all this on the plate of a young man and with all the challenges at home, in 1940 my father graduated as valedictorian of New Haven High School. He was offered a scholarship to Case University in Ohio but was unable to attend due to his family responsibilities. He continued to support his family as he worked the farm, tilled the fields, milked the cows, and slopped the pigs. A role model to his siblings, his work ethic was instrumental to their lives and meaningful to his.

The news, even in the United States was about the war in Europe. His adopted father, Ed, had fought in the last European war. It is plausible

New Haven High School Class of 1940.
Eugene Francis Phillips (top row left).

that his admiration for Ed put him on a course to go into the military. Politicians had vowed that we would never be involved directly in another foreign war. President Roosevelt worked to change public opinion. Everything did change on December 7, 1941. The attack on Pearl Harbor and Hitler's declaration of war four days later, quickly changed American opinion. The internal fight over budget and isolationism ended. The attack on Hawaii had provided an explicit example of how air power could project war far beyond national borders. After the attack on Pearl Harbor there was much discussion in the farmhouse about the war. This farm family had just gotten a radio to hear the news, the newspaper provided images of what they were hearing. All the members of this family were really affected by this news. My father's younger brother, Thom, took black tar and painted scenes he had seen in the paper on the wall of the barn. Planes flying and dropping bombs on the American ships. If that barn still stands, those tar drawings are still there.

The need for pilots became larger and larger. This nation was now fighting in two hemispheres and needed more pilots than ever. It was estimated that 200,000 American pilots would be needed, as well as the training of foreign pilots who were allies. Flight classes grew from scores to hundreds. Potential pilots were brought in from all over the United States. Most recruits had limited or no experience of flying an airplane.

The Air Corps went from 20,503 personnel on July 1, 1939, to 152,069 two years later. The training would increase to 7,000 pilots in 1940 and 30,000 in 1941. By the fall of 1941 the Army Air Corps set sights on training 50,000 pilots a year and then revised the total to 70,000 pilots a year with matching demands for gunners, navigators, bombardiers, ground technicians and of course, flight instructors.

Before January 1939, there were seventeen air bases. By the peak of World War II in 1943, the number had grown to 783 main bases, subbases, and auxiliary fields.

My father had foreseen the need for the U.S. to fight in Europe before the Pearl Harbor attack. Pilot training could take over one year. In January of 1941, Dad enlisted in the U.S. Army. Back then, the U.S. military realized they did not have enough college graduates to achieve the number of pilots needed for the world at war. So, the U.S. government started a program for high school graduates who finished in the top 10% of their high school class, to become qualified as pilots. My father was in this category but, his induction was delayed one year to allow him to enroll into and complete Civilian Pilot Training Program at Harrington's Airport in Mansfield, Ohio. He continued to work simultaneously as a machinist at the Fate Root Heath Company. He could provide money for the family while his younger brothers took on the farm responsibilities. The company produced Plymouth wheel tractors, using designs that originated in the locomotive department.

He successfully completed his civilian flight training and was inducted into the Army on January 26, 1942. Eugene had never been out of the state of Ohio, he had never been on a vacation, and he was about to leave for California for his military training. Young Eugene was twenty years old when he left for Santa Ana, California. He wanted to become an Army Airman. He had the physical qualifications and the mental attitude. Many men who went in at the same time for flight training washed out, but he made his goal. After Santa Ana, he went to King City, California and then Chico, California.

During this time in California, he wrote home to his mother often. The following are some of these letters:

His first letter home:

(Stationery heading)
United States Army Air Corps
Air Corps Replacement Training Center
Santa Ana, California

March 13, 1942
Dear Family,
 I would like to know if you have received the package with my clothes and the letter. Please send the Pereles and my religious medal with the chain on it.

I have been classified as a pilot after going through another stiff mental and physical. Out of my company of 180 men, only a few over a hundred got classified as pilots and some of the others only got several pilots out of a whole company. Out of 3400 men or air cadets only 1700 will be pilots, the rest will be navigators, bombardiers, or washouts; so, you can get some idea of what it takes to be an air cadet pilot. I will be here only a couple of weeks before I will be shipped to a primary flying school where there will be a long chance.

If I knew the address, I might have written to Dad, but it will be more convenient if you will relay these letters to him since I am writing to you all.

Bing Crosby sent his brother to the field Sunday with a group of dancers and other entertainers. Bob Hope will be here tomorrow to entertain us. This entertainment is furnished without Gov't expense.

I was in to see Father Clasby, the Catholic Chaplain and they don't make nicer men. Masses are at 6:15 and 8:15 o'clock. A very large part of the boys here are Catholic. They are also building another Church.

When I was in Columbus, I received $56.00 ration money for the time I was home; I still have over $105.00 plus the time I have been here coming yet.

Thanks to all of you for your letters and if anyone writes. I will try to answer them in what limited time I have. We get up at 5:00 am in the morning, lights out at 9:30 pm, bed check 10:00 pm.

We are doing something almost every minute of the day and when night comes, we don't go to bed. Just fall in. We are also highly disciplined.

Well, it is time to go to bed, so I'll say so long.

—Air Cadet Gene

P.S. The nights are very chilly and the days moderate. Don't think this is sunny Cal. Because it has been raining here half of the time although the residents say it will stop in a few weeks and won't rain again until the latter part of next fall.

In this next letter he asks his mother to send him Pereles. This was a product for constipation. He requests this in many of his letters.

My father asks his mother to relay this information to Ed, who was living in an Asylum. He had become an excessively bad alcoholic and his mother felt it best if Ed was not in the home. In the early 1940s there were no detox or rehab centers for alcoholics. They were put into asylums. Later my dad received a letter from Ed asking him to plead with Elizabeth on his behalf so he could return home. My father did write that letter to his mother. Ed returned home before the end of the war in Europe and was able to be with his family until his death in 1946.

(Stationery heading)
Letter # 2
Aviation Cadet
United States Army Air Corps
Air Corps Replacement Training Center
Santa Ana, California

Santa Ana, California
Saturday, April 4, 1942

Dear Family,
I have just found a little time for writing. They are really pushing us and don't let anyone tell you that a pilot cadet isn't the hardest thing in the service to qualify for.
I have received a full uniform and other equipment necessary for military specification; I will send all the aviation clothes back because I won't be needing them anymore.
We are all very stiff in the limbs due to the shots and vaccinations we received and there are still more to get. Tomorrow, we get the blood test and later more physical examinations.

This field is still being built and it will soon be one of the three largest in the country of its kind. It is only four miles from the Pacific Ocean, and I have been in one blackout already.

The eats are alright, the fellows alright, and there is plenty of allowance for church which we have here on the post.

I will enclose a $5.00 money order for a bottle of Pereles, I have not received any money here yet.

So long
I'll do my best,

—Air Cadet Gene.

P.S. Let me know if anything important happens, the scenery is beautiful here with mountains in the background. We are on parade tomorrow when some movie actors and actresses will entertain.

The Address:
Aviation Cadet Eugene F. Phillips 15074710
Santa Ana, California
Co 24 ACRJC

Another letter dated August 27, 1942:

(This is the only letter written on hotel stationery)
San Carlos Hotel
Corner Fifth and Olive Streets
Opposite Biltmore Hotel
Facing beautiful Pershing square
Los Ángeles, California
Aug. 27, 1942

Dear Family,
I am staying at this hotel, The Carlos Hotel in Los Angeles, California. We are in route to Phoenix, Arizona. One of my

friends has a car and asked me to go along with him. His home is in L.A.

This afternoon one of the other fellows was riding along and I went over into Hollywood and met one of the producers by accident. He showed us through one of the movie studios where we saw Jean Parker and Chet Morris making a scene, he also introduced us. After that I walked over to CBS Studios and watched Shirley Temple make her last broadcast of the season. I must be at Luke Field by 9 o'clock Friday morning. Well, it's time to close, the darn pen scratches too much anyway.

—Always, Gene.

That Friday, he entered Luke Field, Arizona Class J 42 of the Army Air Corps and graduated on October 30, 1942. He received his silver wings and his commission as a Second Lieutenant. He then left for Pendleton Air Force Base, Oregon. After a few more weeks of training, he was handed the keys to a P-38. Second Lieutenant Eugene F. Phillips was now the pilot of the plane of his dreams – the P-38 which had been declared the fastest plane in the world!

Probably the best year of my father's life was 1942. He was doing all the things he had dreamed about. He sent his pay home to his mother to take care of the family. His father living in the asylum due to alcoholism made it a tough time for his family at home. The younger boys would raise chickens for eggs and some to sell. Pigs and cows to sell, and some cows to milk. They would separate the cream from the milk and that paid for most of their food staples. Jim would soon follow Dad's footsteps into the Army. They would eventually end up in the same place after the war ended in Europe.

The U.S. started working very closely with England even before Pearl Harbor was attacked. Once plans are set in place, military leaders will then evaluate how these strategies are working. In World War I there was some use of air power but not to the extent it was going to be used in World War II. Some American pilots like

The P-38 was produced by Skunkworks in California.

Lieutenant Colonel Albert Clark, a West Point graduate and a man who would become a friend, mentor, and confidant to my father, went to England as second in command of the 31st Fighter Group. The 31st Fighter Group was the first American fighter unit in the European theater of operations. Clark would be shot down over Abbeville, France in July 1942 and was a prisoner of war (POW) until April 1945.

As Father was finishing his military flight training, allied leaders decided that the strategies of flying out of North Africa were important. Ground forces had secured Tunisia there and the U.S. had set up an airbase there as well. Tunisia was a great location for an airfield to provide air power over Sicily and the bottom of Italy. On February 21, 1943, Father was sent to North Africa!

In May 1942 Carl Spaatz became commander of the Eighth Air Force and immediately transferred its headquarters to England in

My father in the spring of 1942.

July. The 15th Air Force was established on November 1, 1943, in Tunis, Tunisia and commenced combat operations the following day. The 15th Air Force was formed as part of reorganization of the Twelfth and Ninth Air Forces and activated with a strength of 90 B-24 Liberators and 210 B-17 Flying Fortresses, inherited from its predecessors. From December 1943, thirteen new groups arriving from the U.S. were added to the 15th Air Force, most equipped with B-24 Liberators.

A sample of US Army patches from WWII.

Like the Eighth Air Force in Britain, it was hoped that the Fifteenth would be able to attack Occupied Europe from Italy and the Mediterranean and keep up the offensive when bad weather in Britain grounded the Eighth Air Force. When the allies progressed into Italy, the Fifteenth were able to reach targets in South France, Germany, Poland, Czechoslovakia, and the Balkans which were out of the range of the Eighth Air Force.

During the Second World War the fifteen heavy bomber groups of the 15th Air Force lost 2,110 Bombers on operations. Its seven Fighter Groups claimed 1,836 enemy aircraft destroyed.

World War II was to see large operations with the American invasion of Northwest Africa, but none surpassed it in complexity or daring as Operation Torch, the name of allied invasion of French North Africa, in November 1942. It was the first time the British and Americans had jointly worked on an invasion together. The lessons learned in Africa imposed a pattern on the war. In January 1943 a conference was held among the Allied Forces called the Casablanca Conference. The leaders evaluated the air strategies at this time.

On July 10, 1943, the allies began their invasion of Axis-controlled Europe with landings on the island of Sicily, off mainland Italy, encountering little resistance from demoralized Italian troops. Montgomery's Eighth Army came ashore on the southeast part of the

Two WWII aircraft vital to victory in WWII: the B-17 (left) and the B-24 Librerator.

island while the U.S. Seventh Army under General George Patton landed on Sicily. This also included the North Africa Air Force.

Italy's battles were heavily contested by various insurgencies and Allied Military Forces which waged the battle of the Mediterranean. Ultimately, the Italian empire collapsed after disastrous defeats in Eastern Europe and North Africa campaigns in July 1943. Benito Mussolini was arrested on the order of King Victor Emmanuel III. Provoking a civil war. Italy's military outside the peninsula had collapsed.

Major General Carl Spaatz's of the U. S. Amy's Eighth Air Force was preparing to test the American doctrine of high altitude, precision daylight bombing from the United Kingdom. General Jimmy Doolittle had been assigned after his Tokyo raid, to ready the Fourth Bombardment Wing for service with the Eighth Air Force on July 30. Doolittle arrived in England on August 6 to take on this considerable task. General Dwight D. Eisenhower after conferences with Doolittle and Spaatz built his plan, announcing that he would build the Operation Torch Air Force around a nucleus taken from the eighth with additional units drawn directly from the United States.

After arriving in North Africa, Dad, and his P-38 Fighter-Bomber saw plenty of action. He was a member of the 95th Fighter Squadron, 82nd Fighter Group.

95th Fighter Squadron, 82nd Fighter Group patch.

When he first arrived in Tunisia, the airmen were set up to fly twenty-five missions and then they could go home. Many of them would do U.S. tours for bond drives. Bond drives were a way the American people could support the war effort. However, for my father, that never came to pass. As soon as he finished the first twenty-five missions, he was given a leave but had to stay in North Africa. He then had to start his second round of 25 missions.

His letters home revealed that he participated in the North African campaign including Tunis and Bizerte. The last letter he wrote to his mother, dated August 20, 1943, said he was working for a promotion and stated that he had been on forty-two missions. The letter, written from North Africa, said he saw service in the capture of Sicily and the invasion of Italy.

That Fateful Day

The United States government had received intelligence that the Germans were taking over the Italian airfields. My father's fighter group was ordered to lead the first mass long-range, low-level strafing raid to be carried out in this theater. Seventy-five P-38 aircraft took off on August 25, 1943, to attack an enemy concentration of over 230 enemy aircraft in the Foggia area. Barely skimming over the tops of the water to avoid radar during the long 530-mile flight, they were at the head of the formation of 140 aircraft and arrived on time.

At treetop level, they split off to their various targets. Completely disregarding flak, ground fire and aerial enemy opposition, these aggressive and courageous pilots roared across the enemy fields, strafing enemy aircraft and other targets. In this group alone, they accounted for fifty-five enemy aircraft destroyed or damaged while the mission accounted for over 150 destroyed or damaged aircraft. They dealt a crippling blow at a critical time, right before the Salerno landing of September 3.

The ground fire was intense and the air combat relentless. While maneuvering to protect his wing man, 2nd Lt. James Rudy, my father, was shot down by a German ME109 plane.

Too low to eject, he hit the trees at 300 miles an hour. He was knocked unconscious and severely injured. When he woke up, his plane was on fire. He was able to climb out and begin evasion. He eluded capture, with cuts and burn wounds on his face, for thirty hours. He first hid in a

The German's formidable Messerschmitt ME109.

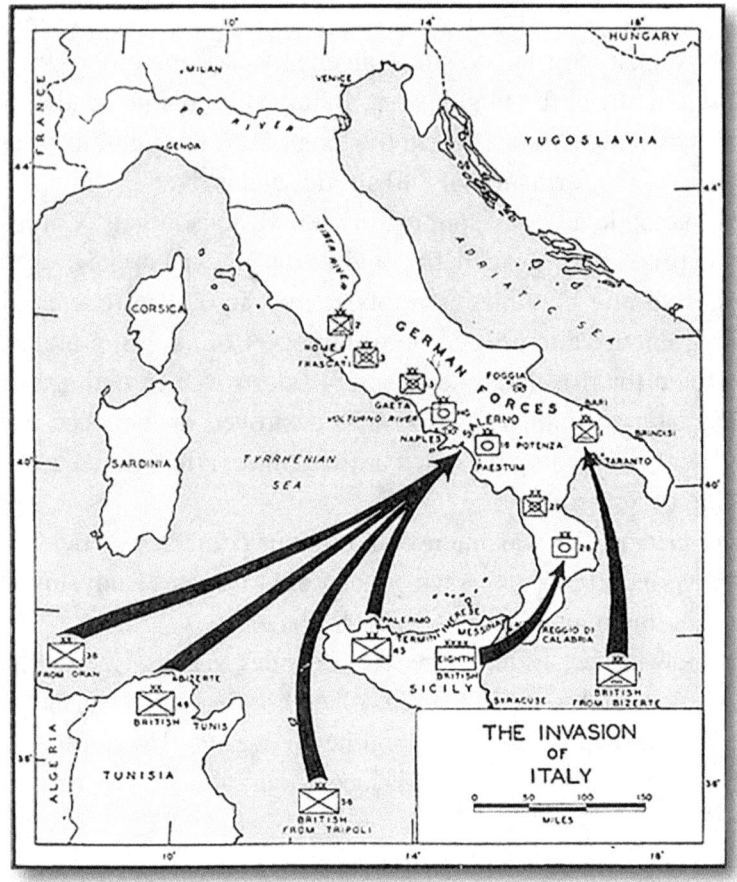

Map of the invasion of Italy, September 3, 1943.

vineyard. Locals quickly found him and took him in for the evening. They treated his burns with olive oil, a precious commodity at the time. But he could not stay. He left before sunrise and continued his fight for freedom. However, he was eventually captured by other civilians and turned into the German Army. The first thing the Germans told you when you were captured was, "for you the war is over."

My father was held in Italian POW camps in Bari, Italy; Chieti, Italy; and in the dungeon in Sulmona, Italy. Train ride after train ride with other POW's took them closer to their destination. Years later he told me about peering through the wooden slats of the train car to see the scenic mountain ranges and the scenic Brenner Pass. My father did not share most things about his time in the War or the POW camp. But he talked about that view from the train more than once. I would learn many of the details I am sharing from research. Each town they stopped in, they were paraded by the Germans down the main streets, to be scorned and spit upon or worse. "These are the pilots that bring death and destruction to your towns and families," the Germans would say as they forced the pilots through the streets.

In a brief telegram dated September 18, the War Department notified Dad's family that he was missing in action. The exact text of the message:

> "I regret to inform you that the Commanding General North Africa area reports your son Second Lieutenant Eugene F. Phillips missing in action since 25 August. As further details or other information of his status are received you will be promptly notified."

On October 10th, he arrived at Stalag Luft III, ninety miles east of Berlin. He was first held with the British prisoners. Because of the burns to my father's face, he wore a beard, which made him look older. When he came into the British section of the POW camp the Brits accepted him as an equal. It was during this time that he questioned the meaning of life as many of the captured soldiers did. Many of the British would spend time discussing deep philosophical topics. This would set him on a path of deep thought for the rest of his life. He would teach me to always respect other countries and people for what they had to offer.

This camp was built just for allied airmen who had been there longer than the Americans. During the twenty-one months that he spent as a POW, the Germans built the south compound of the camp, and all the Americans were segregated and sent there. In this compound, my father met the American who was shot down earlier,

Stalag Luft III POW camp.

Lieutenant Colonel Albert Clark. Clark and Dad had interests in common and respected one another. Their friendship would continue for the rest of their lives.

During the time Dad was in the POW camp, the allied prisoners were digging escape tunnels. A British barrister named Roger Bushell; a member of the Royal Air Force ended up at Stalag Luft III. Bushell was the mastermind of the escape tunnels that he and others decided to secretly dig. They delicately thought through the entire escape and with the help of everyone in the camp put the escape plan into action. They had some prisoners making fake documents, others coming up with routes to freedom and others drawing maps to get there. They sewed civilian clothing from clothing they had. Everyone got involved in the escape in some way. They knew that each man that got through the tunnel had to be with a German speaker or fluent in German. Each group of escapers had a plan and a route to escape. The tunnels were named, Tom, Dick, Harry, and George. They had to dig more than one tunnel in case the Germans discovered one. The escape was set up for 250 men to escape through a tunnel after dark. The timing of the escape would be set for a season of good weather.

At the height of the war, Stalag Luft III held 10,000 Allied prisoners. This prison camp was built on soil that was sand. The barracks were built above ground so if the prisoners tried to escape the German guards could detect it. They also installed devices to listen to sound. The Germans thought this camp above all other camps would stop airmen from escaping. Despite all the German ingenuity to keep imprisoned servicemen from escaping, they had done it anyway, outsmarting the German Nazi military.

During Father's time in the POW camp at Sagan, he did not receive mail from home for a long time. He wrote letters but no response came. Back in Ohio his brother Jim had enlisted in the Army. Jim found this information about why Dad was not receiving mail. The newspaper article read in part:

Nazis Refuse U.S. Mail Bearing Victory Appeal

The Germans are refusing to accept letters to U.S. war prisoners bearing the three- cent "V" stamp and the cancellation legend "Buy War Bonds and Stamps."

The end of the article stated: "The Post Office Department has said the cancellation legend situation will be correct about March 1. Meanwhile, letters to war prisoners should be sent in unsealed envelopes to New York where they will be cancelled by a machine without the War Bond legend."

This mail situation made it worse for the POWs. Their families and loved one's support had been denied them. Many prisoners were depressed. My father told me it would have been better if they were able to work. However, officers according to the Geneva Convention Rules of War, were not permitted to and the Germans followed that rule. However, the Germans did not follow all the rules of the Geneva Convention Rules of War.

The escape plan and the business of this work kept the prisoners' minds busy. Everyone pitched in for this effort. Everyone was given sand that was coming out of the tunnels to disperse. Often it was put into a sock and each POW would walk around with a sand filled sock hanging inside their pant leg and slowly as they walked outside let the sand spill out undetected by the guards. The men slept in bunk beds three high, with slats holding the mattress on the beds. Each guy gave up slats from their bunks to shore up the tunnels. My father told me about how he slept on just a few slats.

In 1963 an American movie titled *The Great Escape* was written and filmed about this camp. The movie starred the hottest male leading actor of the time, Steve McQueen. There were hardly any American escapees. Seventy-six prisoners escaped the night of March 24, 1944. But only three of those escapees made it back to freedom. Fifty of the escapees were shot by the Germans and the rest were sent back to Stalag Luft III. Among those shot by the Germans was Roger Bushell.

By January 1945 the war was leaning toward the allies. Hitler decided to move all his captured military to Bavaria, Germany. He wanted to protect them since he believed he may need them as bargaining chips at the end of the war if Germany didn't win. In late January 1945, extremely late at night, the prisoners of Stalag Luft III marched out of the barracks with only what they could carry. The area was being hammered by a winter storm that night that continued for days. It was the worst storm Europe had experienced in over twenty years. That night was the start of a brutal forced march. This march is featured in the 2024 TV series *Masters of the Air.*

They moved through the night without stopping until noon the following day. They had arrived at a small town called Grosselton, a thirteen hour march through deep snow, sub-zero cold and thirty kilometers (eighteen miles). They were allowed to rest in barns for a short time and then resumed their march six hours later. They marched again into the dark of night and falling snow. The exhaustion and drop rate grew. Seven hours later (twenty-six Kilometers) at 1:00 a.m., they reached a town called Maskau. They were led to a large pottery factory for another rest period. My father contemplated leaving the group at this point, thinking maybe he would be able to survive alone in the forests. However, friends talked him out of the plan.

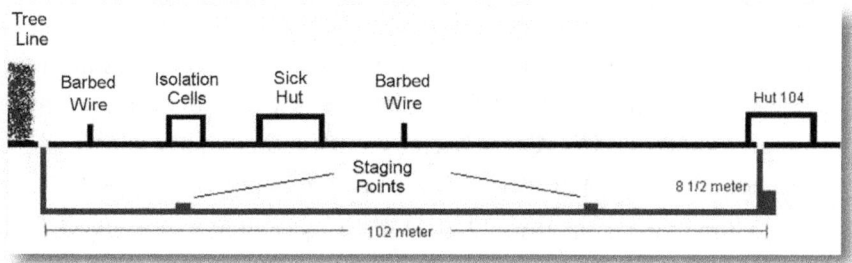

Diagram of "Tunnel Harry" from The Great Escape.

The pottery factory provided a full day of rest. They left the next morning at six. It had stopped snowing but was still bitterly cold. They marched another eighteen kilometers, arriving at a town called Graustein about 6:00 p.m. They rested in barns and chicken houses. Continuing the following morning again at six, they arrived at Spremberg about noon. They were marshalled to a large field and made to stand in deep snow for two hours. Finally, the march to the train station in town was made, which was about sixty miles and forty-four hours of marching through the worst of conditions.

They were loaded into the forty and eight boxcars (named for the capacity of forty men or eight horses it could carry), fifty men to a car. Father would tell many stories about that trip. They were packed so tightly that only one person at a time could sit down. One bucket was provided for water and one other bucket served as a bathroom for the entire car. The conditions were even worse than the forced march they had endured.

The Forty and Eight Boxcar

The train left Spremberg at 7:00 p.m. They had been on the train for twenty-four hours when they stopped in Chemnitz. The doors were unlocked, and cans of meat, margarine and bread were shoved in. However, the train started again before everyone received a ration. They pulled into Regensburg at 2:00 p.m. the next day. There, they were allowed to leave the cars for a few minutes, for the first time in two days.

Back onto the train and moving again, they arrived in Moosburg in Bavaria six hours later. They were left locked in the box cars until the next day. They would not have barracks to stay in and would not have enough food as the Red Cross packages that fed them at Stalag Luft III were not coming to Moosburg. The forced march and the train trip had taken a toll, both physically and mentally. Fights among the men, crying, starving and chaos were only the beginning. At Moosburg, they all lost weight and hygiene conditions became unbearable. Most of the men were covered in lice and filth among conditions less than human.

A display of POWs and the train cars at the National Museum of the Air Force, Wright-Patterson Air Base, in Dayton, OH.

Russian Communist Aggression During January of 1945. The Beginning of The Cold War and the Iron Curtain

When Hitler was moving the prisoners from all the camps to Bavaria, civilian people in Poland and all parts of Eastern Europe were also moving west. Russia was an ally with the U.S. and Britain, but it had become a Communist country during WWI and the Bolshevik Revolution. Russia wanted to take these countries, so the civilian population was moving toward Switzerland and France to escape the Communist Aggression under the Russian leader Joseph Stalin. The Russian soldiers were just as bad as the Nazi soldiers. They murdered whole towns of people, taking what they wanted by force. By the end of WWII General George Patton saw how much of Europe the Russians had taken as the American soldiers were looking to go home. Patton wanted U.S. soldiers to stay and fight to push the Russian aggression back. The American people did not want more war in Europe. However, countries like Poland, Yugoslavia, Bulgaria, Romania, Hungary, and Eastern Germany were now under Communist rule. So as WWII ends for the U.S., European people were in a new war, The Cold War. Times in Europe were beyond comprehension for most Americans at home in the U.S. Currency was changed in these countries. The Communist government imposed their rules on eastern European people. A political boundary dividing Europe into two separate areas became known as the Iron Curtain.

MIS-X Top Secret POW Program

Lost in the dusty, musty recesses of the archives in the Pentagon, random papers so vague they are meaningless, refer to a dark, quiet secret known as MIS-X. In over seventy-five years, since the genesis of the acronym, it is still a mystery. In truth, it was an ultra-secret POW communication, support and supply program that operated full tilt during WWII, and was so successful, it maintained contact with all Eastern European POW camps, sixty-four in all.

The story began with the awesome British intelligence operation, MI-9. MI-9 was born of the 50,000 plus British servicemen taken at Dunkirk. As Hitler ordered all POW camps to be 1000 miles from the English Channel, MI-9 was tasked to accommodate both its prisoners and the vast European front. MI-9, the escape and evasion agency of the POW branch (all services), resolutely dug in, creating no less than thirty-six faux humanitarian aid societies, and commandeered manufacturers under the Official Secrets Act to load escape and evasion materials into goods. They trained hand-picked airmen and soldiers to surreptitiously communicate with special codes should they be captured. Thus, creating an active POW offensive unit. Captives would communicate, escape, evade, and generally wage war on their captors from within. Some escapes were even planned so that the escapees could simply gather intelligence, be recaptured, and then transmit such back to London.

With its involvement in the war in 1942, the Eighth Army Air Force, in preparation for moving its European command to England, was briefed on the exploits of MI-9 and how it was wreaking havoc with captured POWs. General Carl Spaatz was amazed and immediately saw the potential for an American program based on the British success. Ever mindful of the hazard to his flyers, General Spaatz was instrumental in getting British Air Vice Marshall Charles Medhutt to brief Secretary of War Henry L. Stimson in the U.S. about MI-9. Eventually, rather than create a U.S. arm of MI-9 under the Eighth Air Force, they invented a separate, secret unit and it was set up with Eighth Air Force personnel. By October, the German POW camp at Fort Hunt, Virginia, part of George Washington's Mount Vernon Estate, housed several off-limits, high security buildings of MIS-X, America's version of MI-9. It was so secret; it was only referred to by its PO Box number, 1142.

So clandestine was 1142, only a select handful of people knew it existed. And even those few didn't have all the facts. Three cover aid organizations were created to cover the shipment of parcels, some purely humanitarian, but many loaded with radios and parts, electronics, handguns, shovels, photo and developing equipment, cameras, maps, millions in Reichsmarks, compasses, allied and Axis uniforms, printing presses, saws, forged documents, and anything else needed by captive military. Sometimes clandestinely, sometimes overtly, these parcels and their contraband passed by inspectors and censors of the Luftwaffe (German Air Force), Wehrmacht (German Unified Armed Forces), and the SS (the elite guard of the Nazi regime) camp's parcel stations.

Over a three-year period, the trained POW code users (CUs),

reported to London and MIS-X, the setup of camps, staffing and status and identity of prisoners, escape plans and intelligence data. They were also able to advise the U.S. of technical problems on aircraft, impediments with equipment, and dangerous areas for escapees and evaders throughout Europe. One infamous message that made its way out of the camps came from B-17 crewmen who advised MIS-X of critical problems with hatches on the noble Flying Fortress. Within days, the problem was fixed. Such masses of information not only aided the war effort but allowed briefers to give airmen a better chance of survival in event of capture, and a procedure to follow to support or to contact camp escape committees.

Here is an example of how the information was transmitted, as told to me at a Stalag Luft III Reunion by a B-17 pilot and participant:

Those who were pre-designated into the program (higher probability of capture) would write a letter home to a loved one. The known participants' letters would go to Fort Hunt, Virginia. The letters were scanned for a coded date: [March 11, 1943] format of date is NOT a coded letter; [3/11/43] format of a date IS a coded letter.

The numbers in the date would unlock the coded message.

The code was never cracked by the Germans!

Below is a sample of one such coded POW letter to home:

~~March 11, 1943~~ *(indicates not coded)*
3/11/43 (indicates coded)

Dear Aunt Florence,

Life in camp is fine. I have made new friends, and we are able to sit around and talk about each other's history and friends and places we've visited. Since we are no longer a participant in the **bombs** *and shooting of the war, we are able to just talk about it.*

Yesterday we were allowed to have a nice religious service. We gathered some items and decorated the inside of our front **door***. It was a nice time for us.*

This will be a short note this time. I just wanted to be sure and thank you for the wonderful food basket you sent. I'll be **sticking** *by it until it is completely empty.*

—*Love, Tom*

* * *

U.S. and British E&E (Escape and Evasion) agencies, under the guise of the Aide Societies (e.g. The Red Cross), were able to supplant the POW starvation diet and thus saved countless lives. They shipped hundreds of thousands of food items such as coffee, sugar, pate, cheese, oleo, biscuits, canned meats, dried fruit, salmon, and powdered milk. Cigarettes, soap, and coffee created a POW currency with which to trade and bribe guards. Blankets and uniforms became German men's lederhosen and peasant clothes for escapees, fashioned by POW tailors who used razor blades to etch perfect patterns into the wool cloth.

MIS-X hand-loaded many of their E&E devices at worktables in Virginia. Only a small number of items could be handled at the factory in Virginia, as manufacturers could not be sworn to secrecy as had been achieved in England. The small band of MIS-X personnel had big talents. Monopoly and checker boards were loaded with currency, maps, and forged documents. Cribbage boards were radioing and chess pieces. Shaving brushes and other handle-items were full of compasses and money. Decks of playing cards, when stripped of their backs and laid out, became full-color silk maps of Europe. Rubber shoe heels were carved with VISA and official stamps to be imprinted onto the forged papers. It was so successful that Code Users soon communicated that MIS-X should stop sending E&E devices as they were overstocked in the camps. Contacts were so good that POWs knew precisely when to listen to the radio for certain messages.

When the camps were liberated or left, MIS-X was ordered to shut down, smash and incinerate everything. Stacks of loaded goods, records, documents, and POW secret messages were destroyed. Except for a few obscure references from other organizations, nothing survived. So completely obliterated from history was MIS-X, that with the Korean War, imminent as early as 1948, not one person or shred of information was available to activate a similar program less than three years later.

My Mother

My mother, Helen Stella Nadolski, was born on September 22, 1924, the youngest child of U.S. immigrants. She was born at her parents' home in Philadelphia, and capable of speaking both Polish and English. Of the five children born to my grandmother, only two survived. They were my mother, the youngest, and her brother, Tony, six years her senior. When my mother was but two years old, her father left their home forever. My grandparents never divorced but were separated from that time until he died in 1946. My grandmother had not worked outside her home till she forced her husband to leave the house.

My mother was raised by an immensely proud Polish mother, named Henrietta, who worked as a cook and cleaned offices. My mother attended school from time to time but never graduated from high school. She was very smart and capable. It was a shame that she never finished. But my mother did understand the importance of education. She would put education in the highest regard for her children!

My grandmother raised my mother and her brother during The Depression as a single mom. My grandmother had been raised with strong values and in the upper class of Polish society. She was too proud to take public assistance, but she knew that raising her children in the Orthodox Jewish communities in Center City, Philadelphia meant they would be growing up around respect, proper language, and no profanity. My mother was street smart, and those characteristics would serve her, for good and bad, the rest of her life. Her life growing up would touch bootlegging, gambling, running numbers, etc. She'd peel potatoes at restaurants for a nickel and babysit when she became old enough. She would find whatever job she could to make a little money to help. My grandmother, Henrietta, along with her two kids moved from rented room to rented room, sometimes leaving in the middle of the night when they didn't have enough money to pay the rent. When my mother grew a little older, she got a job at the Five and Dime Store. Later, she worked at a dentist's office. Mom was a smart survivor!

After the war in Europe broke out, mother saw an opportunity. When she turned eighteen, she got a job at the Philadelphia Armory as a Purchasing Agent. She did not have a high school diploma, but she bluffed her way into that fantastic job. She wasn't well educated but she was smart. She purchased bullets and other items for the soldiers. She was incredibly attractive and as fashionable as she could afford. She also shortened her name from Helen Nadolski to Lynn Nadel. She only dated officers, believing that was the way to better her situation in life.

The American population in the United States were all invested in the War in Europe. President Roosevelt had established the Office of Price Administration (OPA).

The OPA rationed automobiles, tires, gasoline, fuel oil, coal, firewood, nylon, silk, and shoes. Americans used their ration cards and stamps to take their meager share of household staples including meat, dairy, coffee, dried fruits, jams, jellies, lard, shortening, and oils.

After WWII

My father was finally liberated by General George Patton from his POW camp in Moosburg on April 29, 1945. What he did not know was that his brother Jim was among the troops of General Patton's Army. Not until returning to the States did, he finds out that Jim was there when he was liberated. He reflected however, "It made no difference as Jim would not have recognized me."

During his long incarceration in the POW camp, he received poor care. His plane crash injuries had been severe. He suffered malnutrition and his overall health was at risk. All the released prisoners, along with other soldiers, were sent to camp Lucky Strike near La Havre,

This is an image of ration book and stamps used by American civilians during WWII.

France. They would remain there for two weeks or so waiting on a ship to take them back to the States. My father was there for several months. He spent time on a hospital ship because of his malnutrition and the frost bite from the January death march. On August 5, 1945, my dad was finally on a ship returning to the U.S. While on the ship he got the news that the Atomic Bomb had been dropped on Hiroshima. He knew then that the war was over, and life would be changing back to normal. When American prisoners arrived back in the U.S., they were sent to vacation areas for rest and recuperation, to regain their strength and to readjust to life.

My Parents Meet in Atlantic City, 1945

My dad was sent to Atlantic City, New Jersey, for his recuperation. My mother's family always went to the shore and boardwalk there for several weeks in the summer. They would stay with friends who had a place there, as they could not afford a hotel. Grandmother Henrietta could take a job in Atlantic City if needed. They would do whatever they needed to get to the shore and be able to spend time at the beach.

One serendipitous afternoon, my parents met in Atlantic City. The date was August 8, 1945. They met in a movie theater off the boardwalk. The name of the movie was Rhapsody in Blue, the story of George Gershwin, the composer. Depending on who would tell the story, who sat by whom first is up for discussion, but they sat by each other in the theater. After the movie, Dad asked if he could walk my mother home. She was not sure because he was only a second lieutenant and she liked to date high-ranking officers. She told him it was a public boardwalk and if he wanted to walk with her, he could. Then he asked her if she would like to stop for a soda. When they sat down for the soda, my father introduced himself with a salute and click of his heels. That was the enjoyable icebreaker of that moment.

After enjoying a soda, they walked along the boardwalk and came upon fortune birds. Here, one paid an amount, and the birds would pick a little paper up and that was your fortune. I don't know what Father's fortune read but Mother's fortune said, "You will marry the person you're with." My father had two weeks in Atlantic City so my parents would see each other every day during that August.

My father returned to Ohio but eventually was sent to Texas. He and my Philadelphia girl mother stayed in touch by writing letters. He still had military obligations. He was assigned to Aloe Field in Victoria, Texas where the military put him back in an airplane, a C-45F. Then he went to Perrine Field, Texas, where he flew the AT-6D and the AT-6C. During that year, the romance continued to bud through letters and Dad was promoted to first lieutenant.

During his time in Texas then, my father flew out of the same flight desk as the soon to be famous pilot Chuck Yeager. Chuck Yeager would be the first to fly at the speed of sound. Dad held the fuel consumption record for flying from Los Angeles to New York. The military must have been impressed with his flying abilities in Texas, as he was chosen to be a test pilot for a new prototype plane, the P-82B.

My parents would get back together in September of 1946.

Here is a letter he wrote to her after the September visit:

31 Oct. 1946

Dear Lynn:

The bed springs just stretched under my weight, and it was only 10:30 pm. After a short nap, a good meal and a poor show at the post theater titled, "A Wife Wanted", I'm finally in bed, so as you see, I'm being a very good boy for you. You might appreciate these few lines before I drop off to sleep.

Say, what's that scented stuff you have in your letter? It is liable to lure me to the source.

The day after you left for Philadelphia I flew down to the Gulf and had to remain overnight due to bad weather conditions. Got back on Friday night at about 10:30 pm, went to bed, and started home about nine o'clock the next morning so there, I'm all accounted for.

Darn, the way I feel right now I wish you were here to be the recipient of my fondest affection and passion, legally that is.

The last letter should have informed you about my trip to Cleveland this weekend and the reason, so I won't reiterate. If I don't get that assignment, we'll get a chance to see if it's the person or the uniform you're after. The family wants to meet you so maybe sometime in the future we can arrange to have you visit the little town of New Haven or come out to Cleveland.

Good night, Dream Girl,

—Love, Gene

He was transferred to Cincinnati, Ohio and flew out of Wright

Patterson Airfield in Dayton, Ohio. This plane, the P-82B would be renamed an F-82B just months later. During WWII all fighter planes were designated P for 'pursuit' but after WWII the new Air Force decided to change the designation to F for 'fighter'. During the time he was flying the F-82B, he was also flying the following planes at Wright Patterson, C4-6E, P-82, B-25J, P-61C, B17G, P-61C, C-82A, AT-6F and C-45F. The F82-B was two P-51 planes welded together to look very much like the P-38 he had flown in WWII. It had two fuselages and two cockpits.

My father would fly around the state of Ohio working out the kinks to improve this prototype plane. Dayton is on the west side of Ohio and the farm and family where he had grown up was on the northeast side of Ohio. While he was testing this plane, he'd fly over the farm and tilt the wings of the plane to let his family know he was home. After he landed back at Dayton Airfield, he'd sometimes get a ride all the way back to Plymouth to visit with everyone, of course he was the hero of the moment and had so much to share about the prototype. He was the main test pilot for this plane from March through October 1946 according to his Flight Log Records. Unfortunately, when the day came to introduce the new F-82B to the world, a colonel stepped up to take the glory. My father, who had put the time, talent, and effort into developing the plane was dismissed and the colonel made the final flight. Many of my paternal family members have been to the Air Force Museum at Wright Patterson to see the prototype that my father tested for the Air Force, it has Betty Jo painted on the side, but his family members say it should have been named Helen, after my mother.

The F-82B (formerly P-82B)

Once the standard long-range, high-altitude escort fighter for the U.S. Air Force, the North American Aviation P-82 Twin Mustang was the climax of the famous World War II P-51 Mustang series. North American produced 250 of the double-fuselage airplanes for the Air Force, embracing three versions of the Twin Mustang then in service, the P-82E, P-82F and P-82G. They were ordered too late for World War II, however.

The versatile P-82 made it potentially adaptable to a wide variety of roles—fighter, long-range escort, long-range reconnaissance aircraft, night fighter, attack bomber, rocket fighter and interceptor.

With a speed of more than 475 mph (764 kph), the Twin Mustang had a combat range of more than 1,600 miles (2,574 kilometers) with full armament. Range could be extended using external drop tanks on the wings.

The Proposal

My mother would take a train to Ohio to meet Dad's family in late November of 1946 and that is when my father proposed to her, and they set a wedding date for January of 1947.

Wedding bells rang in Philadelphia on January 18, 1947. My father

This is a photo of my cousins, Uncle Clyde's grandchildren, at the National Museum of the U.S. Air Force at Wright Patterson Air Force Base outside Dayton, OH. Clyde would watch his brother Gene fly this plane over the farm where they both grew up. Many Phillips family members would visit this museum to share the stories of my dad, their Uncle Gene.

had left the military at the end of 1946, but he was allowed to wear his uniform for their wedding. They immediately moved to Ohio. But living in Ohio did not agree with my city-raised, street-smart mother. The job opportunities for Dad were also not great in Ohio at that time. My father loved his family and that area of Ohio, but he was devoted to my mother. Mother missed the city life, and she could see that her new husband was smart and needed more of a challenge.

Adjustments were made. They moved to Philadelphia and lived with my Grandmother Henrietta for a while. This way they could work and save up for a home. My father, coming from a practical family, felt the only option was to purchase a home when they could afford one. They didn't have much money, so as part of their plan to increase his earning capacity, Dad enrolled at a local university to get a degree in Engineering. They found out, soon after the move, that my mother was pregnant.

On Christmas Eve of 1947 my mother went into labor, and my father rushed her to the hospital. My parents were so excited to be welcoming their first child to the world. They had chosen a name for a girl and one for a boy. My father's past POW experience influenced the names they had chosen for a child; a boy would be Roger Bruce Phillips. He would be named for the mastermind of the escape from Stalag Luft III, Roger Bushell. Mother's labor went horribly wrong. She was having a challenging time with the birth. The baby was coming in the breach position and the doctor should have performed a C-section delivery, but he didn't, and things worsened. She finally gave birth to a son. Sadly, Roger Bruce Phillips died at about five hours old from the trauma of a bad delivery. Mother was devastated. The doctor had given her gas to put her out. She never got to see or hold him. She stayed in the hospital recovering from the botched delivery. My father buried his son. My grandmother Henrietta dressed the baby in the handmaid christening gown my mother had made for her first child. Mom would never visit his grave. She only looked forward to having more children.

After burying his first son, Father looked to the sky. He was able

The wedding party, L-R: Mary Sheehan (my godmother); Mamie Sheehan, my great aunt; Tony Nadolski, Mother's brother; Helen; Gene; and Thom Phillips, my father's brother.

to petition the U.S. military to fly in the Reserves. Flying was his love and the Reserves provided extra money. With his stellar flying record, the military wasted no time getting him in. He was back in an airplane by March of 1948. This time he was flying out of the air base in Reading, Pennsylvania, flying the T-6C and T-6D (the T stands for Trainer). He flew each month and was taking classes at Temple University and driving a cab. My parents had saved up enough money to put a down payment on a home in Philadelphia. It was in a neighborhood near the Tacony Palmyra Bridge and across the street from the Magnolia Cemetery.

Because of my mother's difficult labor and delivery, she had pain in her abdominal area. She had a hard time standing up straight from the pain. The doctor was not sure she would be able to conceive another child. She was determined to move on. She got a job working at the Nabisco Factory in Philadelphia taking the hot cookies off the pans. It kept her mind off her abdominal pain. Having a family was important to my mother. She had been the youngest child of parents who lived apart. She was raised by her mother and only visited her father sporadically. Unfortunately, she was also picked on by many in the city who considered her not good enough. My mom wanted to prove she could be just as good as the happiest family she knew. The second most important thing to her was education. She would make sure her husband and children had the best in that regard. Finally, she got some news she longed for, she was pregnant again with me; and I was due in August of 1949.

2

My Arrival and the Korean War

MOTHER WENT INTO LABOR WHILE my dad was driving for the cab company, so their neighbor took her to the hospital. My father met her there. I was born on August 16, 1949, in Philadelphia at Frankfort Hospital (now Jefferson Frankford Hospital), at 11:34 p.m. I weighed eight pounds and three and half ounces, twenty inches long. My parents named me Marilyn Jean Phillips. Marilyn was a combination of Mary (from my cousin Mary Sheehan), and my mother was called Lynn (a short version for Helen). My middle name is a female version of Eugene, in honor of my father. My parents were very happy to see me. Mom made me an exquisite gown which I wore for my christening on September 4, 1949. I was christened at St. Leo's Catholic Church in Philadelphia. My mother's family had not had a baby in the family for fourteen years before I showed up. My father wrote home to his mother in Ohio that I had arrived. I was treated like a princess and carried everywhere. I was always dressed in the most stylish dresses of the time, each homemade by my mother.

I came into this world not knowing that world events would dramatically influence my life. I was born in the City of Brotherly Love.

A city where the Declaration of Independence from Great Britain was signed by the founding fathers of the U.S.

Our first president, George Washington, had lived in Philadelphia during his two terms of office. The Liberty Bell was rung in this town and Betsy Ross had sewn the first U.S. flag in this city. For a brief period, Philadelphia was the capital of the Unite States.

On June 25, 1950, The Korean War broke out. It was termed a police action as the American people had experienced the world wars for too long and too recently. With my father's reserve status, he was recalled to the military.

When World War II ended, the United States accepted the surrender of the Japanese in Korea south of the 38th parallel, while the Soviet Union accepted the Japanese surrender north of that line. Although the Western Allies intended Korea to become an independent democracy, the Soviet Union had other plans.

When North Korea invaded in June 1950, the United States Air Force (USAF) was, in the words of Chief of Staff Gen. Hoyt Vandenberg, a "shoestring air force." In the Far East, the USAF was equipped for the air defense of Japan but had inadequate resources for combat on the nearby Korean peninsula. To increase its strength, the Air Force mobilized its only available resources – thousands of Air Force Reserve and Air National Guard Airmen. Most were World War II veterans and their training and experience proved invaluable to the war effort.

Between 1950 and 1953, the USAF called up 146,683 Air Force Reservists and 46,413 National Guardsmen to fight the war in Korea and fill Cold War needs by increasing forces around the world. This number was nearly equally divided between officers and enlisted personnel.

Reservists and National Guard Air personnel filled roles in every part of the USAF during the war, from combat flying in bombers and fighters, to airlift and rescue units. Included were all ground support jobs at forward and rear bases in the Far East and elsewhere. Mobilization for Korea led to greater equality and cooperation among active duty and reserve forces because Guard and Reserve Airmen played an essential part in the young U.S. Air Force's success as a combat-tested service.

With separate governments established in both halves of Korea, North and South, the Soviets announced their intention to leave the country and challenged the United States to do the same. After training a small national force for internal security in South Korea, the United States departed, leaving only a few military advisors. In the north, the Soviets oversaw the creation of the well-trained and well-equipped North Korean People's Army, complete with Soviet tanks, heavy artillery, and aircraft. After guaranteeing the military superiority of North Korea, the Soviets left in 1949. Less than a year later, border skirmishes between north and south exploded into all-out war with the North Korean invasion of South Korea on June 25, 1950.

The United States was committed to defending South Korea against Communist aggression. Although the United States had no official treaty obligating it to South Korea, President Harry Truman ordered U.S. forces stationed in the Far East, into action on June 27. Three days later, Truman authorized air attacks into North Korea. Concurrently, he began to mobilize reserves for the coming battles.

A letter arrived at our home on March 15, 1951, from President Truman, calling up my father's reserve unit. My mother called the day that letter arrived a "dark day." My father had almost finished his college degree but obviously completing it would be on hold. That letter changed her life drastically, but it also changed mine. I was twenty months old, born a civilian and now it all was about to take a dramatically different direction. My mother, amidst this news, was pregnant again, and due in mid-June.

My father got orders for Turner Air Force Base in Albany, Georgia. As part of the Second Air Force 31st Air Base Group, his assignment would become flying missions protecting the Korean Islands. Mom and I stayed in Philadelphia until her delivery date. Her family in Philadelphia was a great support for her and me.

L-R: Me, Mother and Dad. This was taken just before my father was recalled to active duty. My mother is pregnant.

* * *

The U.S. Air Force was only three years old as a separate service when North Korea invaded South Korea in the summer of 1950. These three years brought significant changes in technology and roles and tactics, marking the beginning of the modern Air Force.

After the U.S. Air Force became a separate service in 1947, it created new blue uniforms. Even so, Air Force personnel during the Korean War continued to wear U.S. Army Air Corps uniforms from existing stocks, including the famed "pinks and greens" clothing and "crush cap" hats from World War II. In some cases, Airmen wore a

L-R: "Pinks and greens" were a World War II nickname given to the uniforms by the soldiers because one of the sets of pants had a pink hue to them. My father in his new Air Force uniform holding me. This photo was taken outside our townhouse in Philadelphia. A WWII "Crush Cap."

combination of Army green and Air Force blue uniforms. This meant that my father had to buy a new uniform. My parents didn't have the money at that time and borrowed it from my grandmother until my father's new status could pay it back.

An interesting result of this uniform change was the nickname "Brown-shoe Air Force." The old Army uniform had brown shoes, while the new Air Force blue uniform had black shoes. So, Brown-shoe Air Force referred to the old U.S. Army Air Forces or to a person who had served in the United States Army Air Force (USAAF).

Although the U.S. Air Force provided the largest number of aircraft, U.S. Navy, Marine and Army Aviation, along with fifteen United Nation (UN) partners and the budding South Korean Air Force, also contributed to the fight. The U.S. force consisted of aviation units from the USAF, Navy, Marines and Army. The small South Korean Air Force started the war unable to contribute combat forces, but with USAF assistance and equipment, fielded combat forces as the war progressed. Great Britain, Australia and South Africa sent combat air units, while Greece, Canada, Thailand, and the Philippines sent airlift units to Korea. Moreover, some of these countries sent aircrews to fly in USAF units on exchange duty.

* * *

My father was assigned to the second Air Force 31st Air Base Group from March to July that year. In August he is assigned to the 308th Fighter Escort Squadron flying a jet, F-84E, at Turner Air Force Base (AFB) in Albany, Georgia. He was able to return home to Philadelphia for my mother's delivery. She gave birth on June 20, 1951, to a ten-pound baby boy, my brother Eugene Lee Phillips. His name Lee was from another WWII buddy of my father. He would be called Lee and not Eugene by everyone. Lee and I were born at the same hospital. My parents were thrilled to have both a girl and a boy. Soon after my brother's birth, my father was sent back to Yokota, Japan, to fly missions defending the Korean Islands. In September he returned to Philadelphia, this time to pack our belongings and move his family to our first military assignment, Turner Air Force Base in Albany, Georgia. What I didn't know was this would be the beginning of many moves for me. I would never know a hometown or being around the same friends growing up.

My first memories of my life are during this time in Albany, GA. I have photos and stories of my life in Philadelphia that my parents shared with me as I got older, but it was in Albany that my first memories appear in my mind. Now mind you, Albany was a very southern town with small homes and dirt roads. My brother Lee, a newborn, slept in a dresser drawer until we had a chance to get a crib set up. We lived close to Turner AFB. Mom, being raised in a big city with a lot of public transportation, did not know how to drive a car. My father had to teach her before he left to go back to Japan. She learned slowly only by making right hand turns. But apparently if you keep making right turns you will eventually go left.

My grandmother Henrietta, Nannie as I called her, was living with us when Dad had to go to MacDill AFB in Tampa, Florida. He took all of us with him. We traveled to St. Petersburg, Florida, not far from Tampa, and stayed in a small hotel near the beach. Nannie was so excited to see orange trees and she loved the beach.

During that year in South Georgia, I got my first scar. Even though I was only three years old I remember the incident. I loved playing in a neighbor's sand box. Usually there were several kids in that sandbox, but that day I was alone. A boy about seven years old wearing cowboy boots on a bicycle rode up to the sandbox and told me to go home. So, I got up and started home. But then he said, "Stop," told me to turn around and lay down on the ground so he could run over me with his bicycle. I told him, "I'm not going to lay down so you can run over me."

Well, he dropped his bike on the ground and came stomping toward me, pushed me down and stepped on me just below my neck. I got up and ran home. I knew he was trouble and the faster I could get away from him the better. By the time I got home, my upper chest was swelling up. My mother realized I needed to go the hospital. She asked what happened and I told her the best I could. Apparently when he had stepped on me with his cowboy boot, he caused a hematoma and they had to operate on me to remove it. It left me with a scar on my *décolleté* that I still have.

* * *

We lived in a neighborhood with lots of pecan trees and because the homes were tiny, we spent a lot of time outside. We would spend time with activities under the shade of those huge pecan trees. The trees also provided us with some tasty treats. When my grandmother

Nannie stayed with us, she would have Lee and I pick up the pecans from the ground and put them in a sack. Then she would spend time cracking the pecans and separating the nuts from the shell, a very tedious and slow process, but worth the time. I still love the taste of sweet pecans.

I remember being outside during the humid summer nights and catching fireflies in a jar with holes punched in the lid. They were so pretty to watch in that jar and flying around the back yard in the dark. I remember the smell of the humid air and a great feeling of fun! It was ridiculously hot in Albany in the summer, and we had no air conditioning in our small rental house. I have photos of Lee and I covered in prickly heat rash. Most of the military families lived around each other since there was no military base housing at the time. I played with the other children in the neighborhood, many of whom, like me, were children of military pilots. During the day we played outside and could hear the jets passing overhead. Those early years defined me. I was keenly aware of my surroundings and picked up a lot of attitudes from my father. We had a small TV in our home, but many families did not back then. Dad loved music and played the harmonica. We sang and danced. My father always discussed the events of the world. His philosophy and attitudes would eventually become mine.

I have fond memories of Albany. I remember celebrating Christmas in November. My father had to be away in December so we celebrated when we could. I had seen wrapped presents in Christmas paper in the closet, where I guess my mother thought she had hidden them. I figured then that the Santa story wasn't all it was cracked up to be. I still felt it was a great time for family to be together and celebrate! What kid doesn't like presents? Mom's family from Philadelphia and some members of Dad's family also came for visits.

*　*　*

The Korean Conflict lasted from 1950-1953. Turner AFB in Albany, GA, became Strategic Air Command (SAC) in 1950 and in July of 1952 the 468th Strategic Fighter Squadron

Albany, GA, and the 468th Strategic Fighter Squadron. My father is third from the left in the first standing row.

Planning to reorganize for a separate and independent post-war U.S. Air Force had begun by the fall of 1945, with the reorganization of the Army and the Air Force.

In January 1946, Generals Eisenhower and Spaatz agreed on an Air Force organization composed of the SAC, the Air Defense Command, the Tactical Air Command, the Air Transport Command and the supporting Air Technical Service Command, Air Training Command, the Air University, and the Air Force Center, as well as the establishment and transfer of troops to the USAF.

The USAF primarily used three jets to fight the Korean War. The F-80 Shooting Star from Lockheed held the line in the initial stages of the conflict, handling a wide array of missions. The North American F-86 Sabre then took control of the skies and dominated over "MiG Alley." But there was a third jet—one that proved to also be very valuable not only in Korea, but for the North Atlantic Treaty Organization (NATO) in general.

The jet was the Republic F-84 Thunderjet. In a way, it makes sense that Lockheed, Republic, and North American all developed an impactful airframe. After all, each of these manufacturers was responsible for a classic, WWII-era plane (the P-38, the P-47, and the P-51, respectively) that arguably filled the same roles as these more-advanced jets did in Korea. The P-38 and F-80 held the line early in their respective wars, while the F-84 and F-86 split the ground-attack and air-superiority duties the way the P-47 and P-51 did before them.

The F-84, however, gets a lot less attention than its contemporaries in discussions about the Korean War. As a ground-attack plane, it played a crucial role on the battlefield. The simple fact is, however, that dogfights sell newspapers. While air-superiority planes were making headlines, ground-attack planes were doing the real heavy lifting — and the F-84 did a lot of lifting in Korea.

The F-84 Thunderjet was the plane my father flew. As small as I was then, Mom hearing and seeing these planes and others overhead, would point up at the sky and say, "There is your daddy!" I didn't really understand what she meant. I probably thought she meant Dad was a bird. The sound of those jets was always the sound of home and safety for me. No matter where I am if I hear a jet, I get an uplifting feeling.

Operation Fox Peter One

I remember one time in particular my mother dressed Lee and I up in our best outfits and took us to the base airfield where we watched my dad walk into the building in his flight suit. He still had his oxygen mask hanging on one side of his face and marks on his face from where the mask had been. He waved to us, and we had to wait for him to finish with debriefing before we could see him and give him a hug. I'm sure he had just landed from some important flight, but I was too small to know what that may have been.

SAC was both a United States Department of Defense (DoD) Specified Command and a USAF Major Command responsible for Cold War command and control of two of the three components of the U.S. military's strategic nuclear strike forces, the so-called "nuclear triad", with SAC having control of land-based strategic bomber aircraft and intercontinental ballistic missiles (ICBMs) and the third leg of the triad being submarine-launched ballistic missiles of the U.S. Navy.

SAC also operated all strategic reconnaissance aircraft, all strategic airborne command post aircraft, and all USAF aerials refueling aircraft, to include those in the Air Force Reserve and Air National Guard (ANG).

On June 26, 1952, the 31st Fighter Escort Wing stationed at Turner Air Force Base was given orders to initiate Operation Fox Peter One. This operation called for the squadron to make a mass air relocation to Japan. With only eight days to prepare for the mission, Turner Air Force Base, under the leadership of Col. David C. Schilling, launched the operation on July 4, 1952, which included movement of 57 F-84G Thunderjets and four transport planes of key administrative and maintenance personnel.

Misawa, Japan, 1953. My father is sitting and looking up, second from the right.

The first leg of the trip was from Turner Field to Travis Air Force Base in California. The air movement made one stop midway into the six-hour and forty-five-minute trip to refuel on the KB-29 tanker. The second part of the journey would involve crossing the North Pacific, and it was determined that this part of the mission would be broken down into three squadrons: 307th, 308th, and 309th. Dad was part of the 308th.

On July 6, 1952, units 307 and 308 left Travis AFB en route to Hickam Air Base in Hawaii. Both units refueled in midair, however, the 307th squadron under Col. Schilling's command was forced to return to Travis after they sustained substantial damage to a piece of refueling equipment. After five hours and twenty-seven minutes the 308th squadron, under the direction of Major Robert J. Keen, successfully landed at Hickam Air Base in Hawaii.

Major Keen was recognized as the first pilot to make the Travis to Hickam flight in a single engine jet employing air to air refueling and the first to lead an entire squadron across the Pacific. This flight was considered the longest mass nonstop flight over water by jet fighters.

On July 7, 1952, Col. Schilling made his second attempt to cross the North Pacific, and this time his team was successful in their midair refueling and landed at Hickam in just under six hours. Col. William D. Dunham led the third (309th) squadron of Thunderjets to Hickam on July 8th.

The jet planes were at full altitude 30,000 to 40,000 feet high. Pilots wear oxygen masks at this altitude. My father's mask lost oxygen. He radioed the leader and requested permission to leave formation and return to base. To stay alive and conscious was going to be a challenge. If he lost consciousness the plane would crash. This situation was dangerous. He took off the oxygen mask to breathe the air in the cockpit as he slowly dropped down in altitude to pop the canopy off his plane so he could breathe and keep control of the aircraft. Dropping down to 10,000 feet in altitude would take about eight minutes. He popped the canopy, and it flew off and he continued to his destination flying a plane with just the front wind shield. It would be like flying the old biplanes or like driving a convertible car. It is very windy. It was a smart thing to do as he saved himself and his plane. He would land and get another plane to finish the mission with the rest of the fighter wing.

After a few days of maintenance on the aircraft, the 31st Fighter Escort Wing resumed their trip from Hawaii to Midway on July 10th. This flight was completed in two hours and fifty-five minutes.

The following day, the troops took off from Midway en route to Wake Island. During takeoff, the unit encountered a large flock of birds (terns, gooneys, and frigate) that were sucked into the powerful jet engines. Even though some 150 birds were lost, none of the fighter jets incurred any damage. It took one hour and fifty-five minutes to arrive at Wake Island. Later that same day on July 11th, the squadron flew on to Eniwetok. This leg of the trip only took one hour and ten minutes to complete.

Spending two days at Eniwetok, the en route maintenance support prepared the jets with two Jet-Assisted Takeoff (JATO) bottles (bottle rockets) to take off on July 13th. JATO bottles were required because of the short runway at Eniwetok. The flight from Eniwetok to Guam took three hours and eight minutes.

From Guam the crew would then fly to Iwo Jima on July 15, 1952. It was on this date that the unit suffered a terrible loss. As Lt. Col. Elmer G. Da Rosa made his approach to land, a section of his aircraft exploded sending the mighty fighter jet earthward. Da Rosa, one of the most popular pilots in the wing, was killed in this incident.

Leaving Iwo Jima on July 16, the Thunderjets flew to Yokota Air Base in one hour and fifty-six minutes. Due to heavy fog and torrential rains, the final leg of the trip was delayed for two days. Finally, on July 20, the 31st Fighter Escort Wing arrived at Misawa after an hour-and-ten-minute flight. Operation Fox Peter One was successfully completed, and the flight would become historical as it was the following:

- First mass movement of jet fighters across the Pacific.
- First mass midair refueling movement of jet fighters.

- Longest mass movement of a complete jet fighter wing by air.
- Longest mass nonstop over water flight by jet fighters. (California to Hawaii)

The flight would not have been so successful had it not been for the dedication and expertise of the en route maintenance teams.

The 31st Fighter Escort Wing would not return to Turner Air Force Base until the latter part of September. The first crew flew back to Turner on September 22, 1952. The remaining crews flew back the first part of October. A reception was given as well as a three-day reprieve, but by late October, the Wing had resumed business as usual at Turner Field.

The sheer magnitude of this accomplishment was sufficient to name the 31st Fighter Escort Wing as the recipient of the first Air Force Outstanding Unit Award. The wing commander, Colonel David C. Schilling, won the Air Force Association Trophy, which was later named after him. This movement included the longest over water flight attempted to that date and was the first trans-Pacific mass flight of jet aircraft. As an encore, on August 20, 1953, Col. Schilling led a flight of eight F-84s on a ten and a half-hour nonstop flight from Turner Field to Nouasseur Air Base, French Morocco. This successful flight culminated in the 40th Air Division of the SAC receiving the Mackay Trophy in 1953.

American Policies and The Cold War

I would grow up not really being aware of how dangerous my father's job was. He would constantly be in the "danger zone." Military aircraft must operate in an array of situations where the threats are numerous, such as in environments that have anti-aircraft artillery, air defense forces and warfare capabilities. During training exercises, military aviation tries to simulate adverse environments as accurately as possible to maintain hazardous levels. My father would never go into detail about dangerous incidents. It was better for my mother and us kids not to know.

When my father got back from Japan in October 1952 we moved to another small house in Albany near the base. My parents bought this house and a new car. This new home was in a housing area known as Pecan Haven. We had previously lived in two different small rental homes around the base from 1951-1952 in a housing area known as Turner City. I was getting used to moving. My parents, seeing that the home they had purchased in Philadelphia was not going to be a permanent location for our family decided to sell the house in Philadelphia. My mom, my brother and I moved back there to get the house sold in 1953, while Dad went back to Japan. He mostly flew missions out of Yokota, Japan. We used the money from that sale to buy a bigger home in Albany. In the new home, I had my own room. The house even had an air-conditioner in the window of the living area. My father liked to invest in buying a home because he felt renting was not financially prudent, from 1949-1955 I would move six times and it was just the beginning.

The other thing I was becoming aware of was that world events and the U.S. presidential administrations would determine where we were stationed and how we lived. In 1952 Dwight D. Eisenhower was elected president of the U.S. He had been the Supreme Commander of the Allied Forces against Germany and Italy during WWII. In 1950 he was selected to become Supreme Allied Commander of NATO. One of the promises he ran his presidential campaign on was to get the U.S. out of Korea. Eisenhower was inaugurated in January of 1953 and The Korean Conflict ended on July 27 of that year. However, he would get the U.S. involved in another conflict that would affect my family's future: Vietnam.

At an early age I would hear discussions that I didn't understand at four or five years old, but I did hear names of leaders repeated over and over. Eisenhower was the name I was hearing. During that year I would learn a critical lesson. One day my mother was looking out the front window of our home in Albany. She stared at a car coming down the street. Her eyes never left that car, but she said to me, "Pray that car does not stop at our house, because if it does it means your daddy is dead." My attention went to that car. It passed our house and we both stared at it until it finally came to a house down the street. My playmates lived there. Mom was right my playmate's father was killed while flying target work in Avon Park. Avon Park was located near MacDill AFB in Tampa. My playmate, her sisters and mother would move away soon after. Back then, many women were full-time mothers. These women and their children would move back in with their parents. I was too young to know what happened to them, but their life and mine changed again. At that early age, I could in no way fully understood that my father's job protecting the U.S. was a family obligation. I did know that we had to keep moving and making changes in our lives.

National and strategic intelligence came mainly from espionage. With the introduction of aerial reconnaissance deep behind enemy lines, the tools of a modern era would contribute to shaping strategy and assessing enemy intentions. They learned that access to accurate and timely information was essential to gain advantage in battle. Command and control came to depend on constantly collected intelligence from a rapidly expanding list of sources to support decisions from the planning stages to their execution.

My father also flew the F-84 Thunderflash. This jet was equipped with cameras only. It was used for reconnaissance, taking photos for information on events happening around the world. No soldier goes out alone, except a reconnaissance pilot. They gather information that is used by the Central Intelligence Agency (CIA) and other military intelligence agencies. These agencies were also as new as the Air Force. Because Dad flew many reconnaissance, day, and night missions, he had top secret clearance. He had access to information that no one wanted the U.S. or the free world to have. He would meet with these CIA operatives. Coming out of WWII, the advance of Communism was a threat to the free world and America. In WWII Russia was one of the allies against Germany and Japan. However, at the end of the war Communist Russia came in and took over almost half of European countries. The people of these countries, Poland, Hungary, and parts of Germany, did not have freedom.

"We must build a new world, a far better world —
one in which the eternal dignity of man is respected."
—President Harry S. Truman, 1945

* * *

The United States dominated global affairs in the years immediately after World War II. U.S. leaders wanted to maintain the democratic structure they had defended at tremendous cost and to share the benefits of prosperity as widely as possible. For them, as publisher Henry Luce of *Time Magazine* said, this was the "American Century."

What Was the Cold War?

The Cold War was the most important political issue of the early post-war period. It grew out of longstanding disagreements between the Soviet Union and the United States. In 1918 American troops participated in allied intervention in Russia on behalf of anti-Bolshevik forces. American diplomatic recognition of the Bolshevik regime did not come until 1933. Even then, suspicions persisted. During World War II, however, the two countries found themselves allied and thus ignored their differences to counter the Nazi threat.

At the war's end, antagonisms surfaced again. The United States hoped to share with other countries its conception of liberty, equality, and democracy. With the rest of the world in turmoil, struggling with civil wars and disintegrating empires, the nation hoped to provide the stability to make peaceful reconstruction possible. Unable to forget the specter of the Great Depression (1929-1940), America now fostered its familiar position of free trade, and sought to eliminate trade barriers both to create markets for American agricultural and industrial products, and to ensure the ability of West European nations to export, to generate economic growth and rebuild their economies. Reduced trade barriers, it was believed, would promote economic growth at home and abroad, and bolster stability with U.S. friends and allies.

The Soviet Union had its own agenda. The Russian historical tradition of centralized, autocratic government contrasted with the American emphasis on democracy. Marxist-Leninist ideology had been downplayed during the war but still guided Soviet policy. Devastated by the struggle in which twenty million Soviet citizens had died, the Soviet Union was intent on rebuilding and on protecting itself from another such terrible conflict. The Soviets were particularly concerned about another invasion of their territory from the west. The United States had declared the restoration of independence and self-government to Poland, Czechoslovakia, and the other countries of Central and Eastern Europe one of its war aims.

Harry Truman succeeded Franklin D. Roosevelt as the American president before the end of the war. An unpretentious man who had previously served as a Democratic senator from Missouri, then as vice president, Truman initially felt ill-prepared to govern the United States. Roosevelt had not confided in him about complex post-war issues, and he had little prior experience in international affairs. "I'm not big enough for this job," he told a former colleague.

But Truman responded quickly to new challenges. Impulsively, he proved willing to make quick decisions about the problems he faced. A sign on his White House desk, since made famous in American politics, read "The Buck Stops Here," and reflected his willingness to take responsibility for his actions. His judgments about how to respond to the Soviet Union had an important impact on the early Cold War.

The Truman Doctrine

Containment of the Soviet Union became American policy in the post-war years. In a statement that came to be known as the Truman Doctrine, he declared, "I believe that it must be the policy of the United States to support free peoples who are resisting subjugation by armed minorities or by outside pressures."

Pilots were used for many purposes during this time. My father, by this time, was also a flight instructor. One of his reconnaissance students was Francis Gary Powers in the early 1950s at Turner AFB in Albany, GA. The name of Francis Gary Powers later would become part of history with the 1960 U-2 spy plane incident. Powers was shot down over Russian air space during a reconnaissance mission for the CIA. In 2015 a movie starring Tom Hanks, titled *Bridge of Spies,* was about how an American lawyer would broker the trade of a Russian prisoner for Powers. Powers would be exchanged for the Russian prisoner as both walked from opposite sides across a bridge.

The presence in our lives of people, like Powers, who were world figures — and those who would become world figures — would continue for the rest of my life. Military life forced me to size up a situation and adapt quickly, and to respect people from all walks of life, even world figures.

My Grandmother's Family Affected by Communist Aggression

In 1913 when my grandmother Henrietta (Nannie), had come to the U.S. from Eastern Poland, she left her father Adam behind as well as her sister, Joanna. After WWI and up until WWII she wrote to them, and they wrote to her. After the Communist Party invaded Poland, at the beginning of WWII, she never heard from them again. She never knew their fate.

This is one story that may explain what happened to them. The town of Katyn in Eastern Poland is an example of truly brutal massacres committed by Soviet leader Joseph Stalin during WWII.

Nazi Germany and the Soviet Union each invaded Poland in September of 1939, having divided the country into separate spheres of influence under the Molotov-Ribbentrop Pact. While the Germans began a massacre of Jews and Poles in Western-occupied Poland, the Red Army arrested and imprisoned thousands of Polish military officers, policemen, and intelligentsia (intellectual leaders) during their occupation of Eastern Poland. Prisoners-of-war and civilian internees captured by the Soviets were placed in several camps in the western part of the nation, run by the Soviet People's Commissariat for Internal

Affairs, or NKVD, a predecessor organization to the modern FSB- camps including Kozielsk, Ostashkov, and Starobielsk.

In April 1943, in the Katyn Forest near Smolensk in the Soviet Union, occupying German troops discovered eight large graves containing the remains of thousands of the Polish Army officers and intellectual leaders who had been interned at the POW camp at Kozielsk. Bodies of the prisoners who had been housed at Ostashkov and Starobielsk were discovered near Piatykhatky and Mednoye, respectively. Collectively, these murders are known as the Katyn Forest Massacre.

An internationally staffed medical commission organized by the Germans excavated the area in early spring 1943. As the excavation progressed, the Germans brought in several groups of observers, including some American prisoners-of-war. This commission determined that the massacre occurred in 1940, when the area was under Soviet control - a determination which was then used as a propaganda tool intended to disrupt the alliance between the U.S., Great Britain, and the Soviet Union. This effort was successful in part, as Polish intelligence sources immediately blamed the Soviets for the atrocities, leading to a break in diplomatic relations between Poland and the USSR.

After their recapture of Smolensk in the autumn of 1943, the Soviet government organized its own excavation. This second enquiry concluded that the Polish prisoners-of-war had been captured and executed by invading German units in August 1941.

The official American response at the time was one of non-involvement. In a June 1943 a telegram to Britain's Prime Minister Winston Churchill from President Roosevelt expressed approval that the British approach to Stalin was grounded "upon the obvious necessity of creating the most favorable conditions for bringing the full weight of the Armed Forces of all the United Nations to bear upon the common enemy...Winning the war is the paramount objective for all of us. For this unity is necessary."

Later, on September 18, 1951, the United States House of Representatives established the Select Committee to Investigate and Study of the Facts, Evidence, and Circumstances of the Katyn Forest Massacre, known as the Madden Committee after its chairman, Rep.

Ray J. Madden of Indiana. The committee assembled records relating to the massacre and its aftermath, including records from the files of the State and War Departments, in addition to hearing extensive witness testimony. Their purpose was to determine which nation was responsible for the atrocities. This story may explain the fate of my grandmother Henrietta's father and sister. However, there were other incidents in Poland that were just as heinous, also committed by the Russians under Stalin.

World War Two ended to give birth to the Cold War. Little did my father know when he marched out of Stalag Luft III on that cold January night in 1945, that his life would become entwined with a new war in that region. The Russians came into the Stalag Luft III camp and destroyed what was left after the Nazi's burned it as the prisoners marched out. However, the tunnels dug by the POWs under the camp survived.

Around the time of the Bolshevik Revolution in Russia, the Baltic Wars, and other political unrest in the area, many of Grandmother Henrietta's family started immigrating to the U.S. She left Poland at age sixteen and came to the U.S. by herself. Her family in the U.S. would eventually introduce her to a Lithuanian man ten years older and they would marry. After eight years of marriage and two children she asked him to leave. As her children grew up and moved into their own places, she lived with them.

My mom was very dependent on my grandmother for help with my brother and I, and with keeping the house in order and clean. Mom had a lot of good qualities but organizing and cleaning were not among them. She and my grandmother would speak Polish to each other when they didn't want my brother and I to know what they were saying. I know they were keeping secrets from me when they did this, and I would often say, "You are *taking* funny." Well, that's how it sounded to me.

With all the moving around Lee and I only had each other most of the time and we became close, as siblings and playmates, and learned to get over our differences quickly.

Life in Albany, GA

I remember my mother taking Lee and myself to the Piggly Wiggly Grocery store in Albany. I never forgot the name of this store because I always thought about the face of the pig on the front of the store! Mom would walk to the store with a red wagon which Lee and I got to ride in. When we arrived at the store, she would park Lee, me, and the red wagon next to the Coca-Cola machine and buy one Coke bottle for us to share. She would instruct us to sit next to the machine and share our soda until she returned. Lee and I would sit as instructed until she finished her shopping. Lee and I did have squabbles from time to time. My mother would load the groceries into the red wagon and Lee, and I would have to walk home.

My parents often entertained the new pilots and their wives at our home. Lee and I would be sent to a room with Nannie as the party went on. We would sometimes be asked to come to the party to be introduced and maybe stay for a while before returning to our room. These were times when we could hear a lot of discussions about world events, and I would again hear names of people and events and missions that Dad and other pilots were involved. Francis Gary Powers and his wife were among the guests. During these events I got a feel for the character of these men. I was taking in a lot of information that would form my view of life. I did feel these men and my father were brave, like the cowboys in the popular TV shows of the time.

Growing up in the new SAC environment had its challenges and interesting stories. The U.S. Government built Air Force Bases for the military and their families. The Strategic Air Command was shortened to SAC. You would hear discussions of a SAC base being built, here and there. SAC was set up to protect the world against aggression of an unfavorable government. The U.S. government was trying to hold down costs by building one building to be used for religious services. It worked like this, On Saturday it was used as a synagogue, on Sunday it was used for Catholic and Protestant services. To do this, there were walls that turned around, or things were moved, so the arch that held the Torah for Jewish services and the altar for Catholic services were made movable. Everything worked well except for the name. The building was named, The SAC Religious Center but sounded like a sacrilegious center. My mother raised the concern with the Base Commander at the time, but I am not sure what happened.

One of the First Air Shows

In April of 1953 my father was promoted to captain. Promotions were important in the military as it meant more money, prestige, and responsibility. By September of that year, he was part of the National Air Show in Dayton, Ohio. He was the command pilot. This show was to exhibit the "U.S. Strength of Power" to our U.S. citizens and the world. The U.S. was a force and a beacon of hope for the world. The U.S. had saved Europe from WWI and WWII. The problem now was the Communist Bloc that had taken over countries in Europe at the end of WWII.

My father was filmed at the Air Show doing a JATO take-off in his jet. JATO stood for Jet-Assisted Take-off because jet engines were added to the plane. The plane takes off at a faster rate using less runway. This film was used for years on TV. In the early 1950s, TV was new and only had limited hours of operation during the day. The TV channel may sign on at 6:00 a.m. and sign off at 10:00 p.m. It would sign off playing the "National Anthem" and a clip featuring monuments including the Statue of Liberty, Lincoln Memorial and others. My father's JATO take-off clip from the 1953 National Air Show was part of that sign-off. Back in the 1950s, 1960s, and even into the 1970s, the movie theaters would feature pre-movie coming attractions starting with the *National Anthem*. The military base theaters that my family and I attended showed this same clip of my father's JATO take-off during the anthem.

There was a movie that came out at the same time as the 1953 National Air Show titled, *Sabre Jet*, starring Coleen Gray and Robert Stack. My father had gotten tickets to this movie, and his brothers, Clyde and Henry, and their wife and girlfriend came to see him in the Air Show and had seats to the movie premier that night in Dayton,

Ohio. My mother, Lee, and I were all so proud of my dad. This was the premiere of the movie, so all the stars were present at the theater that evening. The National Air Show was the pre-event that would lead to all the Air Shows throughout the country for years to come, eventually becoming the U.S. Air Force Thunderbirds.

* * *

My father went back to Japan and returned in June of 1954. When he returned, we took a family trip to Plymouth, Ohio, stopping in North Carolina to visit my Great Aunt Helen and Uncle Charles. The main event of the trip was the wedding of my Uncle Clyde and Mary Ellen. All six children of my Grandmother Elizabeth came for the wedding in Plymouth. My dad was the first of the children to serve in the military. His next younger brother Jim was in WWII, Thom never went into the military, Clyde went in for a short time, and the youngest Henry had just enlisted in the Army the previous November. My father's brother Clyde had been terribly ill when he was a teen and almost died. He had suffered a ruptured appendix that led to other problems. Everyone was here to celebrate this wedding union. People in rural Ohio in the 1950s married young—my Aunt Mary Ellen was only seventeen on her wedding day.

I turned five years old in August of 1954 and started kindergarten in Albany. Mom also put me in dance classes, taking both ballet and tap. I liked both school experiences. I remember a performance my kindergarten class did where my parents attended, and we sang a cute song about six white ducks. I struggled to keep up in the dance class but liked it anyway. Just as I was adjusting to going to classes and not playing with my brother all day, we got a new assignment of duty. My life, my school, my home was going to change again. My father got new orders in January 1955; we were moving to Brussels, Belgium.

Mother had to go to the library to look up Brussels, Belgium. She did not know where this place was and figured she had better study. The more she read the more she realized our family would now be front and center on the stage of world events. This assignment was going to take us over the Atlantic Ocean to a different country. She did not know anything about this country and had never been to Europe herself. My father's assignment this time was with the Embassy in Brussels. Making this move was a big deal. An embassy assignment meant new wardrobes for my parents and a new language for me and my brother.

Just after Father's orders for reassignment came, a letter from the President of the United States arrived in the mail. It read:

> White House
> Washington, D.C.
>
> Dear Service Men and Women and Dependents:
>
> As members of our Armed Forces stationed overseas, you and your dependents are representatives of the American people with the essential mission of building goodwill for our country.
>
> Service men and woman are the largest group of official U.S. personnel stationed in foreign countries. As a result, people form their personal attitudes toward our country and our American way of life to a great extent by what they see and hear about American service personnel and their dependents.
>
> As you serve abroad, the respect you show foreign laws and customs, your courteous regard for other ways of life, and your speech and manner help to mold the reputation of our country. Thus, you represent us all in bringing assurance to the people you meet that the United States is a friendly nation and one dedicated to the search for world peace and to the promotion of the well-being and the security of Nations.
>
> Your President and Commander-in-Chief,
> Dwight D. Eisenhower

When this letter arrived, my mother sat down with me, she read the letter to me and explained what it meant. I knew this move was a big deal but now I had to represent my country and I had better get this right. After all I had been hearing this name Eisenhower from my father and in conversations from all the adults at home and around. I know one thing, when Eisenhower told you what to do, you better do it and do a good job! Remember I turned five years old in August! I was young but this letter would serve me well for the rest of my military life and my life after.

We had to get our first passports, vaccinations and other shots. A few days before the photographer was to come out to our home and take our passport photo, I came down with chickenpox. I was covered from head to toe with pox. The military photographer came to our home, my mother asked him if he had had chickenpox, he replied that he had indeed. Then he looked around and decided to take the photos outside. He sat my mother in a chair with Lee and I on each side. All three of us in one passport photo that would be in one single passport. A few years later in Brussels the fact that all three of us were on one passport became a problem.

We had a thirty-day leave to get ready for this new assignment. My family took a trip to Philadelphia, PA, to see my mother's family. We knew we'd be gone for three years and would not be able to see them for that time. Our household belongings were packed and crated up in Albany, Georgia to be sent to Brussels.

In Albany we packed our mint-green Ford Vedette for a two-day driving trip to Philadelphia. Father, Mother, Nannie, Lee, and I started out on a new adventure. We arrived in Philadelphia on January 30th for our one-month leave. We stopped in Willow Grove where Nannie would live with her son, my Uncle Tony, Aunt Helen, and their daughter Vicky. We then drove into Philadelphia to stay with my cousin Mary and my Aunt Mamie. Aunt Mamie was Nannie's sister.

During this time in Philadelphia, my parents would go shopping for the list of gowns, cocktail dresses, suits, and other items they would need to be properly outfitted for embassy life. My cousin Mary was a year older than my mother and like a sister to her. Mary was also my godmother. Mary was not married and worked at American Telephone and Telegraph (AT&T) in the city. I called Mary-Godno. When I was younger and tried to say Godmother, it came out Godno.

She planned the best parties and trips. She was so excited to have us stay with her and her mother for a month. She would take over. She was very savvy and funny. I knew I was her little princess. She made me feel special. Friends and family came for parties and special events while we were in Philadelphia. We had tickets for plays and musical performances. She also had a TV in her house that never seemed to have problems with static. So much to watch, *The Howdy Doody Show* in the morning was my favorite. The show would open with, "Boys and Girls, what time is it? It's Howdy Doody time!" Lee and I would holler at the TV!

Shopping in Philadelphia was also fun. Mary and Mamie did not own a car. They traveled on public transportation. We would take the elevated train called the "El" and stop to have a root beer and a hot dog in the station.

My parents drove into the city to go shopping. My father bought suits and coats, and ties and shirts. My mother bought women's suits and formal dresses, and I even got a gown, for no special reason, just because.

During one of the days we were visiting, my godmother dressed Lee and I in our coats for a trip to see historic Philadelphia. We visited Independence Hall and saw the Liberty Bell that was rung to declare the U.S. independence from England, the house where Betsy Ross sewed the first U.S. flag, and Benjamin Franklin's grave in the center of the city. My mother grew up in Center City and knew all the famous sites. Lee and I were now old enough to start to understand this remarkable history.

After a month of friends and family events and shopping, the time came for us to leave for Belgium. We left Philadelphia with my godmother Mary. My father drove us all to Springfield, MA. It was a six-hour trip and my Aunt Mamie had packed us lunch. I thought it was so interesting that my Great Aunt Mamie would take all the bread out of the plastic sleeve and make sandwiches, usually bologna and mayonnaise, then she would put all the sandwiches back into the plastic sleeve for us to have lunch!

We finally arrived at Westover Air Force Base near Springfield, MA, and checked into the Westover Hotel, which was a military barracks with a fancy canopy front. We got two rooms; my godmother and I stayed in one and my mother, father and Lee stayed in the other. The next morning Dad drove our car to the New York City Port Authority to have it sent to Belgium by ship. While he was gone the rest of us went into the city to have lunch and do some more shopping. Apparently, my mother needed one more gown. She found this beautiful duchess satin gown and she looked gorgeous in it. When father returned from New York the next day, we took my godmother to the Greyhound bus station in Springfield and said our goodbyes. She was so sad. I guess for her it was like losing her family. She knew she would miss us for the next three years. I was not old enough to understand how long that would be, but she did.

* * *

On Saturday, March 5th, my mother, father, Lee, and I boarded a MATS (Military Air Transport Service) plane at Westover AFB and flew to the Azores. These military transport planes were propeller planes. They were not fancy and didn't have the finished interiors that you would find in civilian airline planes. We stayed overnight in the Azores, a small island in the Atlantic Ocean where the plane could refuel. The next day we boarded a Navy plane to fly to Frankfort, Germany. Navy transport planes had seats that faced backwards.

We arrived in Frankfort, Germany, on March 6, 1955. This was our first overseas adventure! I was about to be exposed to so much more than I had ever known in my short life. The Air Force still being quite new, found the morale of military personnel was better when the family stayed together. The morale of troops was—and is— a constant focus for the U.S. military. Morale is that conditioned quality in the individual soldier and in the unit of command, which holds the soldier, holds the unit, to the performance of duty despite every opposing force or influence. Family members of military that travel with the military members are called "dependents." Sometimes kids in military families were called BRATS, this was an old acronym for British Regiment Attached Traveler. It somehow became associated with military kids like me. In the case of traveling to Brussels, I guess Lee and I were BRATS.

3

Belgian Embassy:
March 1955 – November 1957

CONTAINMENT OF THE SOVIET UNION was American policy in the post-war years. The first significant application of the containment doctrine came in the Eastern Mediterranean. Great Britain had been supporting Greece, where Communist forces threatened the ruling monarchy in a civil war, and Turkey, where the Soviet Union pressed for territorial concessions and the right to build naval bases on the Bosporus.

Containment also called for extensive economic aid to assist the recovery of war-torn Western Europe. With many of the region's nations economically and politically unstable, the United States feared that local Communist parties, directed by Moscow, would capitalize on their wartime record of resistance to the Nazis and come to power. Something needed to be done, Secretary of State George Marshall noted, for "the patient is sinking while the doctors deliberate." Marshall was formerly the highest-ranking officer in the U.S. Armed Forces and credited as the chief organizer of the American military victory in World War II. In mid-1947 Marshall asked troubled European nations to draw up a program "directed not against any country or doctrine but against hunger, poverty, desperation and chaos." The Soviets participated in the first planning meeting, then departed rather than share economic data on their resources and problems and submit to Western controls on the expenditure of the aid. The remaining sixteen nations hammered out a request that finally came to a dollar amount of seventeen thousand million for a four-year period. In early 1948 Congress voted to assist European economic recovery, dubbed the "Marshall Plan," and generally regarded as one of the most successful U.S. foreign policy initiatives in history.

Post-war Germany was divided into U.S., Soviet, British, and French zones of occupation, with the former German capital of Berlin (itself divided into four zones) near the center of the Soviet zone. The United States, Britain and France had discussed converting their zones into a single, self-governing republic. But the Soviet Union opposed plans to unite Germany and ministerial-level four-power discussions on Germany broke down. When the Western powers announced their intention to create a consolidated federal state from their zones, Stalin responded. On June 23, 1948, Soviet forces blockaded Berlin, cutting off all road and rail access from the West. This was known as the first international crisis of the Cold War. It lasted until May 12, 1949. The leader of Russia throughout WWII, Stalin, would die in March of 1953, and Nikita Khrushchev would come to power in Russia.

Arriving in Europe

My family and I arrived in Frankfort, Germany, ten years after WWII ended. We were there because of the situation Europe was in and the American policies of the time. We arrived in a European country with a different look, feel and attitude than the U.S. At five years old, I could sense a difference immediately.

The weather in Frankfort was cool as it had been in Philadelphia. The people at the Air Force base spoke English. We were housed on the base for orientation for a few days. Mother got a resource leaflet that was hand-drawn, typed and then run off on a copy machine. It was not professionally done. My father had his orders and Mom, Lee, and I had ours.

The resource leaflet read:

Welcome to Germany
A Personnel Service Booklet
Prepared & Published by the Personnel Services
7012 PERPRON
Frankfort, Germany

Section I:

You are now at the 7012th Personnel Processing Squadron, APO 757, U.S. Army. Our local address is 30 Wiesenhuetten Platz, Frankfort, Germany.

Our mission is to furnish and/or confirm your station assignment and furnish necessary orders assigning you to your new duty station. We obtain and/or confirm this assignment from the appropriate headquarters (USAF, AMFE, 12th Air Force, etc.) You must have special orders from this organization to obtain travel warrants to your new duty station. Your orders from Camp Kilmer of Westover do not authorize this.

When you return and pick up your form sixty-six and new orders proceed to the train station, U.S., and Allied Ticket Office, Window #seventeen, present a copy of your new orders and a ticket will be furnished to your new duty station. No other mode of transportation is available. Upon arrival at the train station of your destination if transportation is not available telephone the adjunct of your new organization and request same.

After leaving your form sixty-six and a copy of your Camp Kilmer orders with us, proceed to the first floor where billets will be authorized by personnel on duty. You may be billeted some distance from Frankfort, by necessity, due to the small amount of Hotel Space available and the large number (10,000 monthly) of personnel processing it and from the Zone of Interior through this center. The clerk on duty in this office will inform you of the time we wish you to pick up your Sixty-six and the Special Orders which we will publish.

This leaflet went on to tell us about money exchange and military money. Military Payment Certificates, usually called scrip, were only to be used in military installations. It was illegal for us to use scrip with German businesses or with the German people.

It also talked about what uniforms to wear, our mail, cigarette purchases, local facilities, nursery, medical assistance, the American Red Cross, Army Emergency Relief, Air Force Aid Society, restaurants, barber shops, the post exchange (PX), laundry and dry cleaning, theaters, churches, playroom, Frankfort Zoo, and other places we may need to care for families. The last page was a hand-drawn map with hand-lettered places noted. It wasn't fancy, but it was valuable information for a military family on their first overseas assignment.

We would eventually end up in Brussels, Belgium in a pension, a small hotel much like a bed and breakfast. We stayed there several weeks waiting for the newly constructed apartment building we would eventually move into, to be finished. The pension we lived in provided meals and it smelled like soup. I have smelled that soup aroma a few times in my life since then and memories of that pension come back! It was built of brick and stone, and it was very cold. The weather in Brussels had that kind of cold that goes right though you and for the most part the skies are usually overcast.

The Belgians use flowers a lot to brighten their homes, apartments and even their cars. The landscaping around streets and public areas in Brussel's was beautiful. The Belgian people would put flower beds and plants on the simplest street corner. The plants bloomed at various levels and times of the season. Each season they were changed so the areas always looked fresh. I had never seen any landscaping like this in Albany, GA or Philadelphia, PA. Flower planting was all over the

Lee and I standing in front of the spring flowers on a street corner in Brussels.

city, the weather was not the best, so the flowers became particularly important.

We finally moved into our beautiful apartment building on 3 Avenue du Derby. We were close to the American Embassy, located on Franklin D. Roosevelt Boulevard. Most families in the 1950s only had one car. My father took our car to work and my mother, Lee, and I walked to school, stores and to the embassy.

Our apartment building was very upscale. It was brand new, and the Belgian government paid for part of our rent. All the American families with the embassy lived in the building or a building nearby. It was a beautiful residential area of Belgium. Across the street from our apartment building were exceptionally large homes. Landscaping was fancy at every corner of the street and in the backyards of homes. Everything was planted according to height. Smaller plants in the front and larger plants in the back, usually in three levels. We had everything we needed within walking distance of our apartment. If we wanted food or anything from the U.S., it was mailed from family or friends, or we had to drive to an American air base in Germany and shop at the base PX and the commissary.

School in Brussels

I had been in kindergarten in Albany, GA, but then we spent a month in Philadelphia and another month traveling and the pension before moving into our apartment. So, I finished kindergarten in the Belgian School down the street from our apartment, Ecole du Bois de la Cambre. There were no French classes for me and no one in the school spoke English. However, that last month of kindergarten the other American dependent children also attended the Belgian School with me, so there was some communication and friendship. It was a beautiful old building of red brick, probably built in the late 1800s or early 1900s. The interior had large windows and a high ceiling with transoms over the doors for air circulation and a new modern building attached. The modern building did not match the architecture of the original school. I liked this school and found it interesting. My mother would walk me there and the teachers would walk me back to my street and my mother would be waiting for me to cross the street.

One of my American friends was Lynnie. Her father was a civilian American pilot with Sabena Airlines, a Belgian airline company. Her father's nickname was Ziggy, and her mother was Stella. Lynnie was an only child and she and I got along very well. Our parents were friends too. We had them over for dinner many times and we would go to their home for dinner too. Lynnie and her family were Jewish, however, that was a secret, because, back in 1955 Sabena did not hire Jewish pilots. The secret had to be kept or her father would lose his job. Ziggy, Stella, and my mother enjoyed New York bagels, and my mother liked Polish blood sausage and kielbasa. So, whenever Ziggy had flights to New

York he would bring back bagels and sometime Polish sausages for us! My mother missed the comfort food she had grown up enjoying.

My father's position in Brussels was with the Military Assistance Advisory Group, or MAAG. My father was an advisor to The Belgian government. They had purchased the F-84 Thunderjets from the U.S. One of Dad's new jobs was as flight instructor to the Belgian pilots. We were there because of the Cold War and NATO that was headquartered in Paris, France, at that time. My family and I were now on a world stage.

My parents would attend embassy events and parties with friends and enemies of the U.S. We would host parties for other pilots and their families as well as tech representatives and British attachés. My mother purchased a German fine China dinnerware set for twelve and an English Silver coffee and tea service. She also had a silver

My father and the F-84 Thunderflash delivered to the Belgian government.

utensil place setting set for twelve. My grandmother knew that every young girl should have a dowry. During The Depression she started buying one place setting at a time for my mother.

Running into a Princess

One of the British attachés was the former equerry (an officer of the British royal household who attends or assists members of the royal family) to King George VI, Group Captain Peter Wooldridge Townsend. Townsend was sent to Brussels to keep him and Princess Margaret away from each other. The young Queen Elizabeth and her advisors were not happy with the two as a couple. Townsend was divorced and sixteen years older than Margaret. Princess Margaret was the younger sister to Queen Elizabeth.

During the time we were living in Brussels I literally ran into Princess Margaret. I was playing with my American friends in our apartment building, and we were running into the garage to get to another apartment. I saw this beautiful lady wearing an outfit I had never seen. I would later learn that her unusual pants and boots were riding clothes, and those odd pants were called jodhpurs. I recognized Mr. Townsend, a friend of Dad's. I had seen him several times in our apartment. She was lovely and stopped to say hello to me, Lee, and my friends. She was strangely interested in Lee. She picked him up and sat him on a table attached to the wall in the garage vestibule and talked to him. Lee was rather good looking and smart. He often attracted attention, especially from women. Then in typical kid fashion, we went on our way with whatever game we were playing. When I got back up to our apartment that day, I told my mother there was this beautiful lady dressed in these funny pants with boots. My mother knew that I had met Princess Margaret because there was word out that Peter and Margaret were in the building. My brush with royalty!

Cold War Operations

During the Cold War, CIA technical operations included the bugging of the Soviet military's major communications line in East

Germany and the development of reconnaissance aircraft such as the U-2 spy plane. My father delivered the RF-84 Thunder Flash made for photo reconnaissance missions by Republic Aviation Corporation of Farmingdale, in Long Island, NY. This jet was loaded with many cameras. Intelligence-gathering flights were important to the security of the U.S.

Under the Strategic Air Command (SAC), my father's main job in Brussels was not only to train the Belgian pilots but to carry out many Cold War missions dealing in top-secret activities.

An American in Belgium

During that summer of 1955 all the American families in Brussels went to Frankfort, Germany, for a big Air Force event. A few months after returning, mother found out she was pregnant again.

That summer the British School way across town hosted a cookout event to allow interest families to see their facility. After touring the school, most of the American families decided to send their children there. My mother was concerned that the British School was too far across town and that she had no way to get to us. So, Lee and I continued to attend Ecole du Bois de la Cambre. We could walk to school, and she could get to us in an emergency. Lee and I were the only Americans in that school. I started first grade and Lee started kindergarten. Lee was not old enough for kindergarten, but the staff at that school tested my brother and found he was able to handle kindergarten level work, so he started school earlier than most his age.

Entering school with no other American children was like throwing us into water, you either sink or swim. There I was in class for my first day of first grade and no one in the school spoke English. I had to figure it out for myself. It was scary at first. I didn't know how to tell anyone what I needed, I just had to watch. Where were the restrooms? What was the schoolwork? I learned to watch and carefully observe people. A little at a time I slowly picked up some of the French language. I was learning through observation. I learned to read people and I picked up a lot. I picked up on body language and routines. It took me a good year to learn the French language, but I was not getting any grammar to speak of. I was learning to read and repeat words but many times I didn't know what they meant. Of course, I didn't tell anyone. My mother really needed to rely on me for communication, although she spoke both English and Polish, and could manage in Russian and dabble in a little German and Lebanese; French was difficult for her. She never learned much of the language. By the second year there, I spoke like a native Belgian; and I had no American accent when I spoke French. I never lost my ability to speak French and I used this talent later in high school.

In Brussels the school week was Monday–Saturday. We had a lunch break for two hours each day. We would walk home for lunch, never eating at school, then we'd walk back. On Thursday and Saturday, it was only a half day.

My second-grade class in Brussels. I'm standing fourth from the left in this photo and the only American in the class. This was a public school down the street from our apartment building.

My Brother Lee and His Challenges with the French Language

Lee had his challenges too with the language that first year. One day Lee had on an outfit that had straps attached to the pants he could not get unbuttoned, and he didn't know how to ask the teacher, so he just started running back home. He surprised my mother when he got home, but he had to use the bathroom and couldn't get the teacher to understand, and he didn't want to embarrass himself. That was the only solution for him. Mom walked him back to school, and somehow, she got the teacher and principal to understand what happened.

All the Belgian students carried a book bag to school made of leather. There would usually be a pencil case on the front of the flap closure. Many Belgian children had their names on the pencil case. My godmother in Philadelphia sent school bags for Lee and me. They were Walt Disney school bags. Godno was up on the latest pop culture of the time. American pop culture however was not a part of Belgian culture in the 1950s. Lee's bag featured images from the new Disney movie *Lady and the Tramp*. On the pencil case was written "Walt Disney" and below it was cartoon characters of the two dogs from the movie.

On Lee's first day in school the teacher was going around the room asking the children their names and Lee was not sure what to tell the teacher. After all his name was Eugene Lee Phillips, but should he tell the teacher Lee or Eugene? When the teacher came to Lee, he hesitated, and the teacher became annoyed. She looked at his book bag and wrote down Walt Disney. At the end of that week my brother came home with a card reporting how he had performed that week in school. Lee's report card had the name Walt Disney. Again, my mother had to go to school to straighten out the mix up. Mom's family in Philadelphia would hear about this incident from my mother in a letter. We did not call anyone in the U.S. back then, long distance calls were expensive, and the connections were not good. Calling was only used for dire emergencies.

Soon after that incident, the Walt Disney movie came to the movie theaters in Brussels. I was still in first grade, and even though I was in a school speaking only French, I was still struggling with the language. However, my mother and father thought I was doing great. The movie was dubbed in French, and they spoke very fast, and I really didn't understand most it, but my parents thought I did. I did the best I could at that time but was not able to explain it all to my parents.

When Lee was grown up and planning to marry, he and his bride had their reception at Disney World to honor the story of the week that he was known as Walt Disney.

* * *

The Belgian public school had no more than twenty kids in each class. Girls were in classes on one side of the school and boys were on the other side of the school. When an adult entered the classroom, you stood up next to your desk at attention. You stood there in silence until the visitor either excused you to sit and continue with your work or until they left the room. Other than that, the rule of respect for adults, the culture of the class was free flowing and easy.

Each student had a desk, an ink well, a pen holder with a nip and a blotter. We had exercise books that had to be covered and had to be neat. We learned cursive writing with our pens and ink wells. I liked cursive writing very much. If you wrote sloppy the teacher glued the pages together so that sloppy page was not seen. She graded each page as we did them. When you finished your work, you went up to the teacher's desk and she would correct it then. There was immediate gratification, which was great for me. Even though I struggled, this school was fun, and my classmates were truly kind and helpful toward me. I felt appreciated. We had weekly field trips. On one occasion, the teacher asked each student to bring money to school, just change. We all brought the change, and one person was assigned the task of writing down each person's name and the amount of money they brought. Then they counted all the money and we all walked down the street and started shopping as a class. What could we buy for the amount we had collected? We went into several stores, the candy store, the grocery store and finally we decided to buy some Coca-

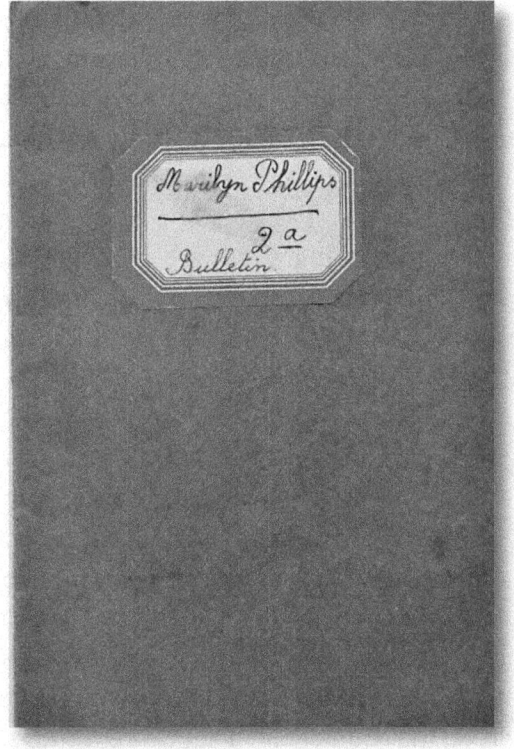

This is a sample of what our school workbooks in Brussel's looked like. This is actually my second grade report card that was sent home each Friday.

Cola. We brought the Coca-Cola back to our class and had to figure out how to divide the drink, so each person got an equal amount. We then poured the beverage into cups and enjoyed our adventure, because this lesson was truly an adventure. It was a great lesson in math, exercise, decision making and kindness. The next day the class as a group wrote a story about our trip to the various stores and purchasing Coca-Cola. It was just a paragraph as this is only first grade. Then we would print copies of this story on our printing device at the back of the classroom. Different students were chosen to help set the type, putting the letters in the correct order, and then printing the story on paper. Each student would then get a copy and paste it into our exercise book and draw a picture to accompany it. So, we learned language arts, visual arts, and had fun! This school system was wonderful.

This public school in Brussels used a Dutch system of education. The population of Belgium is mostly made up of two groups of people, the Dutch-speaking Flemish, and the French-speaking Walloons. I was struggling to learn French, and now we had Flemish classes. This turned out to be helpful for me. Flemish is a Germanic language with some English words.

I was learning what it meant to be an American overseas. I was feeling it too. The kids in my school, like me, were born after WWII. Their parents were thankful to the American people for coming to their aid in the war. I was treated with a lot of respect by my fellow classmates. They knew I had come from a great country that had saved them. We were respected in Brussels as Americans. The Boulevard behind Avenue Du Derby, where we lived, was Franklin D. Roosevelt Blvd. The American Embassy along with many other embassies was on that Boulevard. That Boulevard had been renamed after World War II to honor the American president. The American intervention in the Second World War had changed the course of history for the European people. As an American dependent child in Europe in 1955, I felt that respect and honor for the U.S.

I had made a few friends in school, and I had play dates with them and with the American dependent children too.

Our first Christmas in Belgium was vastly different than what I had experienced in the U.S. On December 6th all the children in the school were ushered into a large auditorium. I did not understand what was going on. I had to wait and see. Finally, after a while a man dressed in bishop's clothing with a miter hat, a pastoral staff, leading a white donkey, walked into the auditorium. All the kids started clapping and shouting out words of joy in French. He went to the front of the auditorium and made a short speech. The crowd cheered again. Then he stayed for a while and walked around talking to several teachers and students. Finally, we were each presented with a gift of cookies and candy. The cookies were in the shape of the bishop, and they were big. I would learn that December 6th is the feast day of St. Nicholas. This is the day that the children in Belgium would receive gifts and candy and cookies. Christmas day was a day to go to church and have a family meal celebrating the birth of Jesus. I would later go to the Belgian department store and have my picture taken with St. Nicholas, dressed like a bishop. Today when I go to my local grocery store and buy windmill cookies, I'm reminded that they're the same recipe as the St. Nicholas cookies I got in Belgium on St. Nicholas day.

This is me at the Belgian department store visiting St. Nicholas.

* * *

One day I arrived at school to see two camels in our schoolyard. The school wanted children to have experiences not just book learning. All the classes came out to see and hear about the camels. After seeing the camels, we went back into class to write a story about our experience. The class wrote the story as a group, we did not each write our own story. Then a group of girls went to the printer to set up the type to print copies of the story for each student. When those were ready, we each got a printed copy to paste into our *cahier d'exercise,* or "workbook" in English. Then we had time to draw and color with colored pencils our own pictures of the camels to share with the teacher.

At the start of my second year of school in Brussels, my parents announced that Lee and I were going to have a new brother or sister in March of 1956. The girls in this school learned knitting, crochet, and cross stitch. Each girl in the second grade had to produce samples of our handiwork with a label with our name and grade, to prove we could master this skill. I remember one day I asked my teacher if she could show me how to use my knitting skills to make a sweater for my new baby brother or sister that was coming. I guess I was always a practical person. Thinking if I was learning this skill, I should be able to produce something useful, not just a sample. The teacher told me that a sweater was too difficult for me at this time, and we were only using string and not yarn. So, I sat down and figured I was only going to do this sample.

In Brussel's we lived in European Christian culture. We are the sum of our experiences. My classmates were diverse. Their parents came from Switzerland, France, Holland, and Africa. I lived on the world stage as a military kid as did many of the people I would encounter.

My love of history started in Belgium. In Brussels, we lived amid so many places of important turning points in history. On the weekends, when Dad was home, our family had historical adventures. I was the oldest and may have gotten more out of these trips than Lee. I could pick up on my father's enthusiasm and history lessons.

One of these historical trips was to the battlefield called Waterloo, just outside of Brussels. The popular saying, "If someone meets their Waterloo," means they will be defeated by someone who is stronger. It originates from a battle that took place on June 18, 1815. The battlefield where Napoleon Bonaparte was finally defeated by the British and the Prussians. This battle ended Napoleon's reign and twenty-three years of Napoleonic Wars in Europe. The Duke of Wellington was the British General who finally outsmarted the charismatic Napoleon. My family and I drove up to the battlefield, a large area of grass and farmland. One area is a very large mound of dirt covered in grass and at the top of this large mound is a statue of a lion. The Lion Mount faces France. This is symbolic that France should never return! At one corner of this large area on the side of the road is a church and in another area of town is a pub or bar. My father's lesson was that Napoleon Bonaparte was so sure he was going to win he had his soldiers in the pub/bar the evening before the battle. On the other hand, the Duke of Wellington had his soldiers in the church praying for victory.

This may not be how the history books portray this turning point in history, but it was what I got from Dad that day. The mound of dirt is made up of the bodies of horses and some soldiers that died that day. The British soldiers' bodies were buried, and the French soldiers' bodies were burned. The mound has 226 very steep steps to where the statue of the lion stands. My father and I walked all the way to the top. Mother and Lee did not make it that far. Lee was only four years old at that time and my mother was pregnant, both grew tired. I remember Father telling me how victory felt that day standing on top of that mound overlooking the Belgian town. The breeze was blowing my hair, and my brave father was by my side. The power of the lion facing France with the strength of a warrior! The battle of Waterloo saw 250,000 men from at least seven nations in action. More than 11,000 were left dead and 33,000 wounded. It was one of the largest and bloodiest pre-twentieth century European battles. Tourism on this battlefield started four days after the battle ended and has continued ever since.

MY FATHER'S SECRETS

* * *

As a family we took many trips to Germany. In Germany there were several American military bases. My father either had business at these bases or we were going to get American items at the Post Exchange. On these trips my parents would try to work in a fun event for Lee and me. One of the fun things we did was visiting German towns and finding interesting stores. Toy stores were exciting places for two kids of four and six. Lee and I were each allowed to get one toy on those trips. German toy stores were the leader in toys for the rest of the world at that time. They had Lego building toy blocks, Steiff brand stuffed animals and puppets. Steiff is the company that invented the original Teddy Bear. It was a German family that started it but inspired by American President Theordore "Teddy" Roosevelt. The first teddy bear was made of mohair and the arms and legs were jointed allowing them to move forward and back. On one of our toy store trips, we purchased a fashionable doll for me and Legos for Lee. The Barbie Doll would later be introduced to the U.S. market in 1959 based on this German doll with the figure of a mature woman. Lego building toys would not come to the U.S. until 1962. By the time we left Europe I had a complete set of Stiff brand puppets and stuffed animals plus my mature figure doll. Lee had stuffed animals and lots of Legos.

In our apartment building lived American military families and a variety of Europeans. My mother made friends with a Belgian woman who spoke perfect English, her name was Gabby. My parents also became close friends with one of the American couples, Alte and John Porter. They had no children as Alte had been in an automobile accident while in high school that left her unable to conceive. John was a dashing pilot who worked with my dad. John had a separate garage from his apartment. We parked in the general parking area under the building. John and Alte's garage opened directly to the street.

One day my father asked me to go with him to see John's new car! It was a 1955 Thunderbird with a removable hard top that he had hanging on the garage wall in front of the car. It could be a hardtop car or a convertible. I had never seen anything like this car in my young life. I still remember that day and that car with excitement. Alte took us for a ride in it at another time. Little did I know I was witnessing a classic car that still demands a good price to this day. My father loved cars and he loved working on the engine. Dad was really checking out that engine and that car, even though he knew it was not a car for a family man.

Mom, Lee, and I spent a lot of time with Alte. I remember she and my mother planned a big dinner party for some of the pilots and attachés from the American Embassy. Lee and I had the job of cleaning the string beans. We did it for a while but found it very boring. Alte and John had a long-haired dachshund named Ibert (pronounced e-bear). Lee and I loved Ibert since we did not have a dog. During that time, when you sent a dog overseas it could be in quarantine for up to six months. My father, who was raised on a family farm with dogs considered that quarantine, animal cruelty.

My parents would also meet and make friends with Marie. Marie was a twenty-four-year-old French woman who lived alone with a full-time maid named Sarah. Marie had survived WWII as a child. Her father was a high-ranking French military officer who was away most of the war helping the French deal with Hitler and Mussolini. Marie had something terrible happen to her as an adolescent. At the end of WWII, Nazi soldiers raped and mutilated young women, Marie may have been one of these victims. Marie was not married and did not work. She was the mistress of a wealthy Belgian industrialist, Ivan. I never knew his last name. He was older than Marie, tall, handsome, and sophisticated. Marie loved children and especially loved my brother and me. Maybe it was because my parents allowed us to be friends with her. Some of the people in the building did not talk to Marie because of who she was, but my mother had experienced prejudice as the child of a single mother growing up in Philadelphia and my father had experienced the prejudice of being an illegitimate child.

Lee and I did not understand any of that, we loved Marie, she was so much fun and had a smile that warmed the heart. Marie allowed

L-R: My mother, Gabby, and Alte with Ibert, her dog. This area of Brussels had beautiful cherry blossom trees lining the streets of this neighborhood. These trees only bloom twice a year—in the spring and autumn.

Lee and I to do things our parents wouldn't. She played with us and took us places. Her Spanish maid, Sarah treated us like we were special guests. On the days when Marie or Sarah would babysit, Lee and I were treated to a fancy dinner. Sarah prepared meals that were served in several courses. We would have a first course, a second course and sometimes finger bowls between courses. Sometimes there were hot towels when we started the meal. Lee and I experienced eating a meal very differently than how we ate at home. At Marie's the meal was part of a wonderful experience, not just filling our tummy. Lee and I looked forward to these dinner events. I remember a particular time Sarah served dinner and then the last course was bananas. Lee and I took our banana and Sarah showed us how to mash it with our fork and add some sugar before we ate it. We had never eaten a banana like that. Sarah had made eating a simple banana part of a dining experience.

* * *

My mother never went to a hair salon. But Marie had slight, blue-tinged hair sometimes and even pink-tinged hair other times in the 1950s. I would go with Marie to her hair salon. I didn't understand about gay men at that time, but I knew her stylist was not like my dad or the other men I had been around. I only knew he was nice to me, and I liked him. When Marie and I walked into the salon he would make a big fuss between the both of us. I did not have my hair done I was there with Marie, and she would treat me to an ice cream or pastry after our trip. I remember she drove a Volkswagen Beetle. The thing that I remember most about that car is that hanging against the interior sides between the front and back windows were flower vases. Often Marie had flowers in those vases. I thought this so strange, but I knew the Belgian people loved flowers. Landscaping with flowers was important to them and so was buying flowers for friends and their homes. This was not an American tradition. Even though Americans had flowers from time to time it was not the same attitude as the European people.

There were days when we could not visit Marie. There would be a long black limousine car parked in front of our building. When Lee and I saw the black limousine, we knew it meant that her friend Ivan was there. That meant we had to make other play plans for the day. Lee and I would meet Marie's friend Ivan from time to time. He was always dressed in a suit with an overcoat. He was very polite to us, and I think he liked us because we made Marie so happy.

Marie's apartment was much fancier than ours. Marie had fancy furniture and the hallway down to her bedroom had a heavy velvet drape. Marie also had a large bed, larger than a double bed. It had a mink bed spread on it. Lee and I did not go into her bedroom often, although Marie let us do pretty much anything we wanted to do. One day she took down all her drapes in the living room so we could build a tunnel to crawl through. Lee and I never had an adult let us do that before or after. Playing at Marie's was the best time ever!

Ivan would take Marie on trips and to fashion shows in Paris and buy her beautiful clothes. On one of Marie's trips with Ivan, she brought us back costumes from Spain. Lee got a matador costume, and I got a peasant girl costume. These costumes were very well made and very ornate. My peasant costume had a thick woolen shirt that was embroidered with beads and ribbon and twine. It had undergarments as well as several layers of overgarments. When we moved to Brussels, the Belgian people were not aware of Halloween the way we celebrate it in the U.S. Our first October there, in 1955, my mother dressed us in homemade costumes, and she took us door to door. We went to the doors of people she knew, and she prepared them for our visit. We didn't go to many doors, and we visited with each couple or family. We were kind of teaching these European people about the American tradition of Halloween. By the second year, 1956, we had the fancy costumes from Marie and all the European people were waiting for our arrival.

Lee and I played with the other military kids whose fathers were there on the same duty schedule and with the American Embassy. There was a vacant lot near our building and the free-range children that we were made use of creatively. We knew Brussels could be dangerous, so we knew how to keep our mother informed of our whereabouts. The older children of the group had set up a tent one day on the vacant lot. It was such fun. I was into building tents and tunnels and making my own space, so this was right up my alley. The older children were picking on Lee. I sided with them to have great access to the tent. I kind of figured if I didn't side with them my access to the tent would be over. Lee came to the tent several times only to be turned away by the older children and I did not stand up for him. He finally reported this behavior to my mother. She called me from the sidewalk near the tent.

Then she took me to a place the other children could not hear her tell me, "You should always stand up for your brother no matter what the other children wanted. Your brother will be there for you the rest of your life and you may never see these other children again." I knew she was right. I knew before she came to get me, I should stand up for my brother. So, I did the right thing and gave up my access to the tent. A few days later I found the tent abandoned and sat in it for a while but without the other children it was not fun!

* * *

Although we were living with high-ranking military families. There weren't many of us. My father was a captain, but there were generals, colonels, lieutenant colonels, and majors. At some of the military kids' birthday parties we were lined up to play party games in the order of our father's rank. I would be near the end of the line. The one big prejudice in the military was rank. The higher you were the more important you were, so I knew where I stood. Of course, the military wives, like my mother were aware of rank too. My father was an extraordinarily talented young pilot that had already seen war and a POW camp. It was about this time in my life that I was beginning to learn what a POW camp was and that my father had been in one. I didn't really understand the whole situation, but I did know it somehow made my dad important. I did not completely understand the dangers of his job. I did remember however, about my playmate in Albany whose father died in the training exercise and never came home.

Lee and the Belgian Family Living in Our Building

The family that lived one floor above ours worked in the diamond trade. They had no children. Lee at the time was adorable. He was a very well-built child, and my mother dressed him in short pants and white high-top leather shoes, like most children his age in the mid-

1950s. Lee was also very smart and could hold intelligent conversations with adults on several topics.

One evening they invited my parents over for cocktails. This couple made a proposal to my parents. They wanted to buy Lee! My parents of course were shocked; but contained their emotions and thanked them for their offer. They then made another offer. They would take the baby my mother was carrying. Again, my parents contained their emotions and turned down the offer. The man finally approached my father to sleep with his wife to impregnate her. My father again contained his emotions and turned them down. They were disappointed and said how much they enjoyed watching our family. My parents shared part of this story with Lee and I when they returned to our apartment. Years later, every time Lee did not get what he wanted he blamed my parents for not selling him. Even my younger brother often did the same. After a while it became a great family joke. I felt bad for these people that could not have children like Alte and John, Marie, and this couple. I learned that in different parts of the world values were not the same as they were in the U.S., and that in some countries people do sell their children for varied reasons.

Almost a Ballerina

I had only taken a few dance lessons in Albany, Georgia before we left, but I loved dancing. I did not take any lessons while in Brussels but on our trips to Germany my mother did buy me a pair of ballet pointe shoes. I loved putting them on and dancing around the room to music. My household did not have a television(TV) because all the shows where in French. We had purchased a German-made Grundig, which was a modern wooden piece of furniture that had a radio and a record player in it. We played music all the time. My father found music soothing. Even though he had grown up in a house with no electricity the first thing he bought when he graduated high school and got his first job, was a radio and he tapped into the electric poles which had been installed down his rural road.

Music was always available for me to dance. One of my relatives sent me a second pair of ballet pointe shoes because my mother told them how much I liked dancing. A retired prima ballerina from the English Royal Ballet lived in our building. She watched my family move around the building as fellow residents but did not know I liked ballet. She contacted my mother at one point and asked if I could audition for the ballet. Mom was under the impression that it would be an audition for classes. When she arrived with two men from the English Royal Ballet Company, she explained that she would watch me walk down the steps of our t building as she sat on her balcony. She told my mother that I carried myself like a ballerina even at my young age. I was excited to dance for these people. I was always looking for an audience.

I put on a pair of my pointe shoes, my mother played a piece of music on the Grundig, and I performed. After the performance I went back to my room, took off my shoes and returned to find out I had been accepted. The ballerina told my mother that I was too young to wear pointe shoes, that I should not start on point' until I was at least 12 or so. I was accepted into the English Royal Ballet Company Children's study, but that meant I would not be living at home. I would be moving into the dorm rooms of the school, but I could come home on holidays to visit my family. Well, that did not sit with my parents. My ballet career ended as quickly as it began.

Nannie Came to Live with Us in Brussels

As my mother's pregnancy got closer to her due date, there was talk that Nannie would be coming to help with the new baby and staying with us in Brussels. There was one obstacle to this plan. Nannie, who had legally immigrated to the U.S. in 1913 at age sixteen and was sponsored by an uncle, never had become an American citizen. For my grandmother to travel to Brussels and return to America she had to finally become a citizen. Nannie who was fifty-nine years old and living in Philadelphia at the time with relatives studied for her citizenship test and became a citizen in 1956, forty-three years after she had arrived at the Port of Philadelphia.

Uncle Henry and the Cold War

One day we had a surprise visit from Dad's youngest brother Henry. Henry had enlisted in the Army before Uncle Clyde's wedding in Plymouth. In fact, Henry had come to the wedding in his Army uniform. Now he had a military intelligence assignment in Germany. Uncle Henry was very smart. The military offered him to go to Officers Candidate School. Henry thought if he became an officer, he may also be recalled like my dad and make the military his career. Henry loved farming and thus turned down the offer. However, he got an especially important assignment in Germany. He and a few other soldiers lived on top of a mountain and intercepted Russian communication radio signals. This was a dangerous position. Had the Russians found out about this location they could have taken out the site. This intercepted information gave America a leg up on what the Russians were doing and provided intelligence for strategic maneuvers in Europe. Uncle Henry stayed with us for about a week. Several days that week he walked Lee and I to school and home. During the weekend we did some sightseeing with him. A few weeks later we drove to his secret location in Germany to visit his station.

The Arrival of a New Sibling

We were preparing for the birth of our new brother or sister. My parents picked out two names, a girl would be named Gina, and a boy would be named Mark Gerard. My mother had been going to Dr. Jacques Bolle, a Belgian physician for her monthly appointments. She would give birth at The Edith Cavell Hospital near our apartment building. My father would share with me the story of Edith Cavell. She was a British nurse during the WWI. She was stationed in Belgium and saved the lives of soldiers from both sides, without discrimination. She also helped 200 allied soldiers escape from German-occupied Belgium. She was arrested under martial law for doing so, accused of treason, found guilty by a court-martial, and sentenced to death. On October 12, 1915, she was shot by a German firing squad. Her execution would receive worldwide condemnation and extensive press cov-

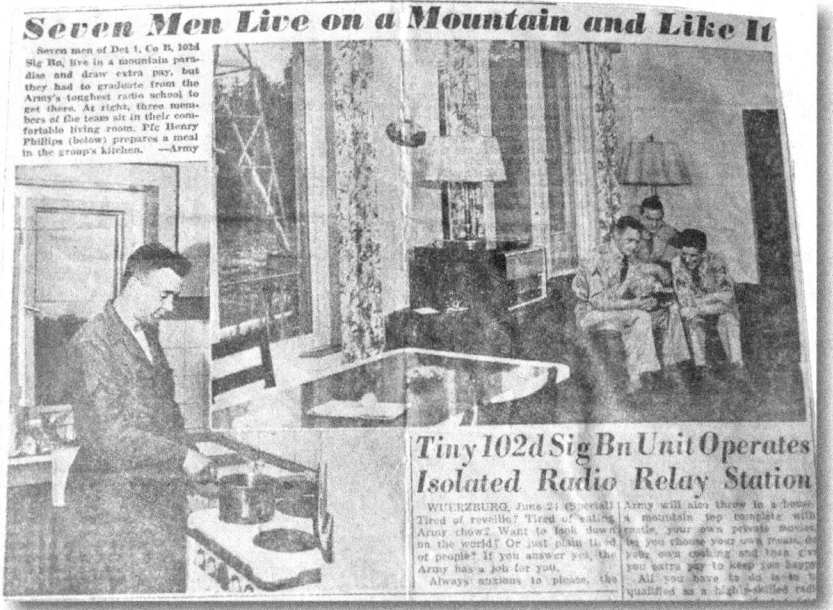

Article in the Stars and Stripes *about my Uncle Henry Phillips and his Cold War assignment in Germany. The day my family arrived to visit him is the day the reporter came to cover this story. Uncle Henry is in the left photo.*

erage. The Belgian people were so shaken by this horrible turn of events for this beautiful and courageous nurse that they started a hospital in Brussels in her name. In 1950 the maternity ward was added.

On March 4, 1956 my mother was talking to a friend that had come over to see the nursery in the alcove of my parents' bedroom. It was beautiful. Marie had paid for everything, and it was the best of the best. All the furniture was white painted wood. Marie would wait until the baby arrived to put up the pink or blue wallpaper. There was a cradle with white fabric canopy. The fabric had small dots and the cradle rocked. There was also a table to change the baby. I was in the living room playing but I could see into the hall and the area of the bedroom where my mother was standing. Suddenly, my mother yelled and separated her feet. Her water had broken. She was upset because it had broken on the new throw rug in the bedroom. She called my father on the phone to let him know. Someone came to watch Lee and I while they went to the hospital.

Our new little brother, Mark, was born at 2:30 p.m. He was the first American born in that hospital. He would have two birth certificates, American and Belgian, neither having his height nor weight on them. In Belgium they list the time of birth, hospital, doctor's name, names of both parents and place of birth. It is also listed that both parents were with the State Department of the U.S., Washington, D.C.

Mother had to stay in the hospital for several days. During that time Dad made sure we got to school and were fed. However, he did not do it like my mother. On the first morning, he fed Lee and me cold rice with milk and sugar for breakfast; we got sandwiches for lunch and dinner. I sensed that I could push things a little with him, so, I decided I wanted to wear my Easter outfit from the previous year to school. In the mid-1950s girls my age wore very full petticoats. These petticoats would make your skirt stand out almost like a ballet tutu. In early March, Brussels is cold and damp. I felt good getting dressed in my fine outfit with the full petticoat and I bounced as I walked. On the way to school, I was uncomfortable and cold. I made it through the day but later regretted my decision.

The next day my father, Lee, Marie, and I visited my mother in the hospital. Marie brought a bottle of the finest champagne, and we all went into my mother's room to see her and my new brother Mark Gerard Phillips. I was six years old, and Lee was four. We were so thrilled to meet our new brother! When we got there Marie opened the bottle of champagne and poured several glasses. Marie lightly dipped her finger in her champagne glass and placed it in Mark's mouth. She thought champagne should be the first thing he tasted! The doctor arrived in the room, and all toasted to the birth of our new baby.

Not long after that, my mother and Mark came home, and we had a big christening ceremony and party. Mark was baptized in a convent church in Brussels where Marie's aunt was a nun. Marie and her gen-

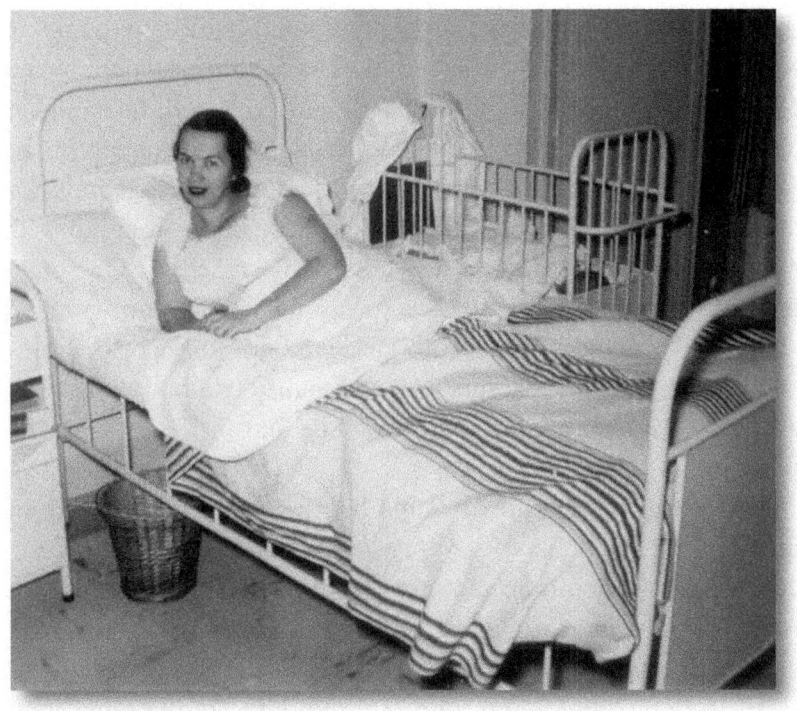

My mother and Mark (in the crib) at the Edith Cavell Hospital.

tleman friend Ivan were named as his godparents. Marie had purchased Mark's christening gown and all to go with it, this included the gown, bonnet, and undergarments plus a hooded cape with sleeves made of sheepskin. The gown and all the extras were purchased at the same shop where Princess Grace of Monaco would purchase Caroline's (her first child) christening gown the following year. Princess Grace of Monaco had been the American actress Grace Kelly before she married the Prince of Monaco. Interestingly, Kelly was from Philadelphia where my mother had grown up. Her father was a builder in Philadelphia, and he frequented the restaurant where my grandmother worked as a cook. My mother admired the Kelly family and could not believe her status in life with this embassy assignment.

Marie was dressed in a designer outfit and a full-length mink coat for the big day. Ivan was dressed in a suit with a cashmere overcoat. My parents were dressed in their best outfits as well. Lee and I were all dolled up in our finest dress up clothes. The Belgian churches were all cathedrals. My father shared that all the cathedrals would take hundreds of years to complete because the men building them had to be in a state of grace to work on the cathedral. Not sure how historical that information is but it was meaningful for me that day.

We had a grand reception at our apartment to honor this blessed event. Many of my parents' friends and neighbors came to meet Mark. It was just another party for Lee and me. Baby Mark slept through most of it.

Mark's christening gown would be used for the christening of all my children and some of Lee's. Mark would use the gown for both of his girls. It would be treasured by my family for a long time. It meant so much to my mother!

Grandmother Nannie arrived on June 30, 1956, and stayed with us in Brussels helping Mom with our new baby brother and us until March 24, 1957. Lee and I had spent a lot of time with Nannie, and we were happy to see her. She was an amazing cook and baker. I always felt special around her.

Cold War Events

Things were not quiet around the world. During 1956 there were several hot beds of trouble perking up. One was in Hungary and the other in the Suez Canal, and there were problems in Yugoslavia too. During the time of Mark's birth, my father was dealing with varying Cold War crises. He had spy trips to Yugoslavia and The Suez Canal. My family would protect a set of clandestine slides from photos he had taken during a car ride in Yugoslavia. This was a mission with several other military operatives. However, all were dressed in civilian suits rather than military uniforms. All I knew was he had the camera set on the dashboard of the car and took the photos secretly. All else was TOP SECRET information of the U.S. government. My father had many secrets that he could not share with us. Mother especially did not want to know for fear she would put him and our family in danger if she slipped. We did know that secrets were part of his job.

Suez Crisis: 1956-57

The Suez Canal was built in Egypt under the supervision of French diplomat Ferdinand de Lesseps. The man-made waterway opened in 1869 after ten years of construction and separates most of Egypt from the Sinai Peninsula. At 120 miles long, it connects the Mediterranean Sea to the Indian Ocean by way of the Red Sea, allowing goods to be shipped from Europe to Asia and back more directly. Its value to international trade made it a nearly instant source of conflict among Egypt's neighbors and Cold War superpowers vying for dominance.

The catalyst for the joint Israeli-British-French attack on Egypt was the nationalization of the Suez Canal by Egyptian leader Gamal Abdel Nasser in July 1956. The situation had been brewing for some time. In the wake of World War II, the Egyptian military had begun pressuring the British to end their military presence (which had been granted in the 1936 Anglo-Egyptian Treaty) in the canal zone. Nasser's armed forces also engaged in sporadic battles with Israeli soldiers along the border between the two countries, and the Egyptian leader did nothing to conceal his dislike toward the Zionist nation.

The Israelis struck first on October 29, 1956. Two days later, British and French military forces joined them. Originally, forces from the three countries were set to strike at once, but the British and French troops were delayed. Behind schedule but ultimately successful, the British and French troops landed at Port Said and Port Fuad and took control of the area around the Suez Canal. However, their hesitation had given the Soviet Union—also confronted with a growing crisis in Hungary—time to respond. The Soviets, eager to exploit Arab nationalism and gain a foothold in the Middle East, supplied arms from Czechoslovakia to the Egyptian government beginning in 1955, and eventually helped Egypt construct the Aswan Dam on the

Nile River after the United States refused to support the project. Soviet leader Nikita Khrushchev railed against the invasion and threatened to rain down nuclear missiles on Western Europe if the Israeli-French-British force did not withdraw.

I never knew what Dad did in Egypt. I did know he had been there on a secret mission. One day two camel saddles appeared in our apartment. They were beautiful! They were on wooden stands and sat about eighteen inches off the floor. They were a new addition to our living room furniture. It was extra seating for all the parties my parents hosted. We would have these camel saddles for years to come.

The Hungarian Revolution of 1956

The Hungarian Uprising was a nationwide revolution against the Hungarian People's Republic and its Soviet-imposed policies, lasting from October 23 through November 10, 1956. Leaderless at the beginning, it was the first major threat to Soviet control since the Red Army drove Nazi Germany from its territory at the end of World War II in Europe.

The revolt began as a student protest, which attracted thousands as they marched through central Budapest to the Hungarian Parliament building, calling out on the streets using a van with loudspeakers. A student delegation, entering the radio building to try to broadcast the students' demands, was detained. When the delegation's release was demanded by the protesters outside, they were fired upon from within the building by the State Security Police, known as the ÁVH (acronym for *Államvédelmi Hatóság*, literally State Protection Authority). Many students died and one was wrapped in a flag and held above the crowd. This was the start of the next phase of the revolution. As the news spread, disorder and violence erupted throughout the capital.

The revolt spread quickly, and the government collapsed. Thousands organized themselves into militias, battling the ÁVH and Soviet troops. During the revolt there were violent incidents; some local leaders and ÁVH members were lynched or captured, while former political prisoners were released and armed. Radical impromptu workers' councils wrested municipal control from the ruling Hungarian Working People's Party and demanded political change. The new government of Imre Nagy formally disbanded the ÁVH, declared its intention to withdraw from the Warsaw Pact and pledged to re-establish free elections. By the end of October, fighting had almost stopped, and the days of normality began to return. Some workers continued fighting in opposition to both the Stalinist regime and the appearances of "bourgeois" parties in its wake. The Hungarian people had asked for help from the U.S. President Eisenhower; however, Eisenhower did not send support.

* * *

Because all the Americans with the Belgian Embassy lived on the Belgian economy, as the military referred to it, all activities outside the embassy were in French. So, every so often the embassy sponsored activities for us American families. There would be bingo and showings of American movies. After a fun time watching a movie and eating popcorn with our American friends, we all piled back into our car. As the automatic gate opened to the streets, we saw young people holding signs and chanting. As our car pulled out of the gate a group of college-age students were waiting for us. They quickly surrounded our car and started banging on it. They had signs and posters and it seemed to me they were mad about something, and they were going to take it out on an American family with two kids in the car. Being the soldier and pilot that he was, Father at first did not want to hurt any of the students. When they started climbing into the back of the car, he saw an opening in the path ahead and hit the gas. We got out of there without incident to the students or us. I was relieved. I did not really understand the meaning of the history and what these students wanted. I feared what these people wanted to do to me and my family. I was in fear for my life, which is likely why I remember the details of those few minutes.

I would later learn all about the Hungarian Revolt. My father explained it to me after we got home, in a very simple way that I could understand. These moments in my life deeply affected me. I could feel their pain. People that had been unjustly treated and dominated by a government that had enslaved them to the point they would risk their lives. They would hurt others to get the help they so desperately wanted. These young people had asked for help from the U.S. and our president did not send what they felt was needed.

Yugoslavia

To curry favor with the leader of Yugoslavia, Josip Bro Tito, the United States supported Yugoslavia's efforts in 1949 to gain a seat on the prestigious Security Council at the United Nations. In 1951, President Truman asked Congress to provide economic and military assistance to Yugoslavia. This aid was granted. Yugoslavia proved to be a Cold War wild card, however. Tito gave tacit support to the Soviet invasion of Hungary in 1956, but harshly criticized the Russian intervention in Czechoslovakia in 1968. While the United States admired Tito for his independent stance, he could sometimes be a bit too independent. During the 1950s and 1960s he encouraged and supported the nonalignment movement among third world nations, a policy that concerned American officials who were intent on forcing those nations to choose sides in the East-West struggle.

My parents had made friends with a family who owned a restaurant that we liked. The restaurant was called the Three Lolli Pops. They had escaped Communist Yugoslavia to get to Brussels. The lady who owned the restaurant was my mother's age. She had survived WWII in Europe as a teenager. Her uncle was a Communist military officer and he wanted to help her, and her husband escape the Communist regime in Yugoslavia. He told her to scrap the plaque off her teeth and put it into her eye. It would present as a strange disease. She and her husband had petitioned to leave Yugoslavia for Belgium. With the apparent strange disease around her eyes undiagnosed they accepted their request. The Communist doctors did not want this disease in the country. She would also receive packages from Yugoslavia with hidden items that were being smuggled out. Jewelry that she could sell in Belgium for money. In Yugoslavia the jewelry, if found, would be kept by the Communists.

I Became Critically Ill

In January of 1957 I had an extremely high fever and was hallucinating. The Belgian doctor the American Embassy recommended came to see me in our apartment. He gave me some medicine and I seemed to get better. It didn't last long. I was sick again within days and my fever was increasingly high and the hallucinations were back. The doctor told my parents I had a bladder infection, and his medicine was not strong enough to help me. He told them this was a serious infection, and I could die from this bladder infection. He suggested my father get me to the military hospital in Germany.

That night my father pulled our car up to the front of our building from the garage, wrapped me in a blanket and carried me into the back seat of the car. I fell asleep and was out for most of the four-hour trip to the military hospital in Frankfort, Germany. When we arrived the first thing, they did was catheterized me. It was traumatic but I was still out of it from my fever. My father stayed until I got into my bed in the children's ward at the hospital. Then he left me there alone. I had no passport, only paperwork he had filled out. The passport that had my mother, Lee, and I on it now presented a big problem. I was an American in an American hospital who spoke both French and English. Germany was still in a delicate state. If trouble had broken out during my stay it could have meant my being separated from my family.

I woke up in a long room with other children. We were in beds along both walls of the room. Most of the children spoke English but some only spoke German. I wasn't afraid of being there alone. I felt better and my fever was gone. A tray of breakfast food arrived, and I ate it.

Later that week, in the middle of the night, a girl was brought into the children's ward. She was put in the bed across from me. She was crying and yelling in German, "*Nein, nein!*" It woke me up and I watched as the staff brought in a huge blanket of ice to lay her in. I eventually fell back to sleep, and, in the morning, she was in a regular bed and sleeping. She didn't speak English or French and I didn't speak German, so I never knew the whole story except for the fact that maybe there was a good ending.

    I did get one phone call from my parents that week. The call was long distance and not a great connection, so it was short and sweet. I was catheterized every day until the weekend when my parents arrived to pick me up. I hated it when they forced that metal tube into my bladder to drain out the urine. It hurt, and the instruments were metal and cold. It was clearing up the infection, but it was a terrible experience for a six-year-old away from her family. When my parents arrived, and they put me in a private room, they were planning on catharizing me with my parents in the room this time. As soon as I realized I had a family there to support me, I kicked the tray of cold metal instruments to the floor. The medical personnel all left the room, and my mother told me they were only doing this to help me. She had not been there all week and she did not understand what I had been through. That day they didn't catheterize me. I was happy about that. The next day we went home to Brussels.

    In February the German doctor and his wife came to visit my family in Brussels and he examined me. In March of that year my parents and I would return to Bitburg, Germany, a couple of times. Each time the doctor would check me again. I would need to come back to the Frankfort hospital again in April for another week. The German doctor that worked in the military hospital wanted to try a new procedure on me. The infection was still there; they could tell by my bloodwork. He wanted to give me intravenous penicillin. Penicillin was not given to children. I was a guinea pig for this medical procedure, but it saved my life.

    The next time I returned they took me into an operating room. I remember walking around the room and then they asked me to get on the table. I did and separated my legs thinking they were going to catheterize me again. To my surprise they told me I did not need to do that they just needed to put a needle in my arm for some medicine. Wow, I was so happy! I didn't care about a needle; I didn't ever again want to have to be catheterized. Years later in my life, after my first child was born and an exceptionally long labor, my bladder was not emptying. They threatened to catheterize me if I didn't empty it. That was all I needed to hear. I got on the bed pan and rocked back and forth until I could feel my full bladder and slowly emptied it.

I stayed in the military hospital for another week by myself just so the doctors could observe me. This was an untested procedure and they wanted to keep me at the hospital so they could see if I had any adverse effects from the penicillin. The experiment worked for me. This time my mother had packed some items to keep me busy during my stay. I had coloring books and games and a loom to make potholders. I made them all week and sold them to the doctors and nurses that took care of me. When my parents arrived at the end of the week to pick me up my mother was embarrassed that I had made money off the people who were taking care of me.

There was one last trip to Bitburg, Germany, to thank Dr. Braband. I was with my parents and our friend Alte. Lee stayed with Marie and Sarah. Nannie took care of Mark. We would meet at the doctor's apartment this time. When we got to the city of Bitburg, my father warned me that there were unfriendly people in Germany that would not like Americans. We walked through an area of the city that was still in shambles; I didn't understand that this rubble was left from WWII. Germany had been divided up after WWII with a lot of rebuilding and adjusting borders for the Free Germany and Communist sectors. The U.S. had military troops there during the Cold War. Parts of Germany were part of the Communist Bloc of Europe.

We finally reached the apartment of Dr. Braband and his wife. We went into a very humble residence, and on the coffee table were some chocolates. The doctor and his wife encouraged me to have some. I did, all the chocolate in Europe is delicious! I got some on my face and when I went to hug the doctor goodbye, I got chocolate on the collar of his white shirt. I felt bad that I had stained his good shirt. I sensed that he and his wife had done without; to provide chocolates for my family and me.

Years later I would find among my father's papers two letters. The first letter (*see below*) was a request from the Department of State asking my father for a reference for Dr. Braband. The second letter (*see next page*) was Dad's reply to the Department of State. My father had written a detailed response to help the doctor and his family get a position with the U.S. Department of State abroad. The doctor had saved my life, but I was also an opportunity for him and his family to have a better life. I never knew the outcome of this correspondence.

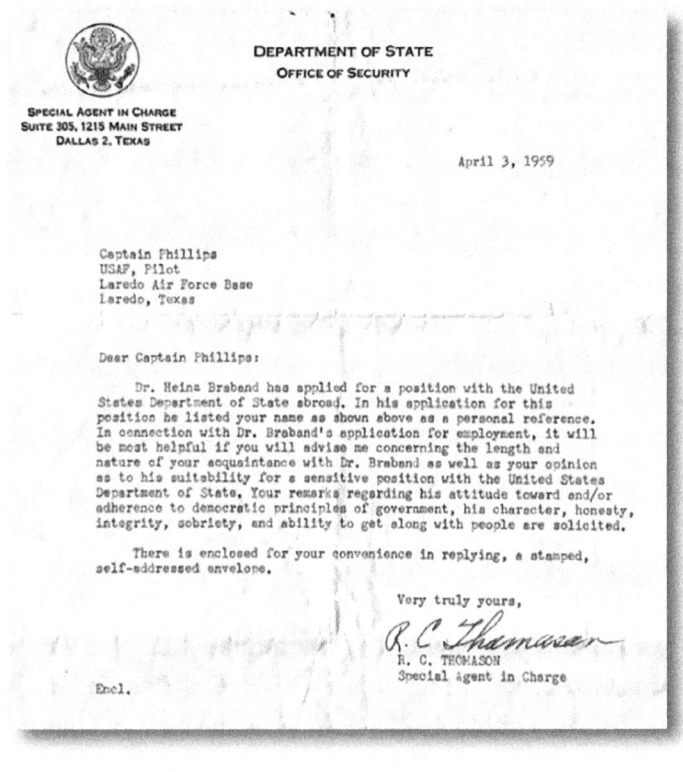

* * *

Leaving their apartment, Dad, Mom, Alte, and I walked back to our car in the Free Germany section of Bitburg. The weather was still cold. Some of the mountain roads we had to travel back to Brussels through Luxemburg were covered with ice. As we were coming down

> Box 187
> Laredo Air Force Base
> Laredo, Texas
> 7 April 1959
>
> Special Agent in Charge
> Suite 305
> 1215 Main Street
> Dallas 2, Texas
>
> Dear Sir:
>
> In response to your request and in the best interests of our government, the following account of the relationship between Dr. Braband and my family, including myself, is submitted:
>
> During a one week period in January 1957 and a one week period in April 1957 Dr. Braband successfully diagnosed and treated a serious affliction (acute cystitis) of my seven year old daughter. His objective approach and job knowledge enabled him to prescribe the necessary remedial action and future preventive precautions which are successful to date. Several previous attempts at other locations in Europe were unsuccessful.
>
> During February 1957 Dr. Braband and his wife visited with my family and I at our home in Brussels, Belgium (my assignment: MAAG-BELUX, American Embassy, Brussels). We later returned several short visits with them at Bitburg, Germany. During these associations with Dr. Braband and his wife (under very informal circumstances) my family and I concluded quite objectively that they were the type of people we would choose as friends.
>
> Dr. Braband takes an especial personal interest in all his patients and works diligently long, hard hours to accomplish a task; his sense of duty and responsibility are unquestionable.
>
> During our discussions he expressed a very unbiased understanding and reflected a very high regard for democratic principles of government, especially as found in the United States of America. He received part of his training in the USA. His character, honesty, and sobriety are above reproach.
>
> The objectivity of this appraisal must be emphasized in that I feel he is strongly dedicated to the best interests of his fellow man and as such would serve as a valued contribution to the organization he has chosen.
>
> Sincerely,
>
> EUGENE F. PHILLIPS
> Captain, USAF

the steep road on the edge of a mountain in Luxemburg our car began sliding, my father lost control of our speed because we were sliding on the ice. He was a very experienced pilot at this point in his life, he had survived WWII and test pilot flights and was a flight instructor. I felt sure he knew how to handle this event. I was sitting in the middle of the back seat of the mint green Ford, looking out the front window of the car and I could see the road turn around the bottom of this steep incline, but we were still very high in the mountains. If we slid off the edge of that mountain, I was thinking that this was going to be the day I died. No one said a word, but I could see my mother bracing in her seat for the fall over the cliff. Alte was next to me, she had been in a bad car accident in high school, but she stayed calm. There were trees planted on the edge of that cliff. A lot of things were going through my head. I thought Dad might have to hit a tree to stop our fall over the cliff.

But just as our car reached the edge of that turn a huge bus pulled up and stopped in front of our car's fated path. This was a bus stop for the folks living in this area. My father maneuvered the car to hit the bus with the side of the car instead of a frontal impact. We spun around, but by a true miracle no one was hurt. We were, however, pretty shaken. The people on the bus came over to help. They called the police and took us into a private home where they offered us a beverage and a place to sit down. The police arrived but did not speak much English. I became the translator for my family because the Luxemburg police did speak French. The policeman asked me my name that day and when I said, "Marilyn," he replied, "Like Marilyn Monroe?" I said, "Yes, like Marilyn Monroe!" I would use that experience, saying the rest of my life, "My name is Marilyn, like Monroe!"

I don't remember how we got back to our apartment in Brussels. But we needed to buy a new car. Our mint-green Ford was irreparably damaged. It's funny how some memories are so clear, and others are not.

Mom talked Dad, a man that had been a POW of the German Third Reich for twenty-one months, into buying a German car. My parents would purchase a 1956 gray Mercedes 360 model. It was a status symbol and usually not something he would be interested in. My city-savvy mother would see the value in this automobile. After we purchased the Mercedes, Father loved the engine and car performance so much that my parents never purchased another make of car for the rest of their lives.

Taking the new Mercedes for a test run, we took a family trip to see the Henri-Chappelle American Cemetery and Memorial in

Belgium. It is fifty-seven acres in size and holds the remains of 7,992 American WWII soldiers. My father would make sure that his children would know the sacrifice of those who gave all in war.

* * *

By early 1957 I started participating in private lessons to prepare me for my first communion. I was the age to make my communion, but Lee impressed the priest who came to our apartment to give me private catechism lessons so much that we made our first communion together. This priest gave private lessons to all the children of the

L-R: My father, Mark, Lee, and me. My mother took this photo of us at the Henri-Chappelle American Cemetery in Hombourg, Belgium.

American Embassy in Brussels. The first communion class was not large, but it was all American kids. My mother would go into downtown Brussels to The Grand Place to get what she needed to fashion our outfits for the occasion. The Grand Place was a beautiful office and shopping area built between the twelfth and seventeenth centuries. It also serves as the central square of the City of Brussels. It is known for its ornate architecture and gold décor and considered one of the most beautiful town squares in the world. My mother found a lace shop and purchased a Belgian lace wedding veil for me. She doubled that veil, and I wore it for my wedding many years later. I also lent the veil to many family members and friends for both communions and weddings, including a daughter-in-law. My godmother in Philadelphia told me to design my dress and she had a dressmaker sew it for me and had it sent to Belgium for me to wear on my big day.

My Mother and the Polish Delegation at the U.S. Embassy Party in Brussels

There was a party at the American Embassy with guests from the Polish Embassy. The country of Poland was under Russian Communist rule as part of The Iron Curtain. My parents got dressed up that evening, and Lee, Mark and I stayed with Nannie. I loved watching my parents get dressed up for these events. They would wear formal evening clothing. I loved clothes, so seeing these tuxedos and gowns and watching my mother fuss with her jewelry, gloves, and stoles or coats was so interesting to me. Father always looked so handsome in his evening attire. I liked watching them leave; I'd be asleep by the time they came home.

My mother said when they arrived at the embassy, she noticed all the Polish guests standing to one side of the room and all the Americans standing on the other. She knew that the purpose of this party was to interact with one another. My mother could speak Polish, and she knew speaking it at the event would be impressive.

Even though my mother had not been raised with many material possessions, she understood class and culture. Raised in an immigrant

L-R: Marie holding Mark, Me, Lee, my mother, and her friend Gabby. This was taken by my Dad at the entrance to our apartment building the day Lee and I made our First Holy Communion.

neighborhood she was exposed to a lot of what to do and not do. She also knew her Polish was of a high standard. So, she walked across the room and introduced herself to the Polish delegates and their wives with great confidence. She started a conversation with the invited guests bringing Dad and other military and civilian guests fully into the party atmosphere. She even translated for Americans who wanted to communicate with the Polish attendees.

Later, Dad told me that Helen Phillips, as he referred to my mom during his sharing, that night was the hit of the event. The Polish delegation invited her to come to Poland to visit. My mother was cordial, but she knew if she went, they may want to keep her there. She did not trust the Communist government to keep their word. They were not known for keeping promises but for doing what the government officials wanted.

Mom and Dad at the American and Polish Embassy event.

Of course, the American Embassy was very pleased with Dad and Mom who had made the event a success! Despite government differences, my mother had brought the people and countries together for one night.

The Polio Epidemic

Polio was a disease first recognized in America in 1894. When I was a kid, we would get a card made to hold dimes and we would fill it and send it into an agency to be used for research to find a cure for the disease. This campaign became known as the March of Dimes. Polio affects the nervous system and can leave people, usually children, with paralysis. Living during that time was scarry to think that this virus could damage us so much. I remember seeing a movie that came out in 1959, starring Danny Kaye, titled *The Five Pennies*. It was based on a true story of a jazz musician whose daughter contracts polio and he leaves his music career to take care of her.

From 1948 to 1955 several polio epidemics occurred leaving many children and adults with disabilities. President Franklin Roosevelt, suffered from a form of this disease. The American population was very aware of polio because of the affected President. The U.S. had started searching for a way to end this disease. By 1955, Dr. Jonas E. Salk and colleagues had developed a polio vaccine. The American Embassy had all Americans get the first dose of the vaccine by needle. Eventually the vaccine was given on a cube of sugar and taken orally. My World Health Organization (WHO) shot record shows I had gotten multiple doses of the vaccine.

* * *

As 1957 was ending so was Father's station at the Belgian Embassy. Mark was not on the passport photo taken in Georgia, so, we each got our own passports to travel back to the U.S. As with military families, we were ready to move again. I had started third grade at Bois de le Cambre and Lee was in second grade. I was quite fluent in French now and could hold my own anywhere. I remember one day in the schoolyard, a Belgian classmate asked me how I would say a word in English, and I could not remember the English word. This shook me, I was forgetting my native language! This happened in September, and by the end of November my family was going back to America.

A few weeks before we left Brussels, I asked my mother who would we be taking back to the U.S. with us. She didn't understand. I said, "Are we taking the maid or the babysitter?" She told me we were not taking anyone with us, only our family. Thinking that I had become a spoiled child, she had me wash the kitchen floor on my hands and knees. I had never done cleaning before, and she wanted me to learn that my life was not going to be like this assignment in Brussels. She also told me that sometimes we would live big and other times not so much. It was a good lesson that day, because our next assignment was in Laredo, Texas.

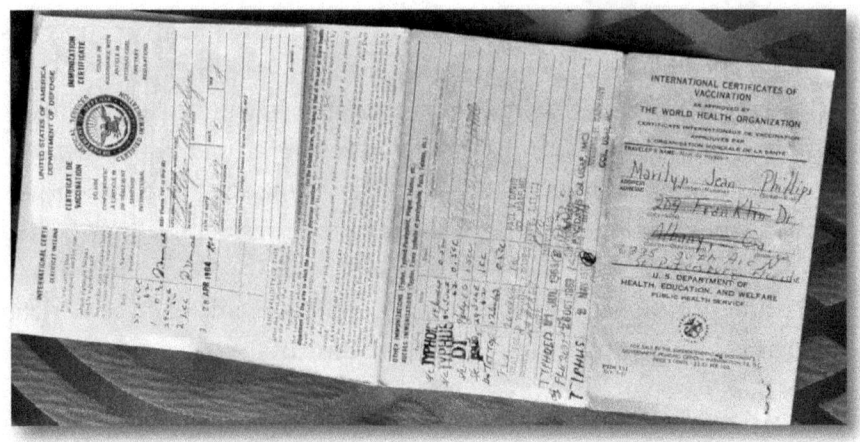

One of my vaccine records. My mother always carried our passports and vaccination records in her handbag. Living in Europe, we needed them each time we entered a new country. We had to stop at the border guard station and show our passports and sometimes vaccination records.

Traveling Back to America

The SS *United States* was an ocean liner built for the United States Lines at a cost of $79.4 million. The ship was the largest ocean liner constructed entirely in the U.S. and the fastest ocean liner to cross the Atlantic in either direction, retaining the Blue Riband for the highest average speed since her maiden voyage in 1952. The maximum speed attained by *United States* is disputed, as it was once held as a military secret. She was designed by American naval architect William Francis Gibbs and could be converted into a troopship if required by the Navy in time of war. The vessel was constructed from 1950 to 1952 at the Newport News Shipbuilding and Drydock Company in Newport News, Virginia. The hull was constructed in a dry dock. The SS *United States* was built to exacting Navy specifications, which required that the ship be heavily compartmentalized, and have separate engine rooms to optimize wartime survival.

The construction of the ship's superstructure involved the most extensive use of aluminum in any construction project up to that time, which posed a galvanic corrosion challenge to the builders in joining the aluminum superstructure to the steel decks below. However, the extensive use of aluminum meant significant weight savings, as well. *United States* had the most powerful steam turbines of any merchant marine vessel at the time.

The interiors were designed by Dorothy Marckwald and Anne Urquhart, the same designers who did the interiors for SS *America*. The goal was to "create a modern fresh contemporary look that emphasized simplicity over palatial, restrained elegance over glitz and glitter." They would also hire artists to produce American-themed artwork for the public spaces. Interior décor also included a children's playroom designed by Edward Meshekoff. Markwald and Urquhart were also tasked with the challenge of creating interiors that were completely fireproof.

Fire safety was critical because of various maritime fire-related disasters aboard vessels including SS *Morro Castle* and SS *Normandie*. Designer William Francis Gibbs specified that the ship incorporates the most rigid fire safety standards. To minimize the risk of fire, the designers of *United States* prescribed using no wood in the ship's framing, accessories, decorations, or interior surfaces, although the galley did feature a wooden butcher's block. During the 1950s and early 1960s the SS *United States* was popular for transatlantic travel. She attracted frequent repeat celebrity passengers, such as the Duke and Duchess of Windsor, along with celebrities like Marilyn Monroe, Judy Garland, Cary Grant, Salvador Dalí, Duke Ellington, and Walt Disney, who would feature the ship in the 1962 film *Bon Voyage!*

By the mid-to-late 1960s, with the advent of jet-powered airliners, the market for transatlantic travel by ship dwindled. The *America* was sold in 1964, *Queen Mary* retired in 1967, and *Queen Elizabeth* in 1968. The SS *United States* was no longer profitable. Unbeknownst to her passengers, crew, or the public, SS *United States* completed her last voyage (Number 400) on November 7, 1969, when she arrived in New York.

The Belgian government gave my parents a choice of how we would travel back to America. Mom had never traveled on a ship so decided that might be interesting. Our family would travel back to the U.S. on the SS *United States*. Our fare was paid by the Belgian government. We would travel first class on the fastest ship in the world. We received an itinerary for the passage across the Atlantic Ocean and into the Port of New York. This itinerary would let us know what to pack for the five-day trip across the Atlantic Ocean in late November of 1957. Mother was preparing Lee and me for what the trip would be like and what we would see when we got to America. Coming into the Port of New York, we would see the Statue of Liberty, which she had shown us in a photo. A couple days later Lee would ask again, "When are we going to see that statue of the lady with the paint brush?"

In our last days in Brussels, we stayed with Marie, as our furniture had been packed and loaded for transport across the Atlantic Ocean by cargo ship. I attended my last day at my school and said goodbye to all my classmates, who told me how lucky I was to go to the U.S. I told them all that one day I would return to Brussels with my husband. I kept that promise; however, I would never see any of them again. In many ways it was sad to leave. My life would become a constant routine of making friends and then leaving.

Those last days at Marie's were sad too. Marie's friend Ivan came over one night while Sarah was babysitting us. Marie and my parents went out to dinner as a farewell to Marie. Sarah answered the door and Ivan asked to speak to me. He showed me a box and opened it to show me a gold watch. He said this watch should be given to his godson Mark when he made his confirmation. It was an expensive gold Omega watch. I felt very grown up to have that responsibility.

On the day we were to leave we packed our suitcases and loaded them into our Mercedes for the drive to Saint-Adresse, France. Saint-Adresse was a small town where Marie had been born. The Port of Le Havre is nearby and where we would board the SS *United States*. This was the port that twelve years earlier Father had left as a former

POW. Marie would write to me years later and tell me when we left, it broke her heart. No one had ever let their children get as close to her as my parents had. Marie would soon leave Ivan. My family had changed her and her life. Sadly, the rest of her life would never be like that wonderful period we all shared in Brussels.

Our trip across the Atlantic in November of 1957 was very rough. The day we got on the ship was wonderful. My parents had cameras and the movie camera ready, so lots of photos were taken. There was a printed manifest document of all the passengers. However, some passengers were not printed on the list. The stewards and stewardesses came into our cabin for questions and anything we may need. They also came in to check on our suitcases. The Duke and Duchess of Windsor were aboard the ship and they had 104 pieces of luggage, and one was missing, and they were checking all the first-class passengers to see if the lost bag was mistakenly put into another cabin.

We had two portholes in our cabin and a bathtub for my mother to bathe Mark, who was only twenty months old. After boarding the ship and experiencing the life vest drill, my family toured this magnificent ship and took lots of photos and movies. We were told by our stewardess that the seas were going to be very rough for our journey the first two days. We walked around the ship for some time and then decided to go down to the bottom of the ship. There was a large swimming pool we wanted to see. We did not plan on swimming since we did not pack swim wear. When we got to the pool, there was one person swimming in the pool. The sea was so rough that as the ship swayed back and forth, I could see the bottom of this swimming pool. It looked way too scary for me, and I was worried about the person who had decided to go swimming.

When we got back to our cabin, the stewardess told us to stay in our cabin the first night and she would bring us light snacks to eat every couple of hours. She told us to keep snacking on crudité and chicken breast. The next morning the sea was better, and we went to the dining room. We were alone in the dining room because most of the other first-class passengers were still seasick from the night before.

Me aboard the SS United States *in November 1957.*

Our stewardess had given us good information. After breakfast we took more photos and then Lee and I went to the decorator-designed playroom for children.

There were several shops on the ship and my mother took Lee and me to look around. Lee was spotted by an English actress, Merle Oberon. She was very taken by him. He spoke about interesting things he had noticed on the ship. A small crowd started to gather, and everyone was impressed with the cute boy and his interesting questions.

Our time aboard the ship and our time with the embassy in Brussels created lifelong memories for me. It was a wonderful time! I would never again live at that level of affluence, but I would reference that time later in my life.

We came into the Port of New York at dawn and my dad had the movie camera ready. My brothers Lee and Mark got to see the lady with the paintbrush and so did I. I remember my mother sharing the meaning of this great statute. For me, I had already stood at the top of Waterloo and felt the power of the lion. I had known people who had lived through war in their European countries. I had walked through WWII rubble in Bitburg, Germany and I had been attacked by angry Hungarian college students coming out of the American Embassy in Brussels. When I saw the Statue of Liberty, a gift to the U.S. from France, I knew probably more than most children my age. I knew the meaning of freedom.

My father picked up our gray Mercedes, and we were off to see relatives in Philadelphia who had missed us while we lived in Brussels. These relatives were anxious to meet my brother, Mark, for the first time. My cousin David had married his girlfriend, Nancy, while we were gone. So, there was much catching up to be done.

The morning we arrived at sunrise to see the Statue of Liberty from the deck of the SS United States. L-R: Lee, Mark, me, and my mother. Father took the photo.

Then it was on to Ohio to attend a family wedding. Aunt Marie's son was getting married. It was a terrific opportunity to be with my paternal family while celebrating a wonderful union. While staying with Aunt Marie, I saw my first basketball game. Her younger son played on his high school team. I remember marveling at the fast pace of the game and going back and forth from one basket to another. I didn't understand the rules of the game or even care about them, I loved the pace and the energy of the crowd!

4

Our New Assignment: Laredo AFB, Texas
December 1957 – May 1959

WE WOULD DRIVE DOWN TO TEXAS. When we left New York, we headed to Philadelphia. When we passed the state line, I was concerned that we did not stop at the border to have our passports checked. My father explained that in the U.S. we did not have to stop at each state because the U.S. was one country, and we had shown our passports in New York. We could drive anywhere we wanted in the U.S. Living in Europe we had to stop at each border.

Dad's first job in Laredo was as a flight instructor for the 3640th Pilot Training Squadron. Laredo Air Force Base provided intermediate and advanced flight training for jet pilots, including pilot trainees from twenty-four countries. The initial host unit stationed at Laredo AFB was the 3640th Pilot Training Wing, initially operating the T-33 in the 1950s and transitioning to the T-41, T-37, and T-38 aircraft in the 1960s.

During our time in Laredo, my father had two titles: Flight Instructor and Administrative Assistant to the Installation Group Command.

Installation Group Command is part of the DoD. It overseas the Air Force readiness ensuring all installations are postured to provide the best support. On March 3, 1958 my father had a temporary duty business (TDY BIS) to Craig AFB, Alabama. The family did not move for this period, only he did.

Craig AFB

In December 1952, Craig AFB added to its mission the Jet Qualification Training Program for selected Air Force pilots in furtherance of the goal of converting to an all-jet Air Force. This function was transferred to Randolph Air Force Base, Texas, in 1958. In May 1958, Craig again began training jet pilots to provide combat effectiveness for the USAF global missions.

As my family was getting settled in Laredo, in a rented home, without our furnishings from Brussels, we lived for two months with no furniture. There was a dock strike in the New York port, which held up our belongings. All we had for that period were the clothes we brought on the ship. My mother just bounced with the challenges. We arrived in time for Christmas, and Mother prepared for the holiday by buying presents for us before we left Europe; but they were not going to make it in time for Christmas. When our family in Philadelphia realized this, Godno went to the five-and-dime store and purchased items for all three of us. She wrapped them in Christmas paper and put them in suitcases, and took the suitcases to the Greyhound Bus station in Philadelphia. Keep in mind that Godno never had a car and never learned to drive. Like all members of my mother's family, they used public transportation. She walked the filled suitcases to the bus stop and on to the Greyhound station.

My father went to the Greyhound station in Laredo and picked up the suitcases. I found the top of a Christmas tree hanging out of our neighbor's trash can. This had probably been cut off the top so the tree could fit in the house. I was thrilled! We put the treetop in a Coke bottle. My mother went out and got some Christmas bulbs and silver garland. The presents were put under that poor little tree after

L-R: Lee, Mark, and I celebrating our first Christmas back in the U.S. This photo was taken in our first rented home in Laredo. I was so proud of the last-minute Christmas tree I found in our neighbor's trash.

Lee, Mark, and I went to bed. We were so happy to have this Christmas in our new location. I remember this Christmas more than most of the others. As military kids with parents like mine, we learned to appreciate whatever we had. We had just moved from a beautiful assignment in Brussels to Laredo with dirt roads and a basic rental home. Many places we lived in we never hung pictures on the walls. We didn't want to make holes in the wall because we were just renters. In Laredo, we didn't have Air Force base housing though we lived in rentals close to the base. We would live in two locations in Laredo before leaving.

MY FATHER'S SECRETS

* * *

Lee and I were very behind in our English reading and writing skills since we had been in school in Brussels learning only French. My parents tried to help with lessons at home. My mother had the Dick and Jane series of readers in Brussels. This time Father insisted we purchase a set of *McGuffey Readers*. These were a series of graded primers for grades one through six. They were widely used as textbooks in American schools from the mid-nineteenth century to the early twentieth century. They were very advanced compared to the Dick and Jane readers. They were awfully hard for Lee and me. We didn't have many lessons at home with these either. But I had great respect for them and would sometimes look through them to challenge myself.

The first school Lee and I attended in Laredo was the Ursuline Academy. I loved this school because, as I said, I was so far behind, I was like a sponge in water soaking up all I could. I also made some wonderful friends. The Johnson family was one of those friends. I met their daughter in my class and somehow our parents got together as well. I had my first sleepover at their house.

Our first Easter in Laredo was at their house. We celebrated Easter with Mexican flare! We had a Mexican Easter egg hunt. They hid eggs; some were hard boiled, and some eggs were just shells with confetti inside of them. When you found one of the confetti-filled eggs you were to crack it over other egg-hunters' heads, and all the confetti would spill out. When all the egg hunting was finished, we had a piñata. I had never seen one before. It was hung in a tree in their yard, and we had to wait our turn to get blindfolded and hit the piñata with a stick. Finally, the candy came pouring out and we grabbed the sweet treats from the ground.

I finished third grade at the Ursuline Academy. The next year I walked to the public school near our second rental home. My parents had a disagreement with the Ursuline Sisters over Lee. He was very smart, and my parents wanted the best education for him. The Ursuline Sisters wanted to leave him back a grade because they felt his English skills and his reading and writing would improve if he repeated second grade. My parents disagreed and sent Lee to another private school where the class size was smaller, and he could get the help he needed to catch up. I went where I was sent. The public school I attended was not good for me at all. I literally learned nothing that year. I had a sixteen-year-old boy in my fourth-grade class. He barely fit in the desk his legs were so long. He was the son of migrant workers, and he was far behind in school. He and I were friendly because we both liked art. The teacher gave us a lot of busy work. He and I spent a lot of time drawing and coloring. To tell you the truth, neither of us benefitted much from that school.

Mother signed me up for dance lessons in Laredo. I had not had a dance lesson since Albany, GA. The classes were expensive, but my mother thought since I loved dancing these classes could provide an opportunity for me. At my first lesson I learned the Mexican Hat dance. The main part of the dance was to hold my hands in a certain way around my waist and walk with a proud stance around the hat. When I got home from the lesson my family wanted to see what I had learned. I showed them the proud walk I took in a circle. I was thrilled they asked me to perform. Mother asked, "That's it? Seven dollars to learn to walk like that?" The family would refer to that day as the day I learned the "seven dollars walk." I continued my dance lessons in Laredo and performed in recitals. I even had one solo in a recital at the officers' club on the base.

That year Lee and I made our confirmation. In the Catholic Church; this is when you say yes to the Catholic faith. Lee and I had been baptized and had our first communion, so now we were confirming this choice of faith for ourselves. I was in the fourth grade and Lee was in third. Since Lee and I had communion at the same time in Brussels, the Laredo church allowed us to do the same. We attended catechism classes at the local Catholic church. Making one's confirmation was a major event in a Catholic family.

My mother's family would use this event to travel from Philadelphia. This time my godmother would come down to Laredo to be my confirmation sponsor, and Nannie would come too. Nannie was living with and caring for her Uncle Tony, who would join her on the trip. The three would travel all those miles on a Greyhound bus. During the time my Great Uncle Tony was visiting for our confirmation he wanted to take a bath in gin. He liked drinking, he liked gin, and he had always wanted to take a bath in it. Uncle Tony had lived through Prohibition in America. He had heard about bathtub gin. During Prohibition people would make their own liquor in the bathtub and then bottle it. Somehow, he thought people were bathing in it. Well, in Mexico the gin was cheap. I remember we bought enough gin for the bathtub and poured it in. Uncle Tony went into the bathroom alone as we all waited outside the door. The bath was over quickly, the gin was not pleasant to be in for any length of time, it burned him almost immediately. It was fun to witness the experiment anyway. We all had a good laugh.

Nannie stayed with us in Laredo for a while, and Godno and Uncle Tony returned to Philadelphia on the bus. I have to say, Nannie's Mexican cooking skills were good. She and my mother could whip out those tamales that I loved!

While living in Laredo my family and I also became familiar with Mexican cuisine. The second house we rented was owned by a Mexican family. They lived in the guest house behind the large home we rented from them. We played with their kids and learned to love their food. My favorite being tamales! We had dinner parties at their home and our home sharing family time together.

One of the fun toys that appeared during that time was the Hula Hoop by the Wham-O toy company. When we played with the kids in the neighborhood we spent a lot of time with that toy.

We purchased a TV in Laredo. We did not have one in Brussels. We watched shows in English and Spanish. There was a favorite show called *Peter Gunn,* but we watched *Pedro Pistolas.* Walt Disney started a show titled *Walt Disney Presents* and introduced *Disney's Wonderful World of Color* during that assignment. Our TV was only black and white, but color TVs were coming soon.

* * *

Laredo is located on the Rio Grande River and traveling to Mexico was easy. As in Europe, we had to pass through the border from the U.S. to Mexico. And as in Europe, we had to have our passports. In addition, my mother always carried our WHO (World Health Organization) shot records. Mom loved shopping in Mexico, just as she loved shopping in European countries. She fell in love with Mexican silver. Mexico has many silver mines and is one of the main providers of silver in the world. My parents were celebrating their twelfth anniversary, and although it was not their twenty-fifth anniversary, my mother talked my father into buying her a silver punch bowl set. Silver is what is used to mark the milestone of twenty-five years of marriage. My mother had been raised in a home with one parent, so her biggest goal was to be married and have a big twenty-fifth anniversary with a party. She figured the silver punch bowl opportunity was one she had to go after now. She got her punch bowl and her twenty-fifth anniversary. But her big anniversary party would come much later, and at a very meaningful time. That beautiful punch bowl, however, would see many wonderful family events for years to come.

* * *

The one problem in traveling to and from Mexico was our Mercedes. There were not many Mercedes in the U.S. or Mexico at that time. Smugglers were looking for different cars to move items like drugs and other things into the U.S. We were stopped and searched at the border each trip. One day the Mexican guard at the border asked my mother what was in her large purse. My mother always carried a large purse because she had all the passports, shot records and other documents, snacks for us kids and wet wipes—as a mother would do. However, this guard was not familiar with large bags and when the guard asked, my mother came back with a smart answer, "I don't know what is in my bag, I haven't been to the bottom of it in years." He yelled, "Dump it out here and now!" I learned then that you don't mess around with a smart-alecky answer with officials. Going from one country to another was a serious thing and not a joke.

***

My father's pilot students were highly rated pilots, and my family became friendly with several of them, including Ronnie Bernasconi. He was a single guy and really took to my parents and us kids. My family would keep in touch with him for quite a while after we left Laredo. Ronnie was a very handsome young pilot, and I had a girlish crush on him. He was raised in New York City, and his father was the head maître de at the 21 Club in New York City.

The U.S. Gets Two New States

When I was born in 1949 the U.S. only had forty-eight states. In 1958 and 1959 the two American territories of Alaska and Hawaii would become the forty-ninth and fiftieth states. President Eisenhower would sign the Statehood Act on July 7, 1958, for Alaska to become a state on January 3, 1959, and Hawaii's statehood became effective on August 21, 1959. Two new stars were added to the U.S. flag. America is not a country that takes land unless we win it in war. Sometimes when we win a plot of land, we may keep part of it for a military base to protect our country and freedom. The people of both Alaska and Hawaii had voted to ask the U.S. for statehood. Both states were also strategic locations in the world for U.S. military bases. Most European countries and Mexico had acquired land in the new world from the 1500s. The U.S. purchased it from these countries.

***

As I finished fourth grade, Father's assignment in Laredo was up, and our next assignment would be Stead AFB near Reno, NV. We left Laredo on May 11, 1959. My family chose to drive to our assignment in Nevada. Dad would wake us up early in the morning and carry us to the car in our pajamas. He always liked getting an early start. The sky was dark, the sun had not come up yet. We would get dressed in the car and only stop for bathroom breaks. My mother always packed food for meals, so that was not a reason to stop. In those years not all highways or roads were paved, and our car was a European model, and it didn't have air conditioning. The car windows would be open, and you could only go as fast as the condition of the roads would allow. The first night we spent in Del Rio, TX, at the Esquire Motel. The second night we stayed at the Mission Motel in Las Cruces, NM. The third night we stayed at the Trails End Motel in Glendale, AR. The next day was going to be a big surprise for us kids.

On May 14th we stayed in the Lamplighter Motel in Anaheim, CA. We were going to Disneyland! Disneyland was new at the time. It opened on July 17, 1955, while we were living in Brussels. This was the first park Walt Disney would open.

Moves were always hard and long. My parents would do the best they could to make some fun for us kids. While we were there, we got to see Walt Disney himself. He loved the small children's section of the park which featured a small train. He was driving the train that day. We got to go on a few rides at Disneyland before going to Knott's Berry Farm, which was not far from Disneyland. It had started out as a family berry farm that had added some old-style rides. It was nothing like Disneyland but had its own charm. My parents were conservative about spending money, so we only spent a little time at each park. My mother was smart and dressed the three of us in colorful outfits. When we entered each venue, she designated a place for us to go to if we became separated. It was always at the entry to the venue, and if we got lost, we could ask for help to get to the entrance and the spot she had set up to meet. She did this every time we were in crowds of people. It was smart and I did it with my own children years later.

MY FATHER'S SECRETS

5

The Sierra Nevada Mountains and Stead AFB
June 1959 – April 1961

THE MILITARY MOVES PERSONNEL ACCORDING to what talents one has and what is going on in the world at that time. In 1951 it was determined that the Sierra Nevada area and forests would be suitable for survival training. SAC had begun the training for its personnel, teaching them how to survive if forced down in remote or unfriendly terrain, threatened with capture, or captured.

Other commands wanted to train aircrews in survival techniques, and in September 1954 Stead AFB became part of the Air Training Command, and the 394th Composite Wing became the 365th Combat Crew Training Wing. After several name changes, the Survival Training School became the 367th Combat Crew Training Squadron.

In January 1958, a small group of instructor pilots from Randolph AFB, Texas, was sent to Stead AFB to determine the feasibility of advanced helicopter training in the area's mountains. On July 15, 1958, the 365th Crew Training Wing was redesignated as the 365th Flying Training Wing (Advanced), concurrent with the relocation of the USAF Helicopter Pilot School to Stead.

Air Defense Command

In 1959 a Semi-Automatic Ground Environment (SAGE) Data Center (DC-16) was established at Reno AFB. The SAGE system was a network linking Air Force (and later the Federal Aviation Administration) General Surveillance radar stations into a centralized center for air defense, intended to provide early warning and response for a Soviet nuclear attack.

Helicopter Training

During the summer and fall of 1958, the USAF Helicopter School was moved from Randolph AFB to Stead AFB and designated the 3638th Flying Training Squadron (Helicopter). The base provided ample facilities and an unencumbered airspace in which to operate the flying training mission. The base had also recently undergone a large building project of all new Capehart Family Housing which lent well to the accompanying military families. Pilots would undergo training in the H-19 Chickasaw and Piasecki H-21 Workhorse/Shawnee helicopters. The syllabus would contain basic transition training and instruments as well as advanced operational techniques in high-altitude confined areas and mountain operations. Training in the HH-43 Huskie was also introduced as that airframe entered the USAF inventory. Pilots from all fixed-wing and rotary-wing backgrounds would also attend the USAF Survival School at Stead in preparation for operational assignments.

Flying training was conducted at Stead as well as an auxiliary airfield, Sky Ranch, located about ten miles east of the base. Several unprepared ridgetop and pinnacle landing locations at altitudes up to 8,100 feet (2,500 m) were located on Peavine Mountain directly south of the base. A similar number of tree-lined spots were in Dog Valley, southwest of Peavine, to conduct confined area landing and takeoff procedures. The area north of Stead to Pyramid Lake was used for instrument training, which was one of Dad's specialties.

The first students to go through helicopter pilot training were rated fixed-wing USAF pilots. In fact, all pilots undergoing helicopter pilot training since 1944 had been rated pilots. In 1965, students were entered into helicopter pilot training having received approximately 120 hours in the T-28 Trojan, but not yet having received their wings. They would receive their wings upon graduation from helicopter training.

The 3638th Flying Training Squadron (helicopter) trained not only USAF pilots but also many from foreign countries. At least a dozen countries, including Japan, Argentina, Pakistan, India, France, Bolivia, and the Republic of China (Taiwan), sent pilots to basic helicopter pilot training as well as instructor pilot upgrading. There was an exchange program with England's Royal Air Force (RAF) and the Royal Australian Air Force (RAAF) for a two-year tour by the exchange pilots. U.S. Marine Corps pilots flying the Sikorsky H-34 Choctaw were given a short course in high altitude mountain flying techniques. Four RAAF helicopter pilots also received several hours of mountain indoctrination on their way from UH-1 Huey training at Fort Rucker and returning to Australia to fly their own Hueys. From 1958 through 1965, the helicopter school trained over 1252 USAF and 384 foreign helicopter pilots.

In support of the Air Rescue Service, which was seeking a better performing aircraft for combat search and rescue missions in Southeast Asia, the school also conducted Lime Light 36, an escalated training program to provide crews for the Sikorsky HH-3E helicopter then deploying. Between August 23 and September 29, 1965, crews and support personnel trained as a unit at Stead. On September 30th, 117 men and six HH-3Es deployed to Udorn Royal Thai Air Force Base, Thailand, and integrated with the three HH-43 crews of Detachment 5, 38th Air Rescue Squadron.

Part of the school included the Instructor Training (IT) Section of the squadron. Experienced line pilots assigned to the squadron to be instructors had to be indoctrinated into the standardized techniques and grading procedures used in the school. This sometimes required some rethinking on the part of the new instructors that had been used to doing it "their way" when in the field. They were reminded about how they handled the controls when they had only five hours of helicopter time and relate it to their students. Standardized procedures were necessary for scoring the student's progress and if a change of instructors might be required.

When we got to Stead, my father was a survival instructor. He had been raised on a farm, shot down and wounded in enemy territory in WWII and spent twenty-one months as a POW. Those qualifications were what was needed in a military survival instructor. His job there also included Base Operations. He served as assistant Base Operations Officer for our entire assignment. Base Operations Officer at Stead meant overseeing the resources to operate the base, installations, camps, posts, and stations of military departments. These resources sustain mission capability, ensure quality of life, and enhance work force productivity and fund personnel and infrastructure support.

Stead AFB was located about thirty miles outside of Reno, Nevada, a.k.a. "The Biggest Little City in the World," in the Nevada mountains. As gambling was legal in Nevada, Reno had a lot of casinos. The base was a self-supporting military town. It provided everything the military and their families needed. We only went into Reno to buy things our Base Exchange did not carry. Our family moved into one of the newly built duplex homes in the officer's housing section at Stead. These homes were all the same. We could see Peavine Mountain from our backyard. The desert mountain terrain was very brown, and we could see the mountains that connected Nevada with California in the distance. There were tumbling weeds at certain times of the year and snow in winter. Lee and I attended school at the base elementary school. Bases were safe and as kids, we had a lot of freedom to walk and ride bicycles.

The base was not close to any city so all of us military kids were deeply entrenched in military protocol. We attended school, shopped at a Base Exchange (BX) for clothing etc., as well as the commissary (grocery store), went to the movie theater, hair salon and barber shop – all on base. The Military Religious Center on any given day could host any religious service, but it looked like a church on the outside. The military provided every need we could imagine.

An Old Buddy from North Africa

One day, not long after we moved to Stead, my father came home to tell us a very interesting story. A man walked up to him at Base Operations and said, "I owe you forty dollars!" He had served with him in North Africa in 1943. The night before my dad's mission to Foccia, Italy, to strafe the airfield, he lent this guy forty dollars. This man recognized him from all those years ago and remembered his debt. The interesting thing is, in that area of Nevada no one carried paper dollar bills, only silver dollars. He had borrowed the forty dollars that night in 1943 to play cards. He paid my father back the forty dollars in silver dollars and he and his wife took my parents out to dinner to deliver the debt.

Catholic Chaplain

My parents made friends with the many other military families, and we also made friends with one of the base chaplains, a Catholic priest, Father John Wizicowski. He was the son of Polish immigrants. He and my mother shared a love of Polish food. She would invite him to dinner with the family often. She apparently cooked very much like his mother. When my Nannie came to visit, Father John was at our house for dinner all the time. I certainly came from a family of great cooks!

Father John became like a family member. My mother loved to sing and became a member of the Catholic choir. My father had been an altar boy in his hometown of Plymouth, Ohio at St. Joseph's Catholic Church, in North Africa and the POW camp in Germany. No matter where we attended mass if there was no altar boy to help the priest, father always stepped up. Lee became an altar boy under the guidance of Father John and became interested in becoming a priest.

My godmother and Aunt Mamie sent him all the items to encourage him. He got a wine glass sprayed gold to look like a chalice and child size robes a priest would wear for mass. For a while, each day after school, Lee would serve pretend mass in his bedroom and all the kids from the neighborhood would come for his pretend mass. Mark would serve as Lee's altar boy and hold a saucer under your chin if you wanted to receive communion. One day Lee was ready to serve the communion and Mark was nowhere to be found, but he showed up shortly after we all heard the toilet flush.

Father John was a fisherman, and he would take Dad and Lee fishing. Mark was still too young. We had some nice fish dinners after those trips. During our time at Stead, Mark was only three to five years old. He was too young for school. He was, however, popular with other kids in the neighborhood. He liked the frontier atmosphere of Stead AFB; and played "Cowboys and Indians" all the time. This was a popular theme back in the 1950s and 1960s. He was always dressed in his cowboy hat and his toy gun belt with a pistol. As Mark got older Lee and Mark became close. They shared a room and talked until they fell asleep at night. Lee and I shared a room until Mark was born. After that I always had my own room. I could hear their conversations at night in the room close by.

Uncle Thom and Family

My paternal Uncle, Thom, and his family lived in Fresno, California. Thom had been in my parents' wedding as the best man. He and his wife Eleanor had left Plymouth, Ohio, after 1945, settling not far from Philadelphia. They came to visit from time to time in Philadelphia. I would play with their oldest child, Mary Kaye. She and I were close in age. When we moved to Stead, we were about five hours away in Fresno, California, and the two families visited from time to time. My mother would always sew dresses for Mary Kaye and her younger sister Patsy. Thom and Eleanor would eventually have six children. Fresno was beautiful and Thom and family had a very nice home, although it only had two bedrooms. The parents had one room and the kids all slept in the second bedroom. The house did have a separate garage with an apartment over it. When we visited, we stayed in the garage apartment. As their kids got older, they took over that space.

The TV Show Bonanza

What would become a very popular TV show started airing while we lived at Stead AFB, *Bonanza*. It had scenes that were filmed not far from us. We lived near the area that the show featured as The Ponderosa. The show starred Lorne Greene, Pernell Roberts, Dan Blocker, and Michael Landon. It was a hit show and aired from September 1959 until January 1973.

1960 Winter Olympics

Another interesting event was the 1960 Winter Olympics held in Squaw Valley, California. We didn't go to the Olympics, but we did watch it on TV. My family was not into sports. The only time my family would watch sports on TV would be the Olympics.

Donner Pass and Lake Tahoe

Stead was located not far from the historic Donner Pass, a 7,056-foot-high mountain pass in Sierra, Nevada. It is one of the most famous mountains in the world, and frequently in the news. It is one of the snowiest places in the contiguous U.S. Lake Tahoe was not far from us either, a breathtaking lake made of melted snow. The water is crystal clear and beautiful. Our family took several trips to Lake Tahoe while we lived at Stead. The views and times at Lake Tahoe were memorable and beautiful. I never experienced anything like it in all the other places I lived. It was cool in temperature and the air was crisp and invigorating.

Living in the mountains was certainly an experience. I remember one day it started to snow. My father came home early and told us that this is the type of snow you can use to make ice cream. He collected the snow himself and then gave my mother directions to cook something up and a while later we had this incredible ice cream made from snow. We were at a high altitude in the mountains, and baking with my mother and grandmother was different because the air was thinner. They had to adjust the baking time, amount of flour and, if making bread, it would rise faster.

Marilyn Monroe and Clark Gable in The Misfits

During our time at Stead, a famous Hollywood director, John Houston, made *The Misfits*. It starred Marilyn Monroe and Clark Gable. I never saw the film crews but there was real buzz in Reno about the famous movie stars! We would hear about it on the local nightly news.

Presidential Election

We got to Nevada in 1959 and by 1960 the talk around our house was of the upcoming presidential election. I remember thinking that I liked President Eisenhower and I felt safe with him. The candidate that my family was talking about was John F. Kennedy. I would wear a Kennedy for President campaign button on my blouse to school. I remember telling my mother, "I wish I were related to Kennedy." She replied, "You are more likely related to Khrushchev, the leader of the Soviet Union." When I thought about it, she was right. My ancestors on both sides came from Eastern Europe and if I were related to anyone it was probably not Kennedy.

California Fire

The Sierra Nevada area between Nevada and California is conducive to fires. Fires have been happening here since 1878, and probably long before that date. The terrain is dry and cool. On a bucolic late-summer day, a plume of smoke was spotted against an overcast cloud ceiling, emanating from a ridge high above Truckee, somewhere near the new Interstate 80 freeway (then under construction).

It was a Saturday afternoon, August 20, 1960, and countless Tahoe vacationers were loading up the family wagons for the trek back to the Bay Area and home. If they'd gassed up their cars, they stood a chance, but a slim one, of getting home. If not, they were probably still sitting at Kings Beach or Tahoe City or South Shore on the following Tuesday morning. At 4:15 p.m. the power went out, and not just in Truckee and Donner Lake; the outage reached from the state line as far east as Carlin and Battle Mountain, to Yerington and

Hawthorne, and naturally, Sparks, Carson City, Minden, Gardnerville, and Reno and Stead AFB. Basically, the northern half of Nevada was in darkness as evening fell that Saturday.

The fire effort was legendary, with firefighters arriving hourly from distant points in the west. Cloaked in darkness, and unsure how long the outage would continue. Harrah's cancelled Jack Benny's show at Stateline (that showroom then only eight months old!) We conserved fuel in our cars, as the service stations were out of business. The local newspaper, with the help of a heavy on-site generator got newspapers onto the street almost on schedule, keeping residents and the tourists held hostage by the fuel shortage apprised of information about the fire and the future. A major problem was created by the huge population of tourists who would normally have left for home, but were now left stranded in Reno, Sparks, and the Lake Tahoe basin and requiring food and housing.

The small smoke column above Truckee and Donner Lake grew with phenomenal intensity, spreading at its base and moving to the east at a speed fast enough to crown across the treetops over the earliest firemen on the scene, forcing them to retreat at a virtual dead-run, in some cases leaving their tools, and at least one Caterpillar dozer behind. The smoke soon engulfed the Lake Tahoe basin.

One radio station in Sparks and another in Reno were able to stay on the air, their audience confined to listeners with battery radios or those willing to run their cars. The Reno Airport continued to function but was hampered by the smoke that darkened the city to virtual nighttime visibility — the airport managers mustered up smoke pots, used liberally as warning devices in the late 1950s around construction sites, and lined them up to form approach lanes and runway and taxiway lighting.

It was named the Donner Ridge fire of August 20, 1960. A disruption to a huge number of residents, tourists, and the economy, and it was devastating to all of us at Stead. The cause was eventually determined to be a spark off the blade of a bulldozer working on the new Interstate eighty high on the mountain above Truckee.

Stead AFB lost electricity for over a week. We could see the fire from our base housing area. Our housing area was in a bowl, a depression in the desert mountain terrain and at the edge of the mountains as I looked up, I could see the fire and smoke. It got close enough for us to have soot in the air. It made a big impression on me. Our neighborhood made the best of the situation. Everyone just set up chairs and tables outside and visited. We had food parties too. The first day was ice cream party day, ice cream was melting in the freezer. Everyone just brought out their ice cream containers from their freezers, set up folding tables and shared with anyone that wanted. The military families learn early on that we are all in this together and we act just like the troops, taking care of one another. By the end of the week, we were having barbecues with all kinds of meat and fish. Some of the dads had gone hunting and had deer meat in their freezers, so it would be added to the barbecue and offered to the neighbors.

Fire Prevention Week

Fire Prevention Week at our school later that year included a poster contest. My mother was always dieting to keep her figure. The impact of the California fire and dieting would become the theme for my poster. I had this idea for a slogan for my poster, "Let's Put Fire on a Diet!" I divided the poster in the middle and had a small campfire properly constructed as my father taught in survival training. On the other side I had a big fat fire eating trees. I was proud of my poster. When we got to the award ceremonies at the base movie theater auditorium, I found out my poster was discarded and never judged. The committee thought it had been done by an adult. I was devastated! It was not fair. However, a local artist saw the poster and asked me to study with his adult class in Reno. I was the only ten-year-old in an adult class with a live model and oil paints. I was in heaven. The days of the artists in the park in Brussels were back. I loved that class and learned a lot! My mother would make sure I continued in art through high school.

Later my brother Lee would use my slogan when we moved to another military assignment. This time my mother did draw it for him. She used my slogan on a paper plate with the small, contained fire in the middle of the plate. Lee won that fire prevention contest and was on the fire prevention float in the parade! The idea of using my work would continue with both brothers through high school and beyond. However, I must give my brothers credit. Whenever I needed help in school, they were always there for me too! Lee was exceptionally talented in math. When he explained it to me it made sense, when the teacher's explanation made no sense to me. Mark was excellent in science and helped me with my biology lab classes from time to time when I was in college.

Girl Scouts

I joined the Girl Scouts in Stead. This was a great program to train young girls in self-confidence (at least it was for me). We wore uniforms, and everyone contributed to different tasks and goals in support of the program. I became the treasurer and took the job very seriously. I was responsible for collecting and keeping track of the dues. I had always had jobs in my family, but never outside my family. We sold cookies door to door on base. We had speakers come in and teach us about jobs in our community. We wore a sash across our uniform and on the sash, we had embroidered badges. These badges represented all the courses we had completed. There were courses you could do in just about anything, at your own pace. I was dependent on my mother to get me to the meetings, but everything else was my responsibility. I enjoyed being a girl scout.

My Turquoise Bicycle

My parents decided Lee and I were old enough to have bicycles. So, our family drove into Reno to buy them. I got to pick out the bicycle I wanted, a beautiful turquoise girl's two-wheeler. I couldn't wait to get my bike home and ride. I loved the freedom my bicycle gave me. The great outdoors of the mountain and desert landscape. It was so much fun to go everywhere faster, feeling the wind in my hair. I loved that bike!

MY FATHER'S SECRETS

I had my fifth- and sixth-grade years at the Stead AFB School; all the Air Force kids attended. It was a good school, and I was finally catching up in reading, writing and arithmetic. I especially loved my fifth-grade teacher. She read to us each day after lunch! She read Rudyard Kipling's *The Jungle Book* and E.B. White's *Charlotte's Web*. After her class I began, for the first time in my life, reading books. The first book I ever read was the story of Helen Keller, and then one about Leonardo DaVinci. I found the lives of people most interesting.

Lee would finally be put back into the grade level he was supposed to be age wise. He had started school in Brussels one year earlier than his age required. Lee wasn't thrilled with school and did not find it challenging. While at Stead Elementary School, he got into trouble in class one day. He found a mistake in the math textbook. He pointed the mistake out to the teacher who did not believe him. When Lee got home, he was terribly upset and shared the story with our parents. My father investigated Lee's claim with several friends who agreed that Lee was indeed correct about the mistake in the math book. He then met with the principal of the school, and they put the question before several experts, and it was found that Lee was right.

The summer between fifth and sixth grade I learned that I was getting Miss Petty for my sixth-grade teacher. I was so upset. All my friends had told me she was a mean teacher. Well, to my surprise when I started sixth grade, I really liked her a lot. I would say she was one of the best teachers I ever had, and I did very well in her class. Years later when I would become an elementary teacher myself, I would try and emulate Miss Petty!

The Stead school was all military kids. You weren't the new kid here. We were all new kids, and we were not racially segregated either. I ran for class president in the sixth grade and won! By then it was obvious that I had no athletic talent. When we'd go out on the playground, I would play hope scotch or jump rope or play on the swings. I tried tetherball a couple of times but after I got hit in the nose with the ball, that was the end for me. However, sometimes there would be ath-

My sixth-grade class photo from Stead AFB School. I'm on the left, fourth down from the top.

letic events by the physical education (PE) teacher and the sports kids would pick teams. I was always the last kid picked. No one wanted me. I couldn't blame them for that. I just wasn't good at sports. With little encouragement to want to do well, I really didn't try either.

One day the PE teacher had us pick teams and a boy named Randy in my class picked me first for his team. When I got in line behind him, he whispered, "Don't worry I've got you covered." I will never forget that gesture of support. I still feel wonderful when I think about it! I know I tried harder that day to play the game. I didn't want to let Randy down.

The family that lived directly across the street from us had a girl and boy. The boy's name was Scott, and he was in my class at school. This family had lived in a lot of places and the boy was interesting and well informed in history and geography. I remember one day it snowed and instead of snowmen, Scott built Easter Island Head Statues on his front lawn. They were tall too. He was smart, and I admired that quality. His sister was more of a wild child with her red hair and impulsive nature. She and Lee played together occasionally. Their mother was a wonderful lady who taught me how to type on a typewriter. My godmother worked for American Telephone and Telegraph (AT&T) and was a very proficient typist, so my mother thought it was a good skill to learn.

Scott also worked in the cafeteria at school. He got to leave class early to go the cafeteria to eat lunch with the other children who volunteered. The kids who helped in the cafeteria got lunch free. I begged my mother to let me volunteer. I thought it was such a cool idea, but she balked at this idea. After some time, I was finally allowed to work in the cafeteria with Scott. I loved it. I sold milk for three cents. Some of the young kids would come in with their money and may have dropped a penny and I could not sell them the milk. They would have to drink out of the water fountain. I always felt bad, but I had to follow the instructions of the cafeteria lady in charge, she gave me orders and I had to follow, in the military that is called chain of command. We learned the atmosphere of the social standards of the community we lived in, the military community.

Living on base, you had to respect the base property. You didn't throw litter on the ground. If it was found that I, or one of my brothers, had littered my father would be reprimanded by his commanding officer. Then I would hear about it when he got home. To this day, if I don't see a trash container, I hold the litter in my handbag or car and then throw it away later. This was an important principle, as it taught me to respect all property no matter if I was on base or not. I realized that military base lessons could be applied to the entire planet.

One of My Father's Flight Student's Visits

My father's flight student in Laredo, Ronnie Bernasconi, had gotten married, and he wanted to introduce his wife to us. They had gone to

Our neighbor Scott's Easter Island Snow creations. Military kids think outside the box!

Mexico City on their honeymoon and then came to Stead to stay with us for a few days. They stayed in my room, and I slept on the couch in the living room. It was fun to meet his wife. She was very pretty! Ronnie would leave the military and their lives became busy with their own children. Eventually we received a Christmas card from the Bernasconi family in New York. Ronnie would become a commercial airline pilot. When friends would come to see us from past assignments it was a way for us to have a sense of normalcy. This did not happen often but made me feel more like I had a world family.

My First Date

I would have my first date while living at Stead. There was a boy in my class and his nickname was Pepper. Pepper's father was of a higher rank than my father. So, I got to go on this date. He really liked me. We were only in the sixth grade. He came to the house and brought me a necklace. The necklace was a heart cut crystal on a silver chain. Pepper walked me to the movie theater on the base. My father of course walked behind us and sat a few rows behind us as well in the theater. It was only the one date, but I kept that necklace for years and eventually gave it to my oldest son to give to his first girlfriend.

New Family Across the Street and Father John

A new family moved in across the street from our duplex. My mother went over to meet them and discovered they had a little girl my age. She encouraged me to go meet her and have a play date. I did but I had a strange feeling about that household. I never wanted to play with the little girl again. Something just didn't feel right to me. I didn't understand what the feeling was, I just never went back to play again.

One incident that left an impression on me, while at Stead, was when Father John was accused of rape. There was a knock on the door of our base house one evening and my parents were asked to step outside. A short time later my mother came back into the living room and pulled me aside. She told me something bad had happened and they wanted to ask me questions about Father John. She told me to tell the truth. That telling the truth was the most important thing. I was about eleven years old at the time. I didn't know what rape was or anything about sex yet. I really liked Father John; he was like a member of our family. He had never hurt any of us, I was worried about him. Something was bothering me. I had been taught by my relatives that priests were close to God and above others. That night as I stood outside my house encircled by the military detectives in civilian clothing answering their questions of, "Did John Wizicowski ever have you sit on his lap?" I answered, "Yes." "Did John Wizicowski ever but his hands between your legs?" I answered, "No." "Did he ever do anything to you that made you uncomfortable?" I answered, "No."

I felt bad about answering the one question that may be bad for Father John. I felt if priests are close to God and better than the rest of us how come God gave me power over a priest? I realized that night that we are all just people, no one is better than anyone else. God loves us all.

Later, I found out that the girl across the street who I had played with once and felt uncomfortable in her home, had accused Father John of rape. Father John would be found innocent of this claim. I would also find out that she had accused others of rape in the past at different cities and bases. Her real mother had died, and she was living with her father and stepmother. I didn't understand why she accused him. Maybe she needed attention? I felt sad for her.

My Friends Next Door

On the other side of our duplex was a family with two daughters and one was my age, and one was older. Ana May and I played dress-up all the time. It was a game where we pretended. We had old clothes from our mothers, and they were dressy items. We'd put them on and pretend we had a secret life. I have to say it was my favorite game. Ana May and I became good friends for a while and got along well.

At one point in time my mother decided Lee and I should take accordion lessons. I always thought it was because of her Polish heritage, as a lot of that culture's music featured the accordion. She rented the accordion instruments, and the female teacher would come to our house. This was not something Lee and I wanted to do, and it didn't last long. However, Ana May liked the accordion. She would talk her mother into letting her take lessons. She went on to become quite good at it. She played in recitals and for entertainment events.

My Ballet Lessons

Mother signed me up for ballet lessons from a retired German ballerina who had married into the American military life. I went to her home for lessons but without a class there and recitals I soon lost interest. I still loved dancing and was good at it but being a kid, I needed the whole experience.

My mother found me my first job while at Stead. After school on certain days, I babysat a girl, Sarah, who was a toddler. She was very smart and cute, and I kept her company and would take her out for walks so her mother could get errands done. It was a fun job. It was nice to make a little money too.

My Father's Promotion and Acceptance of Regular Military and a New American President

A big military event happened to my father while we were in Stead. He was promoted to the rank of major, and the plaque on our house was changed to Major Eugene F. Phillips. He also accepted the status of Regular Air Force. It meant that he would be respected like an Air Force Academy graduate.

The New President

John F. Kennedy won the election in 1960 and started his term of office in January of 1961. When a new administration takes over things change for the country, which means things change for the military and their families. By June 14, 1961, we would need to be at Lowry AFB in Colorado. My father would start Missile Launch Officers' School. Lee and I would miss the last six weeks of school at Stead AFB Elementary. In a military family when it's time to leave you just go. I learned that life is not about me. Life is about what you do for others.

Again, the movers would come and pack up all our belongings. This time however, everything was going into storage. We would live in furnished rental homes until our assignment was finished. We would be going overseas and for this assignment no furniture was needed. We only took our clothes and personal items. My beautiful bicycle was packed up to go into storage. I would not see it again until 1965.

My seventh-grade year of school and Lee's fifth-grade year would be particularly challenging as we would attend three different schools. At this point in my life, I realized that "I'm a nomad." I would never understand growing up in a hometown.

My Father's Ohio Family Reunion, 1961

A big family reunion was taking place in Ohio. I guess my parents figured since we'd be going overseas again, it was time to catch up with family. My grandmother Elizabeth and her second husband, Albin, had moved into town from the farm. Plymouth, Ohio was a one stop light city. Their home was so old, it was hard to determine when it was built. It had a second floor with three bedrooms. I remember she had just cleaned it up and repainted the walls. They had used oil-based paint that was fresh but had an odor to it. I just remember having to stay in a room that smelled of paint, I didn't like it but after a while I got used to the smell. It only bothered me when I came into the room then I'd adjust to it.

My grandmother had a cold cellar where she kept her canning. This cold cellar was dug in the ground and shored up with stones at the back of the home. You had to walk down a circular staircase to get into it, like walking into a castle dungeon. It was narrow but held all her canning. Lee and I loved going into the cold cellar. She would put up peaches, pickles, jams, and jellies. She would let Lee, Mark, and I pick out a jar and eat all we wanted. My favorite were her canned peaches!

Sitting around grandmother's kitchen table was always an enjoyable time with tasty food. Her stove always had an old coffee can on the back where she kept bacon grease. She used that grease to cook everything. We had chores to do as well. She had asked me to go to the empty lot next to the house to pick dandelion flowers. I was only to pick the top of the flower. She was going to use them to make dandelion wine. One night we went to Uncle Clyde's home and in the cellar, he was making liquor and wine from different crops. I got to taste some, but it did not taste good to me at all. My Uncle Clyde and Aunt Mary Ellen had built a home on the farm where my father had grown up.

My father's family was so different from my mother's family. I could experience the difference between city folk and country folk. The farming families were true to themselves. The city families were always interested in the latest fade and trying to impress others. However, both were similar in that they had harsh judgments on some people.

The reunion was held at my Uncle Henry's home which he built just down the street from the original farmhouse. Uncle Henry and Aunt Shirley hosted the event. Their house had one story and a basement underground. Uncle Henry was a farmer and so was Uncle Clyde. The rest of Dad's siblings did not make their living from the land. Henry only grew crops; he didn't have animal livestock. He had a large property just down the road from his brother Clyde. He also had a day job working for R.R. Donnelley and Sons company, called The Lakeside Press, a book printing company.

I can remember everyone arriving from Cleveland (north of Plymouth). Mom had dressed Lee, Mark, and me up in our best clothes. It was a fun day for me, playing and meeting many new cousins. After we had great food and fun, we returned to my grandmother's home for the evening. That night, after I had gone to bed. I heard my parents in the next room arguing, voices raised and firm. I had never heard them fight before. It went on for a long time and several times I thought of going into their room and asking what the problem was. I decided not to and finally fell asleep. The next day, all was fine, I didn't forget the incident, but I figured it was resolved. I never asked them about it.

I would learn twenty-four years later, in 1985, what the argument was about. My father not only had many military secrets, but he also had a personal secret. He had never told my mother he was an illegitimate child. His history taught him that he should be ashamed. My mother found out at the reunion. A relative of Dad's mentioned to my mother that "Gene looks just like his father." My mother commented that she didn't think "Gene looks like Ed at all." He told her that Ed was not Gene's biological father. Knowing Dad never told

My father's family reunion, Ohio, 1961.

her the truth upset her. That night what I heard in muffled voices from the next room was my father thinking that my mother was going to leave him because of who he really was. What he didn't realize is that my mother wanted a family more than anything in the world, she found no shame in him being illegitimate. She had grown up in a shattered family and lived with the repercussions of that in her community in Philadelphia.

It would not be until my mother was in her late seventies and early eighties that she would reveal her true story of growing up with a single mother during the Depression in Philadelphia. She would reveal herself to me a little at a time. I would not know about Dad being illegitimate either until 1985. I would learn to have great respect for my parents who had come through difficult childhoods to have a family and do whatever it took. They had both overcome the harsh attitudes of the community around them. In truth my parents had much in common. Even though they had come from different environments they came from similar circumstances. I learned all my father's secrets, but my mother took some of hers to her grave. She hated going to court, serving jury duty or the like. She would avoid it at all costs. The stories of her father seem to stop when she was about fifteen years old. My guess is there was a custody battle. My grandmother dated other men and brought them home to her one-room apartment. My grandfather Stanly may have thought that inappropriate with a teenage girl in the room. My grandmother never divorced her husband. The last story I ever heard of him was about his death and his burial.

There were many secrets in our family. Secrets from the past and secrets we had to keep now about my father's job and what the U.S. was doing to protect the American civilian population. All these schools he was attending were to prepare him for the part he would play in the 498th Tactical Missile Program, a program so secret, American civilians were not to know about it.

6

Tactical Missile Training: June 1961 – March 1962

THE U.S. AIR FORCE TACTICAL MISSILES, used between 1949 and 1969, were surface-to-surface tactical missiles of the U.S. Air Force. The winged, nuclear-capable Matador and Mace missiles, their units, and personnel proficient in their use and maintenance were stationed in West Germany, Taiwan, Korea, Okinawa, and the United States. My family's new assignment would be to Okinawa.

The training and deployment of these crews were first announced by President Truman in 1951. When President Eisenhower in 1954 learned that operational squadrons of Matadors were being deployed to Europe, he marked a period of combat readiness for the tactical missiles around the globe for over fifteen years. Much of the problem with this history of the 498th Tactical Missile Group at Kadena, Okinawa, was an order by the Secretary of Defense Robert S. McNamara in 1962 during the Kennedy administration. The existence of the TM-76B weapons system in Okinawa "was not to be publicized in any way." Everything was so secret that even the number of military kids in the schools was not to be publicized. During this time, it was not only military secrets expanding, but family secrets as well. Lee and I were instructed not to talk about where we were going or what our father was doing.

Training at Lowry AFB Near Denver

After WWII, Lowry continued to train technicians for all branches of the U.S. military. It was used by the local Navy, and the Air National Guard for practicing bombing and strafing missions and for demolition of unusable Air Force munitions. On June 7, 1951, Lowry's 3415th Technical Training Wing formed a Guided Missile Department. It taught courses in guidance, control, and propulsion for such systems as Matador, Falcon, Rascal, Snark, and Navaho. By 1962, the Department of Missile Training was providing the Air Force with over 1,000 trained missile specialists per year.

Over the years, thousands of airmen trained at Lowry. From 1953 to 1955, Lowry became President Dwight D. Eisenhower's "Summer White House" from which he conducted affairs of state while Mamie Eisenhower, a Denver native, visited with family. In 1955, the USAF Academy was established at Lowry AFB pending construction of its facilities in Colorado Springs. The Academy remained in operation at Lowry until 1958.

Titan Missile Base

On March 13, 1958, the Air Force Ballistic Committee approved the selection of Lowry to be the first Titan I ICBM Base. The launch sites were to be located on the bombing range east of Denver. This was conveniently close to the Titan I manufacturer, the Martin Company (now Lockheed Martin) located in Littleton, Colorado.

Our family would drive from my father's family reunion in Ohio to Denver. We stayed in a local hotel while my parents searched for a furnished house to rent. We would not be living on an Air Force Base in Denver since we would only be there for eighteen weeks before heading to live eighteen weeks in Orlando. From there, the head of the house would be going to Okinawa and my mother, Lee, Mark, and I would go back to Albany, GA, to sell the house my parents had purchased there in the 1950s. My father thought it was a better financial decision at the time. However, with all the moving and needs of the military life, buying became a problem. So, my parents decided to sell the last property they owned, especially since we would be going to the Far East to live for three years.

This year of three schools in one year would be challenging. I worked and took my education very seriously. Lee was very smart but didn't really work as hard at it. Lee's understanding came easy to him, he didn't see much point in doing all the work. For that reason, my grades were always better than his. That worked for me, he made me look good. I knew Lee was smart. He would find something that interested him, and he would explain it to me; he had a gift. He understood things just from looking at them. He would build radios and would see where things were needed. He never read the instructions. One day my mother was knitting, and she was rolling the yarn into a ball to be able to knit from it better than from the way the yarn was sold in the stores. Lee watched my mother for a while. Then he went into his room and with his tinker toy set, he built her a Lazy Susan device that she could put the yarn on, and it would spin so she could roll the yarn more easily. Lee was a born engineer.

* * *

We ended up finding a furnished rental home in the Cherry Hill area of Denver. It was a craftsmen style home and full of old furnishings. It only had one bedroom, but it had a porch and a basement. My brothers got the bedroom, my room was the porch and my parents slept in the basement. There was no air conditioning in this house, but the basement was always nice and cool. This house had some very unusual features. It had a built-in hutch in the living room that went up to the ten foot high ceiling. The bottom drawer of this hutch was a double bed that pulled out into the living room. The house was eccentric but most interesting and I'm sure it had some stories. The washer in this home was an old ringer washer and the dryer was the clothesline outside. The backyard had been a beautiful rose garden at one time that had become very overgrown. It had some interesting rose bushes and other flowering species. Alte and John, from our assignment in Brussels were also in Denver at that time. Alte was into gardening and really got into restoring our garden. She worked awfully hard to clean it up and get it back to its former beauty.

Lee and I had missed the last six weeks of the school year at Stead so, my mother signed us up at the local parochial school to take reading during the summer. My reading was still not up to par, and I think she put Lee in the class for something to do during the day. We had a Catholic nun for a teacher and Lee, and I were the only two in the class that summer. We would walk to and from school each day and some days Alte would pick us up to take us home. Then she would spend the afternoon working in our rose garden.

* * *

My mother called the day Dad was recalled into the military for the Korean War, a dark day. Still, she had turned into the perfect military wife. Her childhood in Philadelphia moving from rented room to room and always making the best of the situation prepared her. This year of moving three times showed her resolve with any situation she was put into. She came through it all with flying colors. She moved, adapted, and moved on. She would not have ever imagined the life she would have with a husband in the military.

While we were in Denver in the middle of the summer, it snowed! My mother woke us up and announced, "It is snowing outside!" Sleepily we responded, "No, can't be. It's summer." Well, it snowed that summer. Snow in the summer can be dangerous. The trees were full of leaves and covered in snow causing branches to fall. We were alerted to stay away from the trees for that reason. Some cars parked on the street under trees were damaged.

Living in Denver, "The Mile High City" as it is called, attracted a lot of visits from relatives on our paternal side. I didn't know most of them. But several came that summer to visit this beautiful city in the mountains. The good thing about family coming to visit is that we got to do things with them too.

The Red Rock Amphitheatre was one of the most outstanding sites to see, a natural setting high in the mountains. Another trip was to the Coors Beer factory. I remember we had an almost private tour the day we went. All the beer was made from the mountain snow water. I always found learning about things and how they were made interesting. Perhaps it was because my mother had come from Philadelphia and always talked about the tours of the famous historical sites and events that started our country in Philadelphia. She had grown up living in rented rooms around Center City and many times would be part of a tour group because her brother was to babysit her, and he'd put her in a tour group while he went elsewhere. She loved the tours. Lee, Mark, and I grew up interested in how things were formed and made and why. Our parents valued understanding where things come from and so did us three kids

* * *

As I grew up, my parents, Nannie, and other relatives started to share their stories and memories. I would start to understand where all these relatives had come from. I would start to get more information on who my dad was and all that had happened to him in the war. He had very somber days. He would call those days his anniversaries. He remembered the day he was shot down in Italy. The day he was liberated from the prison camp. As I grew up, I would ask questions and he would answer with a very philosophical answer. Usually, I didn't understand everything. I did get the impression that the incidents he was remembering were profound to him. He did not share stories but rather lessons with me. One of the first lessons was that adversity is an opportunity to learn. History was important! I started learning that in Brussels.

My grandmother Nannie started to talk about her childhood in Poland. She lived in a convent school there. She talked about how she shared a large room with many girls. She did not have a bedroom to herself. She was born in 1897 and had lived without electricity, just like our father. It was amazing how she could use that old knowledge around the house. I would learn and appreciate some of the things she taught me. If I didn't have any school glue, she would get an egg, crack it open and use the clear part of the raw egg still left in the shell for glue. She had more lessons for me as I grew up. I learned respect for what my family members had learned and the wisdom I gleaned from their knowledge.

* * *

I turned twelve years old that summer. I would start seventh grade in Denver. I walked to Hill Junior High School, a public school a few miles from our house. Lee was still in elementary school. My mother would put Mark into kindergarten. This was the only kindergarten class Mark attended that school year. The kids from across the street also walked to school. They never talked to me. I was once again the new kid on the block. Admittedly, I didn't start a conversation either. They were older and I was still playing with younger kids.

Racial differences were becoming apparent to me through this family. The father and mother were of different races. In the military I was familiar with different races in my classes since I had started school in Brussels. I watched as kids in the school made fun of them and teased them and picked on them. Then I kind of understood why they stayed together and didn't talk to anyone else. I felt bad for them but did not see anything I could do to help.

The school in Denver was like no other I had attended. It was very new, not like the old school I had attended in Brussels or the schools in Laredo or the base schools in Stead. It was very modern and clean and had air conditioning. It had all kinds of classes for electives. I took music classes where we learned to sing. The most interesting thing I learned was in math class. We learned the Base System. We learned base two and base seven along with base ten. Base two is the binary code that is used for computers. Base two only had two numbers, zero and one. So, you counted: 0, 1, 10, 11, 100, 101, 111, 1000, and so on. It was like counting in base ten but leaving out all the numbers you could not use, like two through nine. Base seven was similar: 0, 1, 2, 3, 4, 5, 6, 10, 11, 12, 13, 14. 15, 16, 20, and so on.

From then on when anyone ever said, "What is one plus one?"

Well, if you're in base two the answer is ten! It was challenging, and I loved it. The first time I would think outside the box.

Not long into the school year it was time to move again. By late October we were on our way to Orlando, FL. We would be driving from Mile High city in the mountains to the flat state of Florida and close to sea level.

Tactical Missile Training, Orlando AFB, FL November 1961 – March 1962

Before you knew it, we started the second eighteen-week training course for Dad and another new school for Lee and me. We'd get up at dawn or before so we could get an early start and miss heavy traffic. After several days of travel in our car and stays in local motels, we arrived in Florida. We would settle in Orlando and find another rental home just outside Orlando Air Force Base and within walking distance of schools.

Lee and I attended civilian schools, Lee in elementary and me in Junior High. The group of kids, and the teachers, at Glenridge Junior High School were very warm toward me. They welcomed me into class, and I made friends quickly. I walked to school with kids from

The main gate to Orlando Air Force Base.

the neighborhood. This school had a lot of school spirit. We were the Lions. It so happened, one of the German Steiff puppets I had from Brussels, was a lion. I would take it to school-on-school spirit days, and everyone thought it was funny! It was great to have such unity and commemoratory in a civilian school

Glenridge Junior High School, Orlando, Forida.

* * *

As I grew up, Dad and I spent more time together. I would ask him about his time in the POW camp or about anything historical I may have been learning. He never brought up his war experience except on his anniversary days. He probably always noted those days I had just been too young to notice his somber mood. My mother encouraged me to spend time with him. She had a father that didn't live with her family. She visited her father from time to time until her late teen years. My mother didn't talk much about her broken family and neither did my grandmother. I never talked to my Uncle Tony about my grandfather either. My mother knew how important it is for a daughter to spend time with her father. She encouraged our talks and movie nights. We had several movie theater dates. The movies were biblical or historical and we would discuss their meanings afterward. I appreciated his insight and his time with me. He would always say, "When you are older, you'll understand."

The Cold War Space Race

In 1961, President John F. Kennedy began a dramatic expansion of the U.S. space program and committed the nation to the ambitious goal of landing a man on the moon by the end of the decade. In 1957, the Soviet Union launched the satellite Sputnik, and the Space Race was on. The Space Race was a competition between the two adversaries to achieve superior spaceflight capability. It had its origins in the ballistic missile-based nuclear arms race between the two nations following World War II.

On February 20, 1962, while I was attending Glenridge, all the kids were brought into the gym where several TV screens had been set up. We would watch Astronaut John Glenn's capsule orbit the Earth. The quality of the TV picture was grainy and sitting there in the gym to watch was not that interesting. However, I remember what that moment meant for the U.S. I was not only an American citizen but a military kid. I knew my family was tied to this event. My family was here because of the U.S. missile program. All these events were tied to the Cold War.

My grandmother Nannie, when she heard her son-in-law was going into the missile program said to a family member, "First Eugene flew planes then jets, now he's flying missiles." She almost got it right; except he would not be inside the missile.

* * *

At Glenridge there was a boy in my homeroom class that liked me. We never had a date, but he would always walk me to my classes and carry my books. This school in Orlando was not as sophisticated as the school in Denver, but the school spirit gave this school more comradery among the students and teachers. We had a literature class where we learned poetry, I really liked that class. I had a humanities

Me posing with the Matador Missile in Florida.

class and part of this class was music. The music room had a semi-circle in the middle of the room and tiered seating going up the walls. Desks were on each tier. One day we walked in to find chairs on the tiers and on each chair was a musical string instrument. I immediately walked over to the violin and picked it up. I was a natural and other students picked up the cello, the bass, or the viola! The instructor started teaching us as a group about these string instruments. It was not long before we had formed a small string group and we even practiced outside of school hours.

Again, relatives came to visit while we were in Orlando. This time from my mother's side. My Great Aunt Mamie loved the beach and loved Florida. She had been in my parent's wedding party. She lived with her daughter Mary, my Godno, also a part of my parents' wedding party. They lived in the home Mamie and her husband had bought in 1940. Her husband had died in November of 1948. Godno had never married, but she had graduated high school, and worked for AT&T in Philadelphia. Mamie had not passed the fourth grade. She had worked for years as a waitress. She had learned Yiddish and worked as a companion to older Jewish women later in her life. That is how she had gotten to Florida the first time. Mamie and my grandmother Nannie were sisters, but they had not grown up together. Mamie was born in Philadelphia to a single mother and no father. My grandmother, Nannie was in Poland in a girl's boarding school.

Mamie had driven down from Pennsylvania to Florida with a lady friend. She had gotten a driver's license years before when you could just send in money, and you were sent a license. She only had a few driving lessons before she drove down to see us. It would be her longest driving trip. However, my parents were a little concerned when she asked them what a yield sign meant. Mamie was brave and had a lot of Chutzpah! I always enjoyed spending time with her. She would help build my self-confidence. She told me I was a lot like her, and I could do anything I wanted to do in life.

Albany, GA: April – August 1962

We lived in Orlando until March of 1962. Father had finished his missile training at Orlando Air Force Base. Knowing the family would be going to live in Okinawa for the next three years, my family decided to go back to Albany, GA, where we still owned a home (though it had been rented out since 1955). The family that was overseeing the rental moved away and it was an ideal time to sell the property. Albany was not all that far from Orlando.

Moving back to Albany was the only time I would see a place for the second time in my short life. Lee and I would say goodbye to all our wonderful friends in Orlando. My string music group had a goodbye party for me. My short stay in Orlando was special. I would miss them. Lee and I would have to adjust to one more school before the end of that school year in 1962.

Dad stayed with us for about three weeks, to get us settled in Albany. He would be taking the Mercedes with him when he left. It would have to be sent to Okinawa on a boat and it had to go earlier. He would need the car in Okinawa. He bought us a secondhand clunker car. This car was in bad shape; but he didn't want to spend much money on a car because it was only going to be used for a short period. He rigged the car up with the battery on the front seat. Why we had the battery in the front seat is beyond me, but that is how he rigged it to work. This car had a front bench seat. The passenger side had a hole in the floorboard. I could see the road passing beneath me as we drove. Lee and Mark in the back seat could see the road from the rusted-out floorboards too. This car was to be used by Mom to get to the grocery store or to Turner AFB. Before my father left for Okinawa, a neighbor expressed interest in buying our home. This would make things easier for my mother. She would just oversee the house and anything else before the new owners took occupancy.

We resettled into our house in Pecan Haven Housing area. The whole neighborhood was still full of pecan trees. This had probably been a deserted pecan grove where a developer had built houses. Lee, Mark, and I would pick up pecans and my mother would give them away and even mail them to relatives up north. I remembered the sweet pecan meat taste that I had enjoyed from our last time in Albany. I re-acquainted myself with the same neighbors we had in 1955, the Gary family. Mr. Gary worked at the Coats and Clark Thread Company in Albany. Since Mom made most of our clothes, Mr. Gary would bring us thread for her machine. The Garys had older children with families of their own, but Bruce and Lynn came later for them. She and I were close in age and had played in1955. Now that she and I were in junior high, we'd walk to school together. There wasn't much school left by the time we got settled but I finally finished seventh grade at Albany Junior High School.

Lynn's brother, Bruce, was in high school. He was tall with dark brown wavy hair and handsome. He had an afternoon newspaper route. He drove a motorcycle to school and used that motorcycle to deliver newspapers. Every day the Albany Newspaper Company would drop off the papers at the front of the Gary home and I would go over to help roll the papers and put a rubber band around them. Lynn and I used to do this on our laps. By the time we were finished our upper thighs and hands were covered in black newspaper ink. Bruce would pack the rolled papers up in bags draped on his motorcycle and deliver the afternoon news to the Pecan Haven Housing area.

I had lived in so many rental homes by then that we never painted a room a color I would have liked for my room. One day I came home from school to find that my mother had painted my bedroom a light shade of lavender. This was our home and maybe it needed painting anyway before we could sell it, but for me that meant so much. Purple was my favorite color, and I always had a bedspread with purple and lavender flowers, as was the style then.

That summer was fun! Lee and Mark made friends in the neighborhood. Lynn and I played on her back yard swing, singing songs, and sharing stories. We got close that summer. Sometimes we'd walk to the small diner and have an ice cream float or French fries. I turned thirteen years old in Albany that summer. It was much like what I had remembered from my years there as a young child. My memories of Albany from my early years were more like flashes of moments, or incidents that had occurred. My memory of Albany now was clearer and stronger. The heat and humidity of the night, the cricket sounds hanging on the evening dew. We would sit outside where we might find a cool breeze and enjoy the sounds of the evening. I was older and had a better understanding of life. I had more travel and experiences than most of the kids my age. I had lived in Belgium and learned French. I had lived in TX, NV, CO, and FL, and I had visited my relatives, all immigrants, in Philadelphia, and the rural farmers in Ohio. I had felt the flavors of the U.S. more than most. In Belgium I had witnessed the terrible atrocities to people that had lived through war, and of Communism forced on people by governments that wanted power.

The summer of 1962 was also the beginning of my awareness of the Civil Rights Movement. Albany, in the early 1960s, was a town of about 55,000 people and had a system of legally mandated segregation. In the fall of 1961, the Student Nonviolent Coordinating Committee (SNCC) and the National Association for the Advancement of Colored People (NAACP) joined local activists in creating a desegregation campaign they called The Albany Movement. By December 1961, they had been joined by Dr. Martin Luther King, Jr., and his Southern Christian Leadership Conference (SCLC). On December 16th, King and many others were arrested and jailed following a protest. While King was allowed to leave town soon afterwards, he returned in July 1962 to stand trial. He was convicted, spent two days in jail before being bailed out (reportedly by another famous pastor, the Rev. Billy Graham) and then was rearrested and jailed for two weeks later that month for leading a prayer vigil. On August 10th, he left jail in Albany and agreed to halt demonstrations there.

This movement aimed to end all forms of racial segregation in the city, focusing initially on desegregating travel facilities, forming a permanent biracial committee to discuss further desegregation, and the release of those jailed in segregation protests. Through the course of the campaign, Albany protesters utilized various methods of nonviolence, including mass demonstrations, jail-ins, sit-ins, boycotts, and litigation. Notably, in addition to student activists, the campaign involved large numbers of Black adults of varied class backgrounds.

That summer King's arrival made the national news in newspapers, TV, and radio. My mother's family was concerned. They knew that it was just us kids and her. They were aware of the protests, marches and other activities in other cities and knew it could be problematic to our area. However, all the protesting activity was downtown. There was no danger in our Pecan Haven housing area. The possibilities of problems, however, did loom over us. My mother never stopped us

Our home in Albany and the clunker car we had during our short stay the summer of 1962.

from walking to the diner. I was not aware of the injustice of racism at thirteen years of age. We left Albany when I was five, having just started kindergarten. I had been exposed to many injustices in the world during our time in Europe. That summer in Albany would later play a key part in my career decision after graduating college. I knew about racism intellectually, but I had not really experienced it. I would take a job in 1971 to teach school in a neighborhood where I would better understand racial inequality.

We would sell our home with my wonderful lavender bedroom and sell the clunker car before traveling to Okinawa. Before we left, my mother wanted to visit her family. We would be overseas for at least three years, and they would not be able to visit this station. We would fly from Turner AFB to Philadelphia. We arrived in Philadelphia to visit Godno, her brother David, his wife Nancy, and their girls, Aunt Mamie, Nannie, Uncle Tony, Aunt Helen, and my cousin Vicki. During our stay we went to the Atlantic City, New Jersey, Boardwalk, where my parents had met in 1945, seventeen years earlier. My mother knew the area well. We stayed with friends and went to the beach and did some shopping. My mother was aware that there was not going to be ready-made clothing in Okinawa, so, we stocked up on swimsuits at a factory outlet in Atlantic City. The Miss America Pageant started in Atlantic City and was still held there. In 1969 I would win a Miss America Preliminary Pageant in one of the swimsuits we bought that day.

7

Life on Okinawa: 1962 – 1965

TRAVELING TO OKINAWA WAS A story. My family and I boarded a civilian 707 airplane at the Philadelphia airport and traveled to California. Several relatives from the Philadelphia area went with us to the airport to see us off. We would be the last to board the plane, dressed impeccably as people did when flying in the 1960s. We were the last to board because we were travelling "space available" and at no cost as military dependents.

We landed at Travis AFB in California, deplaned and entered a terminal, following signage that said, "Military Dependents" and "Active Military." We were segregated from the civilian population, but we were not segregated by race. We were being ushered into the military transport terminal. In California we boarded a Navy military airplane. This airplane was part of a Military Air Transport Service (MATS). MATS was supported by the Air Force which combined the resources of Air Transport Command with those of the Naval Air Transport Service. This way the command would be sanctioned by the Department of Defense, and not by either the Air Force or the Navy. MATS moved troops and dependents and government dignitaries all over the world. So, there were multiple locations. We were using the Pacific Coast, Naval Air Transport Wing.

As I walked onto this plane with my first pair of "kitten heel" shoes; the sound of everyone talking was loud because there was no insulation or carpeting. The sound bounced off the metal walls of the plane. The metal floors were corrugated, and I had to be careful walking so my new shoes would not get damaged. I did not remember the Navy airplane we had taken to Europe in 1955. All you could see were metal floors and walls. There were no overhead compartments to put luggage. Thank God the seats with cushions were installed and, on this plane, we flew backwards, facing where we had left. Our airplane was full of military dependents—all women and children. This was a propeller airplane, and once the pilots started up the engines making these propellers whirl, the sound was deafening to my ears. I just had to deal with the noise the best I could.

We flew the first leg of our journey to Hawaii. The first leg was about eleven hours. We arrived in the middle of the night to refuel the plane. We had been asleep before we landed. The Navy crew had all of us deplane and ushered us into a waiting room in a non-military airport in Oahu, Hawaii. The smell of the air in Hawaii was sweet and the sky was so dark. Passengers cannot stay aboard a plane being refueled; we had to wait until that process was completed. After sitting there for about forty-five minutes my mother asked someone how much longer we were going to be in the waiting room. She was told about another hour.

The adventurous side of my mother showed up and she told us since we were in Hawaii, we were going to see more than a waiting room. She took us into the terminal and in the check-in area of the airport were Hawaiian leis made of colorful and varying flowers laying on the counters as decoration. It was late at night and my mother asked if we could have the Hawaiian leis as a souvenir of our time in Hawaii. The staff there said sure, that they would be getting fresh ones soon anyway. Then she took us to a cafeteria, and we had fresh pineapple. We would return to the waiting room to the surprise of the others from our plane with our fragrant leis and happy disposition from our short adventure.

"Wow," said one of the children, "where have you all been?" I said, "We went to Hawaii." They wanted to go too. They were already in Hawaii, but they did not have a mother like mine. None of the others ventured out of that room. We finally got back on our refueled plane and set off for the next leg of our journey. This leg would be about nine hours to Wake Island. During the time we were on the plane the noise of the propellers was loud and irritating to me, there were moments I wanted to jump out of my skin, and no place to get away from it. The only thing I could do was try to ignore it. That worked for a while but then I would finish reading or playing a game with Lee or Mark and the noise would get to me again.

My mother had brought a very large stack of comic books on the plane. My aunt had given them to us in Philadelphia to keep us busy on our long trip. My mother passed these comic books out to all the kids on our flight. The comic books were welcomed by all who were old enough to read, and many who just liked looking at the pictures. On Wake Island we deplaned, refueled, and got back on the plane again. Our next stop was ten hours to the island of Guam. They deplaned us again to refuel the plane. We got on buses this time and were taken to a large dining room. We were served a hot breakfast there. This was the only hot meal we were given during the whole trip. Other meals were boxed cold food, sandwiches, passed out to us by the Navy crew. I was so happy to get a break from the constant noise of those propellers. We were all loaded back on the buses and taken back to the airplane. Our next leg would be about twelve hours to Okinawa. I figured I could listen to that sound for one last leg.

We had been traveling for over forty-eight hours by this point. We were not able to sleep for long. We were in the same clothes we wore when we left Philadelphia. My mother wanted to look nice when she saw her husband again. She had made herself a sheath style print summer dress. I was surprised to see her head to the airplane bathroom about an hour before we landed in Okinawa and change her dress. She also fixed her hair rather nicely. My mother never wore much makeup, only if she was dressed for a formal function. She was beautiful without it. After two days of travel in the air and more hours refueling, waiting to board the plane and deplane, we landed at the airport in Kadena, AB, on the island of Okinawa. Okinawa was an American Territory in 1962, called The Keystone because it was the largest of the Ryukyu chain of islands that trailed down in the East China Sea from the larger island of Japan.

Husbands and fathers were waiting for their families at the airport on the tarmac. I wondered if our father would be as excited to see us again and to introduce us to our new home on the island. My father was forty-one years old in 1962, and he was dressed in civilian clothes, long slacks, and a short sleeve shirt. He had missed us initially as the families deplaned, but I saw him, and ran and hugged him first. Then my brothers greeted him, and finally my parents embraced and kissed. He loaded us into our Mercedes and drove us to a housing area outside of the base. We would have to live off base for a while until an on base house became available. We drove up a hill on a dirt road and arrived at a small house. My father grabbed our suitcases and showed us the house he had rented for us, and we settled into our new assignment. I had my own room with a cot to sleep on. This was not new for me. I had slept on a cot before.

We would start school soon. We decided to rest that day and then go to dinner at one of the island restaurants. When we finally woke up it was twenty-four hours later, when my father told us we had slept for a whole day we could not believe it. The trip to Okinawa had really drained us, more than we knew. We finally did go to dinner at one of the military clubs on the island. It would be my first experience with Asian food. I had a whole plate of spring rolls for dinner. They were delicious, crispy, light, and had just enough vegetables inside to make them a real treat.

As we left the restaurant we drove around the island. Okinawa was truly an island paradise. The colors of everything were bright and the foliage was full. Only the main roads were paved. The rest of the roads were dirt roads and paths. I had lived on dirt streets in Albany and Laredo, but I was now in a completely different culture. On

Okinawa the people were of the Shinto religion. Their customs and attitudes were different. The pace of life was slow and meaningful.

I saw rice patties, small huts with sliding doors covered in paper. The huts looked nothing like any home in the U.S. I saw Asian children dressed in school uniforms. Asian men and women dressed very differently than in the U.S. Women wore dresses that were slim fitting and men dressed in baggy pants. Most Okinawan people were small in stature and slim. They wore wooden shoes, but not like the wooden shoes I had seen in Holland. These were wooden raised sandals. They wore them barefoot or with special socks. The sandal had a thong that held on to the foot between the big toe and the second toe. Okinawan women would carry their babies on their back wrapped in cloth. I could see the baby's little heads bobbing. All these things were new to me and most interesting. Then father took us to see Missile Site #4. He was commander of this site. We drove up to the hill area of the island. The site was dug into the ground. The missiles were large and very impressive, a strong show of force. We had seen the mace missiles in Orlando and Denver. Now we were seeing where they were kept. A few months later would be thirteen days of standoff between Russia and the U.S. called the Cuban Missile Crisis.

Kadena AB History

Kadena Air Base's history dates to just before the Battle of Okinawa in April 1945, when a local construction firm completed a small airfield named Yara Hikojo near the village of Kadena. The airfield, used by the Imperial Japanese Army Air Force, was one of the first targets of the Tenth United States Army seventh Infantry Division. The United States seized it from the Japanese during the battle.

What the Americans captured was a 4,600 foot strip of badly damaged coral runway. It would take the work of the Aviation Engineer Battalion, the U.S. Infantry Division and the Naval Construction Battalion Maintenance Unit to get the landing Division, ready by the fourth of April. By nightfall the same day, the runway could accept emergency landings. Eight days later, and after six inches of coral were added, the airfield was declared operational and put into immediate service by artillery spotting aircraft when the runway became serviceable on Apirl 6th. Additional construction was performed by the 807th Engineering Aviation Battalion to improve the airfield for the United States Army Air Force (USAAF) fighter and bomber use with fuel tank farms, a new 6,500 feet bituminous runway, and a 7,500 feet runway for bomber aircraft, by August.

Kadena airfield was initially under the control of Seventh Air Force, however on July 16, 1945, Headquarters Eighth Air Force was transferred, without personnel, equipment, or combat elements to the town of Sakugawa, near Kadena from RAF High Wycombe, England. Upon reassignment, its headquarters element absorbed the command staff of the inactivated XX Bomber Command. Kadena was used by the headquarters staff for administrative flying requirements.

Upon its reassignment to the Pacific Theater, the Eighth Air Force was assigned to the U.S. Army Strategic Air Forces with a mission to train new B-29 Superfortress bomber groups arriving from the United States for combat missions against Japan. In the planned invasion of Japan, the mission of Eighth Air Force would be to conduct strategic bombing raids from Okinawa. However, the atomic bombings of Japan led to the Japanese surrender before the Eighth Air Force saw action in the Pacific Theater.

The surrender of Japanese forces in the Ryukyu Islands came on September 7th. General Joseph Stilwell accepted the surrender in an area that would later become Kadena's Stearley Heights Housing area.

On June 7, 1946, Headquarters Eighth Air Force moved without personnel or equipment to MacDill Air Force Base, Florida. It was replaced by the first Air Division which directed fighter reconnaissance, and bomber organizations and provided air defense for the Ryukyu Islands until December 1948. The Twentieth Air Force became the command-and-control organization for Kadena on May 16, 1949.

* * *

The Korean War emphasized the need for maintaining a naval presence on Okinawa. On the February 15, 1951, the U.S. Naval Facility, Naha, was activated and later became commissioned on April 18th. Commander Fleet Activities, Ryukyus, was commissioned on March 8, 1957.

While on Okinawa, the 307th was awarded the Republic of Korea Presidential Unit Citation for its air strikes against enemy forces in Korea.

On November 1, 1954, the 18th Fighter-Bomber Wing arrived from Osan Air Base, South Korea. Under changing designations, the wing has been the main USAF flying force at Kadena for over fifty years. The wing has maintained assigned aircraft, crews, and supporting personnel in readiness to respond to orders from Fifth Air Force and Pacific Air Forces. The wing initially was flying three squadrons of North American F-86 Sabre: the 12th, 44th and 67th Fighter Squadrons. The wing flew tactical fighter sorties from Okinawa, and made frequent deployments to South Korea, Japan, Formosa, and the Philippines. In 1957, the wing was upgraded to the F-100 Super Sabre and the designation was changed to the 18th Tactical Fighter Wing. In 1960, a tactical reconnaissance mission was added to the wing with the arrival of the McDonnell F-101 Voodoo and the 15th Tactical Reconnaissance Squadron.

When President Eisenhower took office, he established the Eisenhower Doctrine. It was like the Truman Doctrine. The U.S would protect countries in a weakened state against communist aggression.

Beginning in 1961, the eighteenth Tactical Fighter Wing (TFW) was sending its tactical squadrons frequently to South Vietnam and Thailand, initially with its RF-101 reconnaissance jets and beginning in 1964 with its tactical fighter forces supporting USAF combat missions in the Vietnam War. In 1963, the F-105 Thunderchief replaced the Super Sabres. The deployments to Southeast Asia continued until the end of United States involvement in the conflict.

At the end of the Eisenhower presidency, around 1,700 nuclear weapons were deployed on shore in the Pacific, 800 of which were at Kadena Air Base. The Kennedy Administration would add the 498th Tactical Nuclear Missiles. My father had spent a year in training to learn about these missiles and how to run these missile sites. It would be the first time he would have more than a group of pilots to train to fly or a group in survival training. He would have around 800 men to run these missile sites twenty-four seven.

   I was coming of age at thirteen years old when we arrived in Okinawa. Father was coming into his own as a commander of men. He had his day job, but he also flew reconnaissance missions over Vietnam. One of his skills, that he was particularly good at, was night flying, and he loved it. Night flying was instrument flying. Instrument Flighting Rules (IFR) is the ability to fly an aircraft using only the instruments in the cockpit, rather than relying on visual cues outside the plane.

New Assignment Meant Adjusting to New Schools

   Lee, Mark, and I started the school year in Okinawa in September of 1962. I was in the eighth grade at Kubasaki Junior High School. Lee was in elementary school in sixth grade, and Mark would have his first full year of school in the first grade. Our schools were in various areas of Naha, the largest city on the island and a thirty-minute bus ride. It was not that far but the speed limit on Okinawa was thirty miles per hour.

   I loved school and enjoyed the challenge of learning new things. Lee was smart and just went along with school because he had to attend. Mark, on the other hand, was not thrilled with school. He liked spending time playing with his friends. Mark, like Lee, had been born into military dependent life. He played cowboys in Laredo and Nevada. He liked the moves to Denver and Orlando, still playing cowboys. Okinawa for Mark was a new awakening. The first day my mother put Mark on the military school bus to go to school he got off the back of the bus and wandered around the Okinawan village all day. Part of the Shinto religion was to bury the family members in a family tomb. The Americans called them "turtlebacks" because they looked like large turtles made of stone. Some Okinawan people say they are shaped like the womb of a woman, so people return to the source. These tombs were all over the area where we lived off base. For me it was kind of like living in a graveyard.

Mark had spent the day exploring these family tombs. The Asian people would celebrate the holiday of Obon each year, usually in the month of August, to pay respects to the ancestral line. Obon dances (called *Bon-odori*) are performed during the celebration along with other traditions. This holiday was later featured in the *Karate Kid II* movie that came out in 1986.

Turtleback tomb in Okinawa.

* * *

Living in Okinawa made me aware of different calendars that existed in the world. I learned that diverse cultures mark time in various ways. In the U.S. we used a solar calendar established by Pope

Gregory XIII in 1582, called the Gregorian Calendar. Other cultures marked time by the moon. The Shinto religion uses a lunar calendar. I knew that my Jewish friends also used a version of the lunar calendar.

Each morning mother put us on different buses arriving at different times for school. My bus to junior high school was the first. Lee was on the elementary school bus, grades fourth to sixth. Mark was on the bus for primary grade students, first to third grade. Lee and Mark's schools were repurposed Quonset huts. Quonset huts are a lightweight prefabricated structure of corrugated galvanized steel having a semi-cylindrical cross-section. These huts were used a lot by the military. My school was a former military barracks. Barracks are built to house military personnel. A room that would have multiple bunk beds was now full of desks. The style worked quite well for a school. Our school gym would be another galvanized steel structure that was originally used for the military. It had group showers and a large basketball court

Top: Military Quonset huts.
Bottom: Military barracks.

* * *

We would be back into military life in Okinawa. Even though we lived off base for the first year, we went to church, activities, restaurants, and schools on base for the most part. On Okinawa were all branches of the military. So, there were multiple bases. We shopped in the Okinawan villages from time to time. There was the military Base Exchange (BX) it carried a lot of items from the U.S., that we knew. However, for clothing it didn't carry much. Our only option for clothing was to shop the Sears and Roebuck's catalog. Getting items form the catalogs would take a long time to arrive from the U.S. The best option was to hire a "sew girl." The Okinawan people made their own clothing. If you hired a sew girl she came to your home. You showed her a magazine picture of what you wanted, and she would make a pattern from your measurements. The villages were full of wonderful fabric stores, beautiful silks and linens, cotton, shark skin, anything you could think of. Living in Okinawa, in a way, was like living in Paris during fashion season. Not quite the glamor of Paris, but the design and sewing skill was right up there with the best of Europe.

The Okinawan people worked for many of the American military families. If you wanted your lawn cut, an Okinawan man showed up at your home with a sickle. He would squat down with his sickle and cut the entire lawn by hand. It would take him most of the day. He was then paid a dollar. The military on Okinawa were told not to tip the workers as it would throw off the Okinawan economy. Most Okinawan people squatted instead of sitting on a chair. No chairs existed in their homes. The floors were tatami mats, made of straw. A typical Okinawan home would be a step or two up to the door, slide the door open and take off your shoes. Everything was done sitting on the floor, in a squat or on your knees.

American military families would employ women to clean their homes as well. We had a cleaning lady and a sew girl. The cleaning lady made a dollar a day and the sew girl made a dollar and a quarter, she was paid more because of her education as a seamstress. If you hired a sew girl, you had to provide a sewing machine for her. You could buy a sewing machine for a very good price. Most of them were pirated in China. Piracy was not paying the company for their trademarks.

Racketeering was also one of the problems in off base living. We had to pay protection from being robbed. There was no way around it. If you paid, your home was safe from being robbed; if you didn't pay you were robbed by a naked greased man that could enter your home at any time, usually while you were home and sleeping. He was naked and greased so you couldn't catch him.

We lived in two homes off base before there was a home on base available. They were American style homes built on Okinawa. They looked good on the inside but not too great on the outside. The Okinawan building standards were different from the places I had lived in Europe and the U.S. Some walls were not straight up and down. I don't think the builders used a plumb line. The living room and my parents' room had air-conditioners, but the rest of the house did not. The house was cool because it didn't have many windows. The windows did have had sliding wooden shutters to protect the home during typhoons.

* * *

Typhoons are the Pacific equivalent of hurricanes. During typhoons Dad would have to fly the expensive military jet to a place out of the path of the storm. My mother, brothers and I were left to fend for ourselves during these weather events. Military jets were expensive pieces of the DoD and had to be protected. During these weather events, Lee became the man of the house. He liked being the man of the house and taking care of us.

The island had a lot of gecko lizards. These lizards were small and had feet that could cling to a wall or the ceiling. The geckos were a flesh color and if startled would release their tail. The tail would continue to move after it was released, making the aggressor think it was the entire animal as the gecko ran off and eventually grew a new tail.

Our second off-base house in Okinawa.

These geckos always got into our home. I would go to sleep at night with several on the ceiling of my room and walls. I didn't care they were there, just worried that they may crawl over me while sleeping and startle me. They never did. I left them alone and they left me alone.

Schools the Military Provided for Dependent Children

The military hired civilian teachers to teach in military dependent schools. These were teachers with a sense of adventure. They would get to travel to exotic places. They were housed in barracks with bunk beds. Military families, like mine, would sponsor them. In the barracks, the teachers had no space of their own. For most, it was like being in a college dorm. The military families that sponsored them allowed them to do things with the family and spend time in their homes. The teachers signed up for a year at a time. During that year on their school breaks they would travel to other places in the Pacific, Taiwan, Australia, Hong Kong, Philippines, and Saigon. They lived on military bases with military families, culture, and attitudes. Some who stayed longer than a year did spend their own money to rent their own apartment or dwelling off the military base.

That first school year in Okinawa would be one of my best! We were all military kids, we understood moving and not being from any place. I had the best set of teachers too. Miss Ann Brinkley was my homeroom and English teacher. Mr. William Lacey was the science teacher, Mr. George Jackson taught math, Miss Marilyn Cochran taught history and Mr. Darwin Scales taught literature. Each day we had the same schedule. Every so often we'd go down to the gym and do some exercises. The John F. Kennedy Administration had a physical fitness program that children needed so many days of physical activity along with studies. Occasionally, an Asian woman was hired to teach us Asian style art, like origami. All these teachers were superior teachers. Mr. Scales brought literature to life for me. He was an actor and musician. I could listen to him for hours, he made everything become so alive. He had us read, not at home, but in class, aloud, we all took turns reading. He helped us to learn to read with expression and feeling. He had us read *The Diary of Anne Frank*, Shakespeare, *The Althea Gibson S*tory, and more. He wanted to give us a big picture of what was happening in the world. He told us that he was part American Indian and shared some of the American Indian traditions. Miss Cochran became friendly with my family. She would come over for dinner and we took beach trips too. My family's first Thanksgiving there, in 1962, was in the off-base house. My parents invited all my teachers to have dinner with us. If we had not invited them, they would have been in a cafeteria line at their barracks. So, when families invited them to a home cooked meal it was a real treat.

A big honor that year was being tapped for Junior Honor Society. The Honor Society entered our classroom and asked us all to put our heads down on our desk. The group would walk around the room and tap your shoulder if you were invited to join. I was so thrilled to be tapped. Me, the kid that had no long-lasting friendships, the one who had missed a lot of school to move, got an honor and a reward for working hard at my studies.

By the end of that school year Miss Brinkley and Mr. Lacey were a couple and planning on marriage. He was a sophisticated, smart man from the New York area; she was a southern girl from Georgia. Mr. Lacey was Black, Miss Brinkley was White. In the military culture and the Asian location, it was not a problem. However, they could not return to the U.S.; prejudice was a problem. After the school year I heard they settled in Japan. I was happy for them! Their classrooms were next to each other and when I would see them together, they looked so happy.

History of Okinawa

I would learn about the history of the island of Okinawa. It was not easy to navigate the waters surrounding the island and it also was surrounded by a dangerous coral that could cause dermatitis or even death. The people that inhabited these islands prehistorically had come from China or Indonesia, Australia, and other regions. Later the people of the Ryukyu chain of islands would trade with the Ming dynasty of China. The Ryukyu Kingdom actively conducted trade with Japan and China, as well as the Philippines, Thailand and other nearby countries and was even known to Europeans.

The Ryukyu chain was later taken by the political system of Japan. This heralded the beginning of Okinawa Prefecture. Okinawa underwent some modernization just before WWII, but a fierce ground battle unfolded during World War II. In 1945, as World War II ended, The U.S. had won the island in one of the last battles of the Pacific Theater. The U.S. took control of the island until it was reverted to Japan on May 15, 1972, it went through a different history from that of the Japanese mainland, undergoing heavy influence from the United States.

Leper Colony in Okinawa

National Sanatorium Okinawa Airaku-en was opened in 1938 as a provincial leprosy sanatorium. Okinawa was known as a leprosy-endemic region and was severely stigmatized. Leprosy sufferers there endured extreme difficulties. Under U.S. influence, however, the leprosy prevention law allowed outpatient treatment and social rehabilitation to some extent.

We would encounter mentally ill men on the island who walked the streets naked. We kids referred to them as "Naha Charlies." They didn't bother anyone. They lived in the caves near the main city of Naha on the island. There were all kinds of stories that were floated as to who they were. One of the stories was that they were *kamikaze* pilots who refused to fly to their death. They went insane from the shame they brought to their families. I never knew if any of that was true. They were homeless, living in caves, and forgetting to put on clothes. Some of the braver high school military kids would drop off clothes and food for them near their caves.

Military Life Abroad

When you are in the military living abroad you do not receive your mail to your address but to an APO number. Friends and relatives living in the U.S. would get your APO address and send mail to that address. APO stands for Army Post Office and is associated with Army or Air Force installations. FPO stands for Fleet Post Office and is associated with Navy installations and ships. DPO stands for Diplomatic Post Office and is associated with U.S. embassies overseas. The only way to send an item to an APO, FPO or DPO address is to use the U.S. Postal Service (USPS).

Sometimes when you are career military, your associations with other military personnel continue. The Clark family was one of those for us. My father and Albert Clark had been in the POW camp during WWII. Albert Clark was older and of a higher rank than my father. They got along well and respected each other. Both families had been in Europe at the same time. The Clarks were not stationed in Brussels with us, but they were close by in France. Dad and Clark worked on missions in Europe in the 1950s. When we moved to Okinawa the two families lived on Kadena AB and attended many functions together. Over the years, the two of them attended many Stalag Luft III reunions. Clark would reach one of the highest ranks in the military during his extensive career. General Clark would serve as the Superintendent of the Air Force Academy from 1970-1974. During his tenure at the Air

Force Academy, Clark added many documents and photos of the Stalag Luft III POW camp to the Air Force Academy library. It is one of the largest collection of artifacts and photos outside of Zagan, Poland (where the camp was located). Clark once sent a plane to take Dad to a Stalag Luft III reunion. They would stay in contact until my father's death. After they had both passed away, I would spend time with his oldest daughter Carolyn at the Stalag Luft III reunions.

The Cuban Missel Crisis, October 1962

Defense Readiness Condition (DEFCON) are levels of readiness of the U.S. military to protect the country. Levels are a way of identifying the current threat level faced by the DoD and the United States Military. In peace time the level is five. Level one is pushing the button for the outbreak of nuclear war. During the Cuban Missile Crisis, leaders of the U.S. and the Soviet Union engaged in a tense, thirteen day political and military standoff in October 1962 over the installation of nuclear-armed Soviet missiles in Cuba, just ninety miles from U.S. shores.

In a TV address on October 22, 1962, President John F. Kennedy notified Americans about the presence of the missiles, explained his decision to enact a naval blockade around Cuba, and made it clear the U.S. was prepared to use military force if necessary to neutralize this perceived threat to national security. Following this news, many people feared the world was on the brink of nuclear war. However, disaster was avoided when the U.S. agreed to Soviet leader Nikita Khrushchev's offer to remove the Cuban missiles in exchange for the U.S. promising not to invade Cuba. Kennedy also secretly agreed to remove U.S. missiles from Turkey.

What history does not tell you is that in Okinawa we were on high alert, we were on twenty-four-hour alert to leave the island. We would leave with only what we could carry. What the news back then along with many history books today do not tell you is, the Nuclear Missile Sites on the island of Okinawa during that period were at DEFCON 2! One step away from pushing the button to release our missiles on Okinawa! Nikita Khrushchev had played a masterful game of chess and won.

Years later a Japanese documentary would be made about this period in history and how close Okinawa came to releasing those missiles. This documentary would make it sound like the Americans had put the Okinawan people in danger. However, the Japanese documentary failed to tell about all of the U.S. military, their families, and civilian support programs on the island in mortal danger as well! Sometimes in military life you feel invisible and sometimes history remembers you as invisible. The men who worked on these missile sites wrote a book titled, *U.S. Air Force Tactical Missiles 1949-1969, The Pioneers*, so that their time and work would be remembered. I thank them as a military kid for telling the public of our time and history on this beautiful island.

Moving Into Base Housing

After about a year, there were several homes available on base. These homes were a little better than the off-base housing. We also had the security of the base and did not have to pay the racketeering money for protection from thieves. Our family was invited to view the newly available homes and to pick one to move into. It was nice to live on base. We moved into our home and adjusted to base life. Each home, on base, had a small tori gate on the front lawn that held a sign with the rank and name of the military personal living in that house. We continued to employ Okinawan people to cut our lawn and manage the landscaping, clean our home and to make clothing.

I would have my first real job (outside of babysitting) in the summer between eighth and ninth grade. To work, I needed a Social Security card. My mother filled out the paperwork for Lee and I and we received our Social Security cards in the mail from the U.S. They arrived just before we started that summer. I worked at the Kadena AB Community Center. The center ran a summer day camp program. I worked in the art area as the assistant to the ceramic teacher. She was a military wife. I learned a lot about ceramics, clay, and pottery from her.

Our base house on Kadena AB.
Inset: The tori sign on the front yard with my father's name and rank.

The teacher and I helped the children make pottery or ceramic mold creations. The teacher would pour molds, fire them and the kids would paint them. The ceramics were fired in the electric kiln. Some students would play with the clay and make their own creations of animals, dishes, bowls, or cups. I spent more time with these students. Sometimes these creations would fall apart, and I would play with the clay creations, until they stayed in one piece! I loved working with the kids. The children were young and really tried very hard. My brother, Mark, was in the day camp and I helped him with a platypus duck creation. Mark treasured that small ceramic duck for years. The lady that ran the Community Center, Mrs. Coker, was a military spouse, the wife of Chief Master Sergeant Ed Coker, Dad's first sergeant. I collected my paycheck from Mrs. Coker.

* * *

Growing up in varied backgrounds and cultures gave me an understanding of the world that most kids raised in the U.S. never got. I lived and played and went to school with all races of people. Sometimes we lived on a grand stage and other times in very humble settings. I would learn to make the best of any situation. I knew how to use the finest of things and how to do without most things. After moving onto base housing, I started my ninth-grade school year, with a new bus group! In this bus group were the children of high-ranking officers. The culture on this bus was a little different too. The military kids were exposed to many things. Some of the kids on this bus were not much different in age than the troops manning the missile sites. Okinawa was also a staging area for training. One of the groups that trained on Okinawa was the Army Green Berets group. One of the boys at my bus stop was a mascot for the Green Berets. He trained with them and shared some of the details of hand-to-hand combat. Basically, how to kill another person with just your bare hands. He would go into very gory details while telling me about what he was learning with the Green Berets.

A lot of the military programs had mascots, like my friend at the bus stop who was the mascot for the Green Berets. My brother Lee was one of the mascots for the Jump Training Program. He enjoyed all the physical training, sliding down ropes and being harnessed to ropes while jumping out of the towers. However, the mascots did not participate in the jump from an airplane, Lee was okay with that. Most military on the island had their military jobs and duties and their volunteer obligation to support the military community on the island. My father's volunteer obligation was head of the Boy Scouts for the Far East.

Lee would get involved in Okinawan culture and took judo lessons. There was a funny story around this. My mother went into the village to buy my brother's judo gee, a pair of pants and jacket in white with a belt. My mother never learned to speak Japanese as none of us did because we lived in an American community inside Asian culture. She asked the store owner for a judo suit. The women did not understand what she wanted. My mother knew she had the right name but how come this lady did not understand judo? She was not putting the accent on the right part of the word. My mother was emphasizing the ju*DO* of the word, but in Japanese the emphasis is on the *JU*do. My mother kept repeating ju*DO* until the store owner realized what she wanted. Then they both laughed, and my mother came home with a judo gi.

I remember the long rides and the bus culture. Some girls would sit with boyfriends and they would make out during most of the ride. The bus driver was always an Okinawan man. Sometimes the girls would be dating a young military guy, and he would dress in civilian clothes and ride the bus with us. We all knew what was going on, but no one ever tattled, and the bus driver didn't care or didn't know. The cool kids sat in the back of the bus and the rest of us in the middle or the front.

Our family became friends with the Durbin family. Mark and Robby Durbin were in the same class in school and our houses on base were close. The boys were pretty much inseparable. They were similar in look and build. I was at the same bus stop as the Durbin sisters, Beth and Candy, both seniors. Beth was a merit scholar finalist and in the homecoming court that year. Candy was on the yearbook staff and in the National Honor Society. Both beautiful and smart. They were popular kids!

The singing sensation from Liverpool, England, The Beatles, hit it big around the world. I would see them for the first time on the TV in our base house on *The Ed Sullivan Show*. I was at that age of being in love with these guys. All us teenage girls had a favorite, and mine was Paul McCartney. I had bought Beatle fan magazines at the Base Exchange and cut out all the pictures of Paul and taped them to the back of my bedroom door. I thought Paul was so dreamy!

There was another singing group from Liverpool, called the Liverpool Five, and they had made their way to Okinawa to perform for the military and us kids. Beth and Candy went to the concert. They even got to meet the guys after the concert! At the bus stop the next day, they told us all about the time they had, they even claimed they had dates with these guys while they were on the island. I was younger than them and my parents were not interested in my attending the show.

It was fun to hear them tell their stories and I felt closer to Paul McCartney by listening.

I had Beatle records too, unlike many of the girls in America, my records were pirated versions of the real things, produced in China. China made a lot of knock-off products that the military and family members could easily get in the Okinawan village shops. The list of pirated products available in Okinawa included many items, even sewing machines.

During my ninth-grade year, the McGuire Family lived down the street from us. Gay and I were the same age and rode the same school bus. She was an only child. Her mother and my mother got along well. They had a lot in common. Both liked to sew, cook, and bake. Gay was showered with attention at home. Gay and I enjoyed art too. She was very smart and helped me with my Latin homework. Latin was a tough language for me, and she seemed to get it easily. Gay loved to read books and I learned a lot form her. She would discuss the books she had read. I remember she got me to read the book, *Bridge to the Sun* by Gwen Terasaki, the story behind the bombing of Pearl Harbor. Gay and her family would move back to the U.S. before us. We would visit them in their home outside of Washington, D.C., the following year when we would return to the U.S.

I joined the Catholic Youth Organization (CYO) that year. It was a fun organization. We attended Catholic Mass together, talks on Catholicism and Christian morals. We also sponsored dances at the church and outings. We met at the Officer's Club for business meetings. I became the treasurer for a while. Sundays were fun! My family would go to Catholic Mass in the morning, always at the earliest service. Then we'd go to the Veterans of Foreign Wars (VFW) Club off base for brunch. Then we would go back home or do some sightseeing or visit friends of my parents. If we visited friends, we would have to sit the whole time and listen. It made us very patient kids. Every Sunday night was dinner and entertainment at the Officer's

Club. The meal was several courses, from appetizer to dessert! The entertainment varied from acts from the U.S. to local entertainment. These were good family times.

One family Sunday adventure, we went to see a Habu-Mongoose fight. This was an Okinawan sport. A Habu is a venomous aggressive snake, and a mongoose looks much like a ferret or mink. Mongooses live in many parts of the world, and they can kill venomous snakes. We went into a room like a ring theatre with seats that came up the walls so everyone could see into the ring on the dirt floor. People were making bets on which one would win. Then they let them loose, and they fought until one was dead. Not something I was interested in watching again but did find it interesting to understand the Okinawan culture.

One of the seasonal events I loved was a festival called Boys Day! If the Okinawan family had a male child, they would fly a koi fish windsock for every male child in the family. The koi windsock symbolizes strength. I loved car rides on the streets of the off-base area where the Okinawan families lived and seeing all the brightly colored windsocks flying from a single pole. The more boys in the family the higher the pole. I was fascinated with the beautiful windsocks of fish. Perhaps because windsocks at airports had always been interesting. I was quite taken by this Okinawan culture and its very different attitudes on holidays and life in general.

We were living on an island that seventeen years before during WWII had been a battlefield. Sometimes we would hear explosions go off. There were bombs and mines that had been buried in the ground during the war and were rusting, deteriorating and would sometimes explode. We were not to go exploring in certain areas as these devices may still be buried and dangerous. There was an incident one day when we were living on base. We heard a blast and found out later it was a military kid that had gone into a restricted area. Sadly, he died of his wounds. Sometimes people die from a war, after the war is over.

My life would revolve around the school bus stop. The bus stops in the morning and the ride home. Occasionally, there were Okinawan protesters in the streets and when our bus would pass them many kids on the bus would sing the U.S. National Anthem as loud as we could when we passed the protesters. The U.S. had won this island in WWII in a three-month battle that took many American lives. More men died in the battle for Okinawa then on Iwo Jima. Okinawa was the last battle of WWII before the Atomic bomb was dropped on Hiroshima and Nagasaki. A glimpse of this horrific battle was portrayed in a 2016 movie named *Hacksaw Ridge*.

President John F. Kennedy

One morning in late November of 1963, I woke up and walked down the hall, to see my father watching the news in the U.S. on TV; mind you, we were halfway across the world and in a different time zone. It was Saturday morning in Okinawa. It was November 23, 1963, and the news was that President Kennedy had been shot. I had loved this president and started praying for him to live. My father was watching the news knowing that his assignment at Kadena was linked to this president. My understanding of this news was different than his understanding. He knew that this event could change things for us. I had not put all that together. We later learned that the President had died of his wounds and that we had a new leader, Lyndon B. Johnson. The new President did not change anything that affected us. We would finish our assignment on Okinawa.

Part of a United Service Organization (USO) Theater and TV Production

In an overseas assignment the USO was important to the military families and the young men and women serving their country. The USO organization provided entertainment for the troops. Lee wanted to try out for a part in one of the plays that the USO was putting on and it required two children. I agreed to read with him for the part, but I was not interested in being in the play. My mother talked me into doing it for him. The play was Thornton Wilder's "The Happy

Journey to Trenton and Camden," a one act play with no scenery. It was about a mother, father, and two kids on a trip from Trenton to Camden, NJ, written in 1931. The USO was producing three different one-act plays for this season. Lee and I auditioned, and I was picked to play the part, and they took Lee because it worked. I had learned a lot about acting from my experience in the Denver Hill School and it continued in Orlando at Glenridge reciting poetry. Mr. Scales, my eighth-grade literature teacher at Kubasaki Junior High, taught me so much about making literature become real. I liked poetry and my part in the play required I recite, the "Star Light, Star Bright" poem.

Our play would get the best reviews of the three one-act plays performed that year. Armed Forces Radio and Television asked if they could produce our play to be seen throughout the Far East. It was a lot of work to make this production for TV. We spent hours blocking the scenes for the TV audience. It was also more fun to perform for a live audience. The TV live performance of our play was very well received throughout the Far East. We had inquiries, asking if this was going to be a weekly show. The director of this play was a GI who worked for the USO. He was going back to New York after this military assignment was finished. He wanted me to try out for a part in a new play on Broadway that needed a child my age. My parents were not interested in the idea. I really didn't enjoy acting and I never pursued that career.

Coming of Age in Military Life

As I turned fifteen years old, my father signed me up for drivers' education classes. It was not run by the school but by military personnel. My father's first sergeant, Chief Master Sergeant, Edward Coker Sr. He and his wife had a son Edward Jr. who was in my grade at school. Edward and I also rode the same bus to school and were in the CYO (Catholic Youth Organization). Edward was tall and good looking, an altar boy at church and an only child. He was smart and had so much confidence. The Cokers were a Black family. I worked for Mrs. Coker at the youth center. Sergeant Coker would pick me up

The USO cast of Thornton Wilder's "The Happy Journey to Trenton and Camden," a one act play. Lee is on the left and I am on the right along with the actors that portrayed our parents in the play.

for drivers' education classes with Edward in the back seat and I would sit in the front. During the classes we primarily watched films about driving rules and regulations. We watched safety movies about driving motorcycles and learned about bad accidents. When we practiced actual driving, we would use military vehicles from the motor pool, including heavy trucks that were stick-shift. On top of all that, several students would go out at the same time. We would take turns driving, while the others sat in the back seat of the truck. The boys were better at this than I. Eventually I did learn to drive that massive stick-shift truck and passed drivers' ed.

I developed great friendships with all the kids in CYO. Edward and I really had a lot in common, we both liked poetry and went to the same school and church. We attended CYO outings and danced at the CYO dances at the church hall. Edward was one of the cool kids. I may have been noticed at school, but I never felt like a cool kid. Edward also befriended my brother, Lee. They would hang out at our house.

Our family would make friends with another family on the island, The Chiu family. They were not in the military and lived off base. They had two children: a son in college in America and a daughter named Rosa, who was two years older and also at Kubasaki High School. Rosa was in her junior and senior year of high school during the time we met them in Okinawa. She was voted "Most Likely to Succeed" in her senior year. Mr. Chiu was a pilot. He and Dad got to know each other from the flight desk. There may have been more the two men shared, although I can't say with certainty. Mr. Chiu worked for CAT (Civil Air Transport) Airlines. CAT Airlines was a cover for the CIA. As I mentioned earlier, Dad did a lot of reconnaissance flying, that may have been their connection. Reconnaissance is acquiring intelligence. Pilots that acquire intelligence can work closely with the CIA.

We often attended mass together, then went out for brunch. One weekend we met up with the Chiu family and their oldest son who was home from Columbia University in New York. He was telling us about his experience of attending college, as well as some of the fun and interesting things about being Chinese in the U.S. The story that I remember was the one where he and some of the other students took a trip to visit some of the southern cities, like New Orleans and Atlanta. On one of the bus rest stops, he told us, "The bathrooms are marked, 'White' and 'Colored.' I knew I was in trouble if I went in either one." I don't know what he did that day, but I never forgot the dilemma that situation presented him. I was familiar with racial problems in Albany, but this was another perspective of the problem.

My family would fly to Taiwan and meet up with the Chiu family at their second home there. That home was much nicer than their home in Okinawa. They took us out to eat at a real Chinese restaurant. We went up to the top floor of this restaurant and were seated at a large round table with a lazy susan built into the middle of the table. The food would come out of the kitchen and be put on the turning tabletop. If you wanted a certain food, you turned the moving piece and took what you wanted. The plates we were given were small and you just ate and then took another dish until you were full. I sat next to Mr. Chiu, and he taught me to use chopsticks that day. The food was vastly different from the Chinese food we eat in the U.S. There were all kinds of sea creatures that did not look appetizing to me. My favorite dish that day was steamed buns!

This is when I learned of Mrs. Chiu's story. Mrs. Chiu was born into a very wealthy Chinese family around 1921, the year that the Chinese Communist Party was founded. Her family supported Jiang Jieshi, alson known as Chiang Kai-shek, to become President of China. He would battle Mao Tse-Tung and the Communist Party from 1937-1950. Jiang Jieshi was fled to Taiwan in 1949, and Mao Tse-Tung took control of mainland China. Her family lost a lot when their land, house, money, and personal belongings were taken from them in mainland China. Mrs. Chiu met her husband during this time, married him, and started a family. In her youth, Mrs. Chui was considered one of the most beautiful women in China.

* * *

One of the reasons my family took the trip to Taiwan was to adopt a Chinese baby girl, as did many of the military families during that time. I would learn many things on this trip, one is that in Chinese culture it is important for the first child to be a boy. If the first child is a girl, she would be left on the sea wall to wash out to sea. We took a trip out to the beach to see the sea wall where many babies had been left. My family would visit three orphanages that day, to look for baby girls. I was fifteen years old, and I found these orphanages hard to experience. There would be rooms for infants crying or sleeping in cribs. The orphanages had too many babies for the staff to properly care for. The orphanages we visited were run by Catholic nuns. It was hard to see room after room of cribs with babies. My parents finally decided on a baby girl they liked. There were medical tests these babies had to pass once the choice was made. We did not return to Okinawa with a baby girl. The medical review would take a week or so. Sadly, the baby my parents picked did not pass the medical tests. Her mother had a venereal disease leaving this little girl with problems that would lead to an early death. My mother was devastated but was happy for other families that had success adopting those beautiful Chinese babies. My parents had lost children before, it never got easier.

Some Friends Lasted a Long Time, Some a Lifetime

My father had 800 men under his command as Missile Site Number Four Commander and as Unit Commander of the 498th Missile Maintenance Squadron. There were two of these men that became close with our family. Robert (Bob) Lathrop was an integral part of the field maintenance team. He had married in May before coming to Okinawa. His wife Peggy stayed behind to finish nursing school in Orlando, FL. Once Peggy arrived, they found a house off base; Bob no longer had to live in the barracks. My mother found a job for Peggy working at the base nursery. Peggy made friends with many of the Okinawan children in her neighborhood off base. She and another American even planned outings for the children. When Peggy and Bob eventually got orders for his next assignment, the Okinawan villagers lined the streets with gifts for the Americans who had shared their time and attention with the kids of this village. Peggy would describe this farewell event with much heart when she shared it with me many years later. The Lathrop's would follow us when we moved back to the States. We would stay friends with them until my father's death. Bob would pass away after my father and Peggy; her daughter and granddaughter would attend my mother's funeral.

Another one of Dad's men was Richard Selle. Selle, as he was called in the unit, fell in love with an Okinawan girl. She was beautiful and they got along well. Richard was Catholic and as their romance continued, they started attending the Catholic mission church off base with the tatami mat floors. She fell in love with Selle and with Christianity and converted to Catholicism. My family was invited to the wedding. We all dressed and showed up at the mission church for the ceremony. The only part I remember is that she was so late to the service that at one point we were concerned it might not happen at all. Her family was not happy about her conversion from the Buddhist religion to Catholicism. We heard her brother had tried to kill her the night before the wedding and was holding her at home to try to keep the wedding from happening. They did marry that day, and lived in off-base housing. She would travel to America with her husband, and they would have three boys. I don't know if she ever flew those three carp fish windsocks from a pole in the States celebrating Boys Day. The Selle family stayed in contact with us and even came to visit us in America.

Summer Sewing Class

Our last summer in Okinawa my mother signed me up for a sewing and pattern making class at a local Okinawan business that trained Sew Girls. I loved the class and took to it with ease. I learned to sew like the skilled Sew Girls that had made all our clothing.

New Kubasaki High School Building

By 1964 the military started building a proper high school, no more second-hand barracks! In my final school year at Kubasaki we moved into our new building. It was my tenth-grade year, 1964-65. It was a beautiful state-of-the-art building, especially to those of us who had been in the barrack buildings. We were the Kubasaki Dragons. Kubasaki was a true melting pot of all races and many different religions. We didn't share the prejudices that existed in the civilian population State-side. President Harry Truman had signed an executive order on July 26, 1948, banning segregation in the Armed Forces. Our families were in the military, and we understood that to defend a country, we all must work together. That is what makes the U.S. military strong.

State-side civilians didn't have to work as a unit, like in military life. Most had lived in the same city growing up. When I would be State-side, I would get asked, "Where are you from?" I never had an answer they understood. Even when I would tell them, "I'm from everywhere and nowhere," they would ask me what place I liked best or what town I was born in. They were always looking for a reference to a place, but I had none they could understand.

Kubasaki High School Sports

In high school one of the great pastimes was football. There was only one high school on the island. Who would our team play? The military had that problem solved. Depending on what branch of the service your father served in, you were a supporter of that team. I was an Air Force kid, so my team was the Falcons. I was a Kubasaki Dragon *and* a Falcon. Some Army kids were the Eagles and others were the Knights. We played football games with the kids at our school. On the Thursdays before games, we wore our school spirit buttons. Kubasaki had one pep rally for all three teams, and we cheered our team as the pep rally featured our three different cheerleading squads, in smart cheer routines. The football players got to wear their football jerseys to school that day. We would pass kids in the hall and tell them our team was going to beat their team. Everyone enjoyed the competition.

I was on the drill team for the Falcons. A regular military drill sergeant volunteered to train us in drill routines. He worked us like his troops. Some girls complained or quit, but most took on the challenge. I was one who took on the challenge and it paid off later in life when I had to face difficult times. That drill sergeant taught me that I can handle more then I think I can.

In the tenth grade we had Physical Education (PE) in our new high school facility. We had some PE prior to the new school but it was spotty, borrowing the military training gyms for our recreation classes. When we got to the new high school, we had regular PE classes. We moved into the school before parts of the school were finished, like the gym. So, we worked around that by playing games outside. I was not athletic at all, so my grades in PE were not great. With a D grade in PE, I received a notice that I was no longer eligible for the Honor Society. My mother went to the principal to fight for me, but it was of no use. I was crushed!

My Father's Concern for My Welfare

My father had the daunting task of commanding 800 men, some who were away from home for the first time, working around-the-clock shifts. This task was even more critical since he was overseeing these troops on missile sites. One of the problems prominent with the men was getting into trouble while off duty. Some of that was getting into fights in bars. Other problems could be getting venereal diseases. Now, any time there was a problem day or night our house was called. Many of the problems and fights were late at night. My father would take calls from the military police. I could hear one side of the conversation from my room. I would later hear my parents talking about it too. I got the gist of his job. I was also aware of the military guys that played the part of high school kids riding on our buses. I never shared that with my father. He took the responsibility of his job seriously, as he did everything. He was serious about how he worked with his troops. He wanted the best for them. He often felt the military police were too hard on the guys. I'm sure he came from his own experience and his deep faith.

I was coming of age at fifteen and my parents, especially Dad, wanted to keep me out of trouble. He didn't know how exactly to handle it. There were training documentaries films for the military covering everything from how to do the job to how to stay out of trouble. There were documentary films produced by every branch of the service about venereal diseases (VD). The Marine Corps film was apparently one of the most explicit. The rule at that time in Okinawa was, if you had VD more than two times, you had to report it to your commander. Prior to the third exposure, you could go to the base hospital and get a shot of penicillin. Some of the troops did not want to face their commanding officer so they would go to the Okinawan doctors. Some of these doctors were charlatans who shot them up with Brylcreem, which looked like penicillin but was a hair product for men. So, the illness got worse and then they had to go to the base hospital with a bad case of the disease, and of course Dad would find out. Because of all that, I was on the list to see the Marine Corps film on VD. Thank goodness, my mother talked him out of it. My father did have the proverbial talk with me about sex and the dangers of venereal diseases, again coming from his childhood experience. I knew that he loved me very much and always wanted the best for me. I loved and respected my father, and never wanted to let him down.

Mark Learns a Lesson

One day my mother walked into our base house to hear Mark and Robby reading aloud. As she got back to Mark's room, some of the words she heard disturbed her. Mark was reading about risqué behavior. She stormed into the room and asked where he had gotten this book. Mark and Robby were truly innocent. They told my mother that there was trash on the curb at Colonel Tate's house and they found the book. When my mother picked it up, she saw that it was a diary. It was Sharon Tate's diary. My mother did not know Sharon Tate. Linda Tate was in high school with me and was one of the people at my bus stop. I didn't know her well. She was like me, quiet and kept to herself. My mother took both boys down to Colonel Tate's house and knocked on the door. Mrs. Tate answered, and my mother showed her the book and told her the boys found it in the trash pile on the curb. My mother pointed out that since it was a private diary, maybe she would want to keep it. Mrs. Tate agreed and thanked my mother and the boys. My mother thought of this as a lesson for the boys to do the right thing.

The diary belonged to Colonel and Mrs. Tate's grown daughter, who was not with them on this assignment. For years my family thought Mark had found the diary of Sharon Tate the famous actress, but that was not so. The name apparently was not that uncommon.

MY FATHER'S SECRETS

8

Next Assignment: MacDill AFB, Florida

NOT LONG AFTER THE TATE family moved to their next assignment, my father got his new orders too. He had requested an assignment in the northeastern part of the U.S. I was hoping to go to Bryn Mawr College for women in Pennsylvania, so that move would have been ideal. My mother always talked about this college, and I thought she wanted me to go there. Plus, both sides of my parents' families were in the northeast. When his orders arrived, our new assignment was MacDill AFB in Tampa, FL. No one was thrilled with this news at the time. We didn't know what the future held for us. I knew that I had two more years of high school, and my plan was to go to college. Neither of my parents had finished college; heck, my mother never even finished high school, but I didn't know it at the time. The military had given my father a college equivalency status for his military training and the college classes he attended in Philadelphia.

My parents purchased a small Mazda car while we lived on base. It was the first time we had two cars in our family. We were not going to take the small Mazda back to the U.S. They decided to buy another Mercedes car while we were on the island. We could get a better price when buying overseas. Our family went to the Mercedes dealership on Okinawa and ordered the new car to be delivered to the Port of New York after we arrived back in the U.S. My father was eyeing the two-door models, but I reminded him that he had a family and we needed four doors. He agreed. It was the first time I was included in an important family purchase. I felt very grown up that day.

* * *

Many military families were good to the Okinawan people. We provided a lot of employment for the people on the island. Long after I left in 1965 it would be returned to Japan. More movies would be made about the island and a study of the people there would bring notoriety to this island paradise.

On May 15, 1972, upon reversion of Okinawa to Japanese administration, the two organizations were combined to form Commander Fleet Activities, Okinawa. With the relocation of Commander Fleet Activities, Okinawa, to Kadena Air Base on May 7, 1975, the title then became Commander Fleet Activities, Okinawa/U.S. Naval Air Facility, Kadena.

Lee, Mark, and I would finish school in 1965 in Okinawa. My father had to report to MacDill AFB on July 27th. We would fly out of Kadena AB. I have a strong memory of standing in that airport terminal, thinking, "I will never return to this beautiful island and the wonderful people and friends I'd made here." Like all our other assignments, that precious time was over and it was time to move on. We flew to Hawaii. This time we flew as a family on a jet—not a propeller airplane. We were going to stay at Fort DeRussy on the Hawaiian island of Oahu. We were excited to spend time in Hawaii, after all we had only been in the airport on the trip to Okinawa and in the middle of the night.

Fort DeRussy was not a lavish hotel at the time. We checked in and were shown to a room that had been a barracks. It was a large room and in a corner of the room was a toilet and sink. There was no privacy in the room's set up. The soldier showing us the room assured us that for privacy there was another bathroom down the hall with showers and a private toilet.

We had lived on Okinawa for three years and I had become accustomed to the slow pace and the Asian attitude. On Oahu the speed limit was fifty miles-an-hour, and the pace was fast. After the first few days I began to cry, it seemed for no apparent reason. My parents didn't understand what was wrong with me. I was fifteen years old, becoming a woman, with hormones raging. The pace of this life was overwhelming for me. I really needed to adjust to everything, because we were going to be on a faster pace in the States. Slowly, I adjusted. We had a great time in Hawaii visiting all the sights on Oahu and experiencing a real Hawaiian luau on the beach in Waikiki. One of the outstanding sights we would visit was the Pearl Harbor Memorial. This was the place that so many American men had died. It was an attack that led to the U.S. involvement in WWII. In a way, it was part of the reason I was living in a military family.

Back in the U.S.

We landed in San Francisco in the middle of the night and had a problem finding a place to stay. We ended up finding a room at the Saint Francis Hotel, a beautiful upscale hotel that was also a historic building. We rarely stayed at places this nice. The next day, Dad's brother Thom, who lived in Fresno, CA, came with all six of his kids to visit us at the hotel. We toured the sights in San Francisco and had a nice welcome home with family.

After that visit we flew to New York, where we would pick up the Mercedes ordered in Okinawa. It was the latest 1965 model 220S and again it was a shade of gray. While there, the 1964-65 New York World's Fair was in full swing. The city built a huge stainless steel art statement to mark the Fair, named the "Unisphere." Many buildings and structures remain from that world's fair today including the Unisphere. The theme of that year's World's Fair was "Peace through Understanding."

We drove to Philadelphia to visit our maternal family, and then to

Washington, D.C., to check on Father's military records. We stayed with Gay McGuire's family. I could tell Gay was going to do well in this environment. She seemed to be right where she needed to be. She was planning to attend Georgetown University and then go on to law school. Unfortunately, during college our families lost touch. However, I would later hear that Gay did get her law degree. I don't think she knew that I was a big fan of her goals.

As a military family overseas, we had to maintain a U.S. address. We had friends in New Jersey, Harriett and Dick Fenimore. We had met them through my godmother, who had worked with Harriett in Philadelphia for AT&T. A military family could use a U.S. address for lower taxes. We had used this New Jersey address thinking we'd return to New Jersey when Dad retired. In fact, we had a New Jersey license plate on the first Mercedes we bought in Brussels. We had that plate from Laredo, TX, to St. Petersburg, FL. All those years, I thought I'd be going to college in the northeast. When the orders came for us to move to MacDill AFB in Tampa, I didn't know what my future would look like.

History of MacDill AFB, Tampa, FL

By 1941 construction was completed on Southeast Air Base, Tampa, later named MacDill Field in honor of Colonel Leslie MacDill. The field became MacDill Air Force Base after the establishment of the USAF in 1947.

On the second of January 1951, the 305th Bombardment Wing was activated at MacDill AFB and became the second SAC wing to receive the B-47 jet bomber. Operational squadrons of the wing were the 305th, 364th, 365th, and 366th Bombardment Squadrons. Initially training with Boeing B-29 and B-50 Superfortresses, the 305th also received its first Boeing KC-97 Stratofreighter later in 1951. Following this, the group began training heavily in its new dual mission of strategic bombardment and aerial refueling. It was not far outside of MacDill AFB in Avon Park that our family friend had lost his life in target practice in the early 1950s.

In June 1952, the 305th upgraded to the all-jet Boeing B-47B Stratojet. The wing continued strategic bombardment and refueling operations from MacDill and deployed overseas three times. Air Defense Command (ADC) became a major tenant unit at MacDill in 1954 with the establishment of a mobile radar station on the base to support the permanent ADC radar network in the United States sited around the perimeter of the country.

During 1961, MacDill AFB joined the SAGE system, initially feeding data to Site DC-09 at Gunter AFB, Alabama. After joining SAGE, the squadron was redesignated as the 660th Radar Squadron on March 1, 1961.

In 1966, the AN/FPS-26 was modified into an AN/FSS-7 submarine-launched ballistic missile detection and warning radar, part of the Fourteenth Missile Warning Squadron. The first attempt to close MacDill AFB was made in 1960, when the impending phaseout of SAC's B-47 bombers caused it to be listed as surplus and slated for closure. However, the Cuban Missile Crisis of 1962 highlighted the base's strategic location and its usefulness as a staging area. As a result, the cuts were stayed, and the base repurposed for a tactical mission with fighter aircraft. In response to the crisis, the United States Strike Command was also established at MacDill as a crisis response force; it was one of the first unified commands, a command that draws manpower and equipment from all branches of the U.S. military.

In 1962, MacDill AFB was transferred from SAC to Tactical Air Command (TAC). Bomber aircraft remained home-based at MacDill until the 306th Bombardment Wing's transfer to McCoy AFB, and SAC continued to maintain a tenant presence at MacDill through the 1980s, using their alert facility as a dispersal location for B-52 and KC-135 aircraft. But for all practical purposes, the 1960s marked MacDill's transition from a bomber-centric SAC base to a fighter-centric TAC installation. Under TAC, MacDill AFB remained a fighter base for almost thirty years, but other changes went on in the background.

Upon MacDill AFB's transfer to TAC, the twelfth tactical fighter wing (12th TFW) was reactivated on April 17, 1962 and assigned to Ninth Air Force. Initially, its only operational squadron was the 559th Tactical Fighter Squadron. The mission of the 12th TFW was to prepare for tactical worldwide deployments and operations. Until 1964, the wing flew obsolete Republic F-84F Thunderjets reclaimed from the ANG (Air National Guard). In January 1964, the wing was chosen to be the first Air Force combat wing to convert to the new McDonnell Douglas F-4C Phantom II.

The wing was soon involved in F-4C firepower demonstrations, exercises, and ultimately, at the Paris Air Show. The conflict in Southeast Asia was escalating, and throughout 1965, the wing supported Pacific Air Forces Contingency Operations by rotating combat squadrons quarterly to Naha Air Base in the Ryukyu Islands. The 12th TFW began its permanent deployment to the first Air Force expeditionary airfield at Cam Rahn Bay Air Base, South Vietnam, on the sixth of November 1965.

The 12th TFW combat squadrons initially scheduled for deployment to Vietnam were the 555th, 557th, and 558th Tactical Fighter Squadron (TFS). Ultimately, the 559th TFS took the place of the 555th when the squadron was diverted to a second TDY with the 51st Fighter-Interceptor Wing at Naha Air Base, Okinawa, followed by a reassignment to the 8th TFW at Ubon Royal Thai Air Force Base, Thailand. Still later, the 555th was assigned to the 432d Tactical Reconnaissance Wing (TRW) at Udon Royal Thai Air Force Base.

On the seventeenth of April 1962, the 15th TFW was activated at MacDill and assigned to the ninth Air Force. Operational squadrons of the wing and squadron tail codes were the 12th and 15th TFWs which constituted the 836th Air Division at MacDill AFB on the first of July 1962. Initially equipped with the F-84F Thunderjet, in 1964 the 15th TFW was subsequently upgraded to the tail-coded McDonnell Douglas F-4C Phantom II.

The mission of the 15th TFW was to conduct tactical fighter combat crew training. The wing participated in various exercises, operations, and readiness tests of TAC, and trained pilots and provided logistical support for the 12th TFW. Reorganized as a mission-capable unit at the time of the Cuban Missile Crisis of 1962, it returned afterwards to a training mission.

With the departure of the 12th TFW in 1965, the 15th TFW became the host unit at MacDill with the unit's mission becoming a formal training unit for F-4 aircrews prior to their deployment to Southeast Asia. The wing deployed 16 F-4s to Seymour Johnson AFB, NC, during the USS *Pueblo* crisis in 1968.

In 1965, the wing deployed its 43rd, 45th, 46th, and 47th Tactical Fighter Squadrons to Southeast Asia, where they participated in the air defense commitment for the Philippines from Clark Air Base and flew combat missions from Cam Rahn Bay Air Base in South Vietnam and Ubon Royal Thai Air Force Base in Thailand. Members of the 45th TFS achieved the first U.S. Air Force aerial victories of the Vietnam War.

★ ★ ★

As my family and I packed into our new vehicle, we drove down to Florida from The Big Apple. Although MacDill AFB was in Tampa, we would stay a few miles away in Orlando initially. We drove to St. Petersburg and stayed at a motel there for about two weeks while we checked out housing. MacDill had base housing, but it was close to Tampa Bay and the bay was so polluted in 1965, that the area smelled. In fact, the Hyde Park area of Tampa Bay had been a very high-class area at one time, but now most of the homes were boarded up and abandoned because of the smell. We also heard the high school I might attend in Tampa was not sure to get its accreditation renewed. So, we ended up looking at homes in St. Petersburg. St. Petersburg and Tampa are just across the bay from each other. It would be a drive for my dad, but he was willing to do it to have a home and a school for his family in a better setting. He also decided it was time to buy a home again. He was possibly getting close to retirement time. He had been in the military since 1941 with one year out.

My father would take his post at MacDill as the Commander of the 15th Organization Maintenance Squadron. He would organize the airplane hangars and oversee the maintenance of the planes as well as pilot training. He had experience with fighter planes and jets, and had been a participant in Fox Peter One, the first in air refueling of F-84 fighter jets. He had been trained in the U.S. Missile system, had been the commander of 800 men at the Okinawa missile site, and had flown missions over Vietnam while we were in Okinawa. Now, I can understand why he was sent to MacDill.

We ended up buying a home in St. Petersburg, in Holiday Park because it was the highest area of Pinellas County. Always a farmer boy, he understood you always lived on high ground. Lee and I enrolled at Dixie Hollins High School. Mark would attend Tyrone Elementary School. We bought a brand-new model home and again lived without furniture until the storage company that had packed up our home in Stead AFB in Nevada could get our furniture and belongings to St. Petersburg. Our things arrived. and along with them my turquoise bike. I had missed that bike and did ride it from time to time, but I turned sixteen years old that first summer in St. Petersburg and bikes were a thing of the past. I had already learned to drive a car, although I wouldn't get a car for another three years. Fortunately, we were also the owners of two Mercedes vehicles, which was good. My father had to drive to Tampa, and we were in a neighborhood that was not convenient to walk to the store or schools, so Mom would need a separate vehicle.

Lee and I would start school at Dixie, in a section of Pinellas County called Kenneth City. It was named for the first superintendent of schools for Pinellas County, Dixie M. Hollins. The school was opened in 1959 as the South County Comprehensive Vocational high School with more than thirty vocational, technical, and business programs. Two of these programs were an advanced art program and a program for elementary teachers. I signed up for both. In the state of Florida (at that time) there was a requirement that I had to have a course called "Americanism vs. Communism." It was a rule I could do nothing about. I probably knew more than most of the teachers in this course. I had certainly lived in and around this subject and I had a dad whose whole job was to protect the world from Communist aggression. Strategic Air Command (SAC) was created for just that purpose.

Part of the school was air conditioned, and part was not. I had been on the drill team at Kubasaki and joined the drill team at Dixie. The school teams were The Rebels. I thought this was an odd mascot name at the time, after all we were an integrated school in the south. All the schools I had attended around the world had been integrated and we never had a mascot name that honored a difficult time in history. Nothing I could do about it; I just went along. Our drill team was called The Reb-Belles. Our majorettes wore the rebel flag on their outfits and so did we.

This school, unlike Orlando, was not that welcoming. There were many cliques, still I would find a group of friends. My mother was checking out the public bus transportation system in St. Petersburg for Lee and me to use to get around the city. On one of her trips, she met a young girl named Hari Katz. Hari and I were introduced and soon became friends. Hari introduced me to others. She was into singing and piano. I even attended some of her recitals. She had a terrific voice. Peggy Owens was added to the group. A house was built across the street from our home and a large family moved into it. There were two daughters around my age, Lillian and Linda Traugott. Most of us were juniors and soon some started dating. So, boys were added to this group. high school was fun with this group.

We had beach days that summer break. Once I used the pattern-making skills I had learned in Okinawa to create patterns for matching outfits for each couple. Lillian, Linda, and I found Hawaiian print material in different background colors. Each couple wore a different background color. The girls in long Hawaiian-style dresses over our swimwear and the guys in Jams, a popular name at the time for boys swimming shorts. All the girls sewed using my patterns to make the outfits for themselves and their boyfriend. We thought we looked so cool.

As new families moved into our housing development, new kids were added. This included another military family across the street, the Waddel family. A new home was built behind us and the Henderson family moved in. They had one son and one daughter, Virginia. She was one year older than me and attended Boca Ciega High School. Because she was a senior and had attended Boca Ciega the last three years, she was allowed to finish her senior year and graduate there. Because we attended different schools, we would become better friends when we were both at junior college in the years to come. It was good to move into a new housing development with new people looking to make friends.

I would do well in my art classes. I was winning prizes and selling my art. I was starting to get recognition in school. I made a friend in art class, Vicky Leland. We discovered we had a lot in common. Vicky was not a part of our group, she had lived in the area and gone to school with all the local kids at Dixie. She was Homecoming Queen in her senior year. She was an artist and a beauty. Our families also connected, and both of our mothers enjoyed sewing. Vicky was one of four daughters. Each one was prettier than the last. Her family would help me find my place in the St. Petersburg community.

I was also taking a French II class. I of course had a leg up on the rest of the class. I had spoken French in Brussels and the French teacher had noted my pronunciation was like that of a native French speaker. Dixie's French teacher entered me into the yearly French Declamation Contest representing Dixie Hollins H.S. I participated in this competition in my junior and senior years, taking first place each year. I enjoyed the recognition and becoming a part of my new community. This was a first for me. There would be no next move. My time as a military kid was ending. I would be here for a while, so fitting into this community felt right.

9

My Father's Retirement:
May 31, 1966

BY THE END OF MY junior year in high school my father would retire from the Air Force and leave MacDill AFB. This would happen suddenly. I never really knew why. There was discussion of his commanding officer being extremely difficult to work for. My father kept coming home with headaches. Sometimes people are stretched to their limits. He went to San Antonio, TX, to do what was needed to retire as a pilot. He loved flying and would miss all the challenges of those jets. He was forty-five years old when he retired. He would never fly military jets again. However, he would continue flying civilian planes. He had the opportunity to fly commercial airlines, but he was not interested in the job. He told me he did not want the responsibility of all the souls onboard the planes. Pilots refer to passengers as "souls."

As mentioned earlier, my father served his country from 1941-1946 as a WWII fighter pilot and as a POW in Stalag Luft III. He left the military in 1947 but enlisted in the reserves in 1948, being recalled to active duty in 1951, serving until 1966 continuously. He had flown forty-three missions out of North Africa with the Fifteenth Air Force of the Army Air Corps in 1943 before being shot down during a strafing mission over Foggia, Italy—a mission at the turning point of WWII. He was in Stalag Luft III during the Great Escape and endured the winter march from Stalag Luft III to Moosburg in January of 1945. He was a test pilot upon his return from Europe in 1946, being the main test pilot for the F-82. He would test the new F-84 jets and fly missions over Korea from 1951-1953. He would participate in Fox Peter One, the mission to refuel jets over the Pacific Ocean. His service in Brussels included a lot of Cold War missions. Many of them I would never be able to get information about because they were top secret. His flying in Laredo, TX, and Stead Air Force Base outside of Reno, NV, would prepare pilots for Vietnam. He served during the golden age of flight. He had been the commander of a nuclear missile site on Okinawa. A leader of men under his command, he took his job seriously, always trying to do what was best for all involved. He was ready to wind down and enjoy this beautiful state and great weather, to spend time with family and friends. His time for fighting the good fight was over.

* * *

I was growing up and getting ready for my last year of high school. My life would have more impact from the military than both my brothers'. Lee would be at the same high school for four years. Mark would have most of his education in St. Petersburg. Every military-raised kid has a distinct experience. The press likes to show the military person coming home and surprising family members. That scenario is only part of the experience, so much more goes into us. In many ways I would take-on the fight. I had not been a member of the military. Many kids raised in military families join the military when they are of age. We are comfortable in that environment. We grow up on defense. We understand the importance of protecting our country. I would understand the importance of protecting my country and the cost of protecting my country.

Military families are only about one percent of the population. Once I was in civilian life, I realized many people do not understand the military and what it does. Many don't appreciate what the military does for them because they take their freedom for granted. My mother would make sure I understood how important it is to have an education. I would graduate from high school in June of 1967; and although my mother had filled my head with the possibility of schools like Bryn Mawr, that was not going to be for me. I would start St. Petersburg Junior College that summer. It was one of the top ten junior colleges (JCs) in the U. S. at that time. Vicky Leland and I started JC (as we called it) at the same time and went to orientation together, and we would both still be living at home. JC was not far from our housing area and since I didn't have my own car, one of my parents would drop me off in the morning and pick me up in the afternoon. I would spend a lot of time in the Student Union Building (the SUB), or the library.

Vicky worked a part-time job as an usher at the Bayfront Center Arena and Theater. This was a large complex located on the Bay near downtown, it was opened in 1965. She told me about a job opportunity, and I got a job too. The Bayfront Center would call you when they had events, and you could let them know if you could make it or not. Vicky and I would usually usher in the higher priced seating area. In the late 1960s when you sat someone, they tipped you. It was not a huge tip, but a quarter or a dime was nice to have. I would work at the Bayfront Center for the two years I attended JC. Some of my best memories from that job were working the Ice Capades and walking the world-renowned pianist, Liberace, from his dressing room to the stage. Liberace wore extravagant costumes, played the piano, and told funny stories. I was seating people in the front row seats that night and got that privilege at the last minute to go to his dressing room, knock on the door, and tell him it was time to go on stage. I walked with him to the bottom of the stage. As he walked the steps up to the stage, the spotlight hit him, and the crowd went wild. His audience was so large they put him in the arena not the theater.

* * *

My brother Lee would find a red used 1960 Ford Falcon car during my second year at junior college. It cost $500. We split the cost and shared the car, and my parents paid for the insurance. Lee was in his last year at Dixie Hollins. He was working and so was I, but we worked well together, sharing that red car.

I would drive alone for the first time. This was a problem because I had no sense of direction. I would know one way to get to school and one way to get to my job. I would drive back to my house to get to my next destination. My family would laugh at me when they would see me drive into the driveway and then back out again to go in another direction. Little by little I learned ways to get from one location to another without going back home.

Lee got a job at the Bayfront Center in the concession stands. He worked there during his four years of college. He was running the concession business by the time he finished college. Lee would get his engineering degree in four years. He did not take the job at the Bayfront Center offered him. He had a lot of great friends and connections from working there. His work ethic and resilience gained him a lot of respect.

* * *

Mark was always the class clown until sixth grade. Mark, like Lee, was very smart and found no challenge in the classroom. So, he enjoyed being a funny guy. His sixth-grade teacher changed all that. I went with my mother to a conference with this teacher. She saw that Mark was smart but not interested in doing the work. She told us that Mark needed to set a goal in his life before he would get serious about his studies. She and our parents would help my brother find his passion. He started volunteering at the hospital as the only male candy striper. He volunteered at the science center too. He eventually found a job at a veterinary clinic. That sixth-grade teacher changed my brother's path. Mark took his studies more seriously. His path would have many challenges, but he achieved his goal of graduating from medical school.

***

One spring Lillian Traugott and I were trying to get a job at the community center for the summer. While we were there these ladies asked me if I was interested in being in a pageant. It was the Junior Sun Goddess Pageant. I took the application home and discussed it with my parents. It turned out to be a wonderful experience. I would go to many practice sessions and the result was being presented at the St. Petersburg Yacht Club with my father escorting me in a white gown. Before my father retired from the military, Mom had hoped to have my coming out debut at the Officer's Club at MacDill AFB. Unfortunately, that year it was cancelled. So, this opportunity the ladies at that community center gave me was a tremendous gift. Lillian and I did not get the job that summer at the community center. I had gotten something much more.

Bay Pines Hospital, St. Petersburg, FL

Bay Pines Veterans Hospital, National Cemetery and Administrative Services is a multi-function area for U.S. Veterans. It is in a charming area off the Gulf of Mexico. The Bay Pines VA Healthcare System is a level one tertiary facility. Originally opened in 1933, the medical center is located on 337 acres approximately eight miles northeast of downtown St. Petersburg. Bay Pines National Cemetery is sited on the grounds of the Department of Veterans Affairs Medical Center at Bay Pines, between St. Petersburg and Madeira Beach across Tampa Bay from Tampa.

In 1968 Vicky called me one day and said they really needed girls for a pageant at Bay Pines Hospital. 1968 was the height of the Vietnam War, and the hospital was full of injured soldiers. Each year the Jewish War Veterans Auxiliaries 246 of St. Petersburg and 383 of Tampa held a beauty pageant competition. This was the seventeenth Annual Miss Bay Pines Pageant. Each contestant would bring a gown and a one-piece swimsuit. All the contestants were presented as a group in our gowns and then individually we walked through the audience. Each injured soldier was given a card to vote for their favorite contestant. We were presented again in swimsuits as a group then individually we walked through the audience of injured soldiers in swimsuits. That part of the competition was the most popular.

Miss Bay Pines

MARILYN PHILLIPS, 18, a St. Petersburg Junior College student majoring in elementary education, was named Miss Bay Pines of 1968 at the 17th annual contest sponsored by the Jewish War Veterans auxiliaries 246 of St. Petersburg and 383 of Tampa.

Brunette Miss Phillips of 6335 30th Ave. N. was selected from 12 other contestants March 30 at the Bay Pines Veterans Hospital recreation hall.

Vicki Leland was first runner up and second runner up was Cookie Crawford.

Bette Orsini of The Times staff was master of ceremonies for the event attended by patients at the hospital.

These young, injured soldiers came in walking, walking with assistance, in wheelchairs, or on stretchers with IV bags. All the cameras were on us contestants. It should have been on the audience. My memory of that night is of that audience. They were packed into that auditorium. We were an evening of entertainment for these brave men. When we each walked in swimsuits, we got plenty of whoops, hollers, and whistles! The guys went crazy and loved that part of the competition. After all the soldiers cast their votes, it took an hour to count all the ballots. At the end of the counting, I would be crowned "Miss Bay Pines." That night my father, who attended the pageant with my mother, would tell me that was the most important pageant I would ever participate in. I had been chosen, not by a panel of judges like all the other pageants, but by each member of the audience. It was an idea by a group of caring volunteers who did something that night to boost the morale of these injured soldiers. Dad was right, it would take me many more years to see the wisdom of his words.

There was one appearance I made as Miss Bay Pines that year (see newspaper clipping next page). It was a photo shoot at Bay Pines for Fire Prevention Week. This photo shoot would be featured in the *St. Petersburg Times Newspaper*. It started off the full week of activities on Fire Prevention at Bay Pines. In Nevada when my fire prevention

The queen of Bay Pines V.A. Center, Miss Marilyn Phillips, indulges the world of fire fighters to control the spotlight during observance of fire prevention week which got underway Monday at the Center. The week's activities are featuring fire drills, fire prevention classes, and the showing of films on fire, its origin and control. Miss Bay Pines is a freshman at St. Petersburg Junior College majoring in elementary education. The lucky Bay Pines fireman waving to onlookers is William Cramer. This afternoon at 2 p.m., the Seminole Volunteer Fire Dept. will join the fire fighters from Bay Pines in a simulated fire disaster drill. The general public will be welcomed to observe this demonstration.

poster was disqualified, I was heartbroken about the whole thing. Now, I was getting my recognition for that effort at a different time and place. There I was in my smart plaid orange suit with a fire hat on my head posing with a fireman on the back of a fire truck!

Job Opportunities During College

Clothier John Baldwin opened a small shop in St. Petersburg, FL, in 1947. The business grew, and in 1951 he opened his flagship location at Fashion Corner, Beach Drive at Second Avenue. His womenswear shop catered to wealthy locals and tourists in an elegant atmosphere. The focus was on service. He opened nine shops throughout Florida and in Myrtle Beach, S.C. In addition to womenswear, Baldwin eventually sold menswear, lingerie, shoes, and furs.

Vicky introduced me to this very high-end clothing store in downtown St. Petersburg. Mr. Baldwin would very often purchase an ad for his store on the inside front cover of *Vogue* magazine. At this time Mr. Baldwin had stores throughout the state of Florida and his business was growing. In the late 1960s high-end women's fashion was purchased with models wearing the couture. I was one of these models. I would put on the fashion that was picked by Mr. Baldwin or his assistant and walk around the shop or model for just one customer. This was a Saturday job for me.

I had many jobs while in junior college. Living at home provided me with more free time since I did not do my own laundry, cook, or clean—my mother or Nannie did those chores. I even did volunteer work at the St. Petersburg Science Center. They had classes there, and since I was considering becoming an elementary school teacher, I volunteered to help with the classes. The Science Center was a non-for-profit organization founded in St. Petersburg in 1959 by William Guild and Nell Rodgers Croley. It was the first science center of its kind in the world, and it operated on donations and grants. Its mission was to inspire interest in and to promote the understanding of all sciences. I would make friends at the center and learn some interesting science, like the reproduction of sea urchins. My brothers Lee and Mark would also become involved volunteering at the Science Center.

I also had a part-time job at the Colony Shops retail store in Pinellas Park Shopping Center for a year. Colony Shops were all around the St. Petersburg Tampa area. It was a growing chain of stores for young women. They carried upscale clothing lines that were popular at the time, Lady Bug, John Roman handbags…and more. I worked there in sales and sometimes the manager would put me in the latest fashion. When customers came in, they would often buy what I was wearing. I learned a lot from that manager about sales. While I was there the first credit cards were introduced to pay for your purchases. We had a machine that you had to put the credit card in and then run the imprint of the card number. This worked well for a while then the credit card companies started supplying us with books of bad credit cards and you had to look up every card before you could ring the sale. That took time and slowed down the line of customer sales. If I found a bad credit card, I did not give it back to the customer. I had to call in the store manager to handle the situation.

Graduating Junior College

In the spring of 1969, I graduated from St. Petersburg Junior College. Once I started college, I never took a summer off. Hari Katz and her friends were all away at universities. Lillian and Linda had moved away from the Holiday Park neighborhood. Peggy was going to school elsewhere. It was just my friends at school and the people that lived around our area. Vicky's modeling career was going strong. She did a lot of work for the *St. Petersburg Times* newspaper.

I had started college at the University of South Florida St. Petersburg Campus. There was a program for Elementary Education majors called "The Block Program." It meant that all our classes were blocked out for us. All members of this program would spend two years going to local elementary schools in the morning and then university classes in the afternoon. Our two-year time in the classroom helped to prepare us for our own classroom.

Dad's Retirement Jobs

My father was working for businesspeople and corporations in the St. Petersburg area that owned private planes or jets. He flew for Milton Roy Company among others. Flying all single-and twin-engine type aircraft of general aviation, especially Beechcraft 18, Twin Bonanza, Cessna 310, and Piper Aztec. He flew air ambulances, transporting bodies to locations for hospital care. He was a well-known figure at Albert Whitted Airport in downtown St. Petersburg. The city's airport sits on the edge of downtown, overlooking Tampa

Bay. The airport provides various aviation services including fueling, storage, parking, maintenance, flight training, charter and rentals, avionics, and sightseeing tours. In addition to general aviation, the airport also supports Civil Air Patrol, Johns Hopkins All Children's Hospital, Bayflite Medivac, and other medical transport services. This airport was next to my University of South Florida (USF) satellite campus and the Coast Guard base on the bay. If you look down from the air it is also across the bay from MacDill AFB.

During this time, we got some sad news from Ohio. My grandmother, Elizabeth, had suddenly succumbed to an aortic aneurysm. My father, being the oldest, would need to travel up to Ohio to take care of the property and financial needs. I could not go because of my college classes, so Dad and my brother Mark drove up to Ohio to settle my grandmother's farm property. I would visit her grave many years later. She and Ed were buried together in the family plot in Plymouth, Ohio. They had a beautiful double headstone and at the foot of the headstone was Ed's World War I military stone that listed his name and the unit and battalion he had served in with in the Argonne Forest.

My Father's Concern for His Only Daughter

My father was home a lot. He also reminded me that he had my best interest at heart. He waited up for me if I was out on a date. If he found an article in the newspaper of information he thought I should know he'd write a letter to me with the article and leave it on the dresser in my room. Many times I didn't understand why he found this information important for me, but I read the letters and articles anyway. Mostly I knew he loved me by making the effort and taking the time to write those letters. When I was younger, he would always say I would understand when I was older. He was right; as I grew up, I did understand more about the world, society, and social interaction. He taught me to be cautious and pay attention to my surroundings. His concern for me taught me that. Young people are vulnerable, and I had more awareness than most because of his concern.

The following is one sample of a letter Dad wrote to me. It was one of many he would leave on my dresser while I was in high school and college:

Dear Daughter Marilyn,

Historical human aspiration for immortality is a manifestation of the greatest Love, Love for God. Human behavior in this life that subordinates all other love and activity to the love of God is fundamental wisdom and the most fulfilling behavior. Such behavior seems to warrant the greatest beauty and glory of this life. In answer to the prayers of your parents, you seem to have acquired such wisdom and beauty in this life.

Too often in life I have been guilty of procrastination; However, your religious activity has prompted this expression of gratitude to a loving and gifted daughter before it was too late. The best of intentions is often interred with our bones. To grateful parents you are a flower of creation. That provided much happiness and love. You had a happy exemplary childhood which was most gratifying to loving parents. Your school years and subsequent evolution to adulthood were well disciplined according to the tenets of Catholicism. Therein was the source of the Wisdom and hope for a fulfilling life. It was also a source of wisdom, for example on the part of your parents. The church has historically taught us the value of self-discipline.

Although life is not without trial and tribulation, may you always find beauty in this life.

—Your loving father

* * *

During college I had classes that required field trips. Dad would insist on coming with me. At first, I balked at this idea. But he convinced me that it was in my best interest. My botany field trip to the Ocala Forest with the class proved to me that he was right. My father drove my friend and me. It was a cabin used by hunters with an area for hunting dogs. It was nice enough. The teacher separated the boys and the girls. The boys stayed in the hunting cabin and the girls in a large tent. My father had my friend and I sleep in the car. My father slept in a sleeping bag on the ground under the back bumper. The first night the boys found a local bar and got drunk and went into the girls' tent looking for trouble. When they came by our car, the guys started to shake it, then one of them noticed my father on the ground in the sleeping bag and they left us alone. After that experience, I never questioned him again. The second field trip was to Miami for a teachers' conference. My professor thought this was a valuable experience for upcoming teachers. My father drove me to Miami and stayed with me. He was right again. This professor was inviting the girl students to his room. After those instances I learned to protect myself from vulnerable situations. My father knew he had taught me well. Soon he realized he no longer needed to go with me.

Miss America Preliminary Pageant

In the fall of 1969, just after starting USF, there was an opportunity to enter a Miss America Preliminary Pageant. Most people don't know that the Miss America Pageant, along with preliminary competitions, make it the largest scholarship foundation for women in the world. I needed money for college tuition and had done well in other pageants. I was eligible for the First Miss North Tampa Pageant since I lived within a seventy-five-mile radius of Tampa. Tampa was growing in population, and North Tampa was where the USF main campus was located. The preliminary was held at a stripmall in Tampa. The final round would be held at the Curtis Hixon Hall. I would be one of twenty-five contestants for the first preliminary round, and was picked in the top ten. I used what I had done before, poetry, from a book titled, *It's Hard to Be Hip Over 30 and Other Tragedies of Married Life* by Judith Viorst.

At age twenty I could not relate to her poetry, but I had recited poetry in the USO play in Okinawa, competed in French Declamation

Contests in high school, and in college I competed in poetry competitions. Yes, I could act! That night was my night to shine. The judges loved my talent, and by the end of the evening I was crowned Miss North Tampa, having worn one of the swimsuits we had bought in Atlantic City in 1962 before we left for Okinawa.

I was the first Miss North Tampa. There was another pageant in the area, the Miss Tampa Pageant. The girl who won the Miss Tampa Pageant was in school in North Florida and could not make very many appearances. I was kept busy and loved every appearance. I was the focus of numerous articles in the *Tampa Tribune* newspaper. I attended art exhibitions, was featured in photo shoots for the latest fashions, and the *Tampa Tribune* journalists did stories about our pageant and my going to Orlando to compete in the Miss Florida Pageant.

* * *

The largest event in Tampa is the reenactment of the capture of Tampa Bay by the pirate, José Gaspar. The story of Gaspar's life and career vary, especially with his origin. Most agree that Gaspar was born in Spain about 1756, served in the Spanish Navy until turning to piracy about 1783, and met his end in southwest Florida during a battle against the United States Navy in late 1821. The extravaganza, "Gasparilla," began in 1904 when Miss Louise Francis Dodge, society editor of the *Tampa Tribune*, and George W. Hardee, then with the federal government in Tampa, conspired to promote the City of Tampa in a fantastical celebration. I was front and center on the City of Tampa float in the daytime parade in downtown Tampa in January of 1970. The seven-mile Gasparilla Parade is held on the last Saturday in January. There was a day parade and a night parade, and I was featured in both. A photo of me on the float graced the front page of the *Tampa Tribune*. I went to numerous balls and political events and many smaller parades.

Next Was the Miss Florida Pageant

The pageant officials were getting me ready to compete for a full week of rehearsals, luncheons, and dinner events. The schedule of events with dress codes for each event was given to each contestant. Some events required us to wear hats and others requested casual attire. Everything we did had a dress code. When we arrived, we were taken to motels in the Orlando area. There were two contestants in a room. A driver and a car moved us from one event to another. It was like we were under lock and key. We also had a woman chaperone who would take care of our needs. Our driver and the pageant officials were the only men we had contact with that week. I was not even allowed to see my brothers or parents. Everyone had a name tag. Even my parents! My brothers' name tags simply said, "Brother."

The pageant was held in June in Orlando, FL. The winner of the Miss Florida Pageant would go to Atlantic City, NJ, to compete with the pageant winners of all fifty states and territories of the U. S. for the crown of Miss America 1970. During pageant week my photo along with several others made the front page of the *Orlando Sentinel* newspaper. The paper thought I had a chance to make the top ten. Alas, I would not make the top ten, and that would be my first and last try for Miss America. I could have tried to win another local pageant and do it all over again, which some girls did. That was not in the cards for me.

I did have one other opportunity to travel. The Gasparilla Ball Queen, Miss Tampa, and I, Miss North Tampa, would travel to Barranquilla, Columbia, in South America. Tampa and Barranquilla are sister cities. We three were invited to participate in the Queen of Seas Pageant in Santa Marta, Columbia. It was almost a week of activities. We would be competing with all the pageant winners of various pageants in South America. The head of the North Tampa Pageant and the mayor of North Tampa would travel as our chaperones. The consulate of Barranquilla in Tampa would make the arrangements and give us a list of events and suggestions on wardrobe. The three beauty queens and the two chaperones would board a plane at Tampa Airport. In 1970, Tampa Airport was so small, boarding your flight just required walking onto the tarmac and up the stairs into the plane. We would takeoff from Tampa on an Avianca Jet and fly over Cuban air space. This was a real treat to see Cuba from the air. It was beautiful, an island with pastel colors and turquoise ocean. I had lived through the history of the Castro regime and the Cuban Missile Crisis. We only had the privilege of seeing Cuba from the air because we were on a Columbian airline that had permission to fly over Cuban airspace.

We arrived in Barranquilla during daylight hours and were ushered into taxis. We were taken to two different hotels. The first stop we dropped off our chaperones, and the second stop was us girls. I was a little concerned when this happened. It did not turn out to be a problem. All the girls from South America were in the same hotel. The three of us shared a room. It was a beautiful Spanish colonial architectural style hotel. The outside of the hotel was spectacular, the inside rooms were basic with no frills.

The first day we rested and had a leisurely breakfast. We had an overview tour on a bus of the city and area. That evening we dressed for dinner. We were taken to a beautiful building downtown where we were introduced to our Columbian navy escorts for the rest of that week. They did pair me up with a naval officer who spoke perfect English. Each of the queens participating in the pageant had an escort. Each queen gave a speech at each event. I had not been told about the speech and had nothing prepared. My escort agreed to teach me a speech in Spanish that I memorized and used at each event where a speech was required. I was very thankful to him for his help. At that first event we were each given a key to the city of Barranquilla and other mementos of the city. There were about forty girls from all parts of South America and us three from Tampa.

We were each given an itinerary of events and times. My schedule for the next day had a luncheon event at noon. I was dressed and ready and in the lobby before noon. That was the day I learned that noon was not the time we were leaving but the time we were supposed to start getting ready. We left at 3:00 p.m.. There was a Maybelline room that we could go to have our makeup done at no cost. They did a fabulous job of making us up, way more makeup than I would have ever worn back in the U.S., but here it was normal.

The next evening, we were invited to a dance with an orchestra, several tables of liquor and food. Each table had full bottles of liquor and mixers to fix our own cocktails. Licorice liqueur was on each table. This was to aid in digestion, and we had it almost every night. I tasted everything but never drank to get drunk. It was just the way I was raised. I knew how to make a cocktail or two last all night. The ballroom was not air conditioned. When I was asked to dance it was not for one song but rather the full set. I could easily be on the dance floor for twenty minutes or more. After a set I was sweaty and ready for a break. I left the party around 1:00 a.m., but it went on until four in the morning. My two roommates knew the drill since the Gasparilla Queen was from a Hispanic family in Tampa, and Miss Tampa had lived in the Tampa area all her life. They were both more familiar with the customs than I. I was the military kid who knew you had to be ready on time and prepared, which was not the case here in Columbian culture.

At one event they had us walk through the crowd of people chanting our names. They had left a long path for us to move through, and I put my head down and walked through the crowd. After I got to my station, I noticed the girls were walking with a lot of "attitude" and raising one arm and getting the crowd to respond to their word which most of the time was "*viva Columbia!*" My Navy escort asked me if I was ashamed of myself. I told him no, not at all.

He said, "But you put your head down like you were." Wow, that was a wake-up call for me. I never did that again. I walked with attitude and held up my arm and declared, "*Viva Columbia!*" for the rest of the trip. My memorized speech also got stronger, and so did the cries of *Viva Columbia* after each speech! I was catching onto this culture of pride and charisma. Of course, none of us Tampa girls won the pageant, but we were not expected to win. We were there for diplomatic reasons—showing our support for a sister city and enjoying the festivities of Latin culture. There were many wonderful events during that trip, and a lot of political discussions went on during those events. I was raised to understand political diplomacy. The letter my mother had read to me before we left for Brussels from

President Eisenhower—my actions represented my country to other places and cultures—dictated my actions during that trip. I always spoke and presented myself to the best of my ability. I never indulged in any actions that would make Tampa or the U.S. look bad.

I returned to Tampa after the wonderful trip and settled back into my studies at USF. I had the rest of that year to hold onto my Miss North Tampa crown before crowning the next queen in November of 1970.

Photo of me the night I crowned my successor, the second Miss North Tampa, November 1970.

My Friend Gets Married

Vicky was getting married to one of the *St. Petersburg Times'* photographers and moving to Texas. I was one of the bridesmaids at her wedding. Her mother made her wedding gown. She was married during the winter in St. Petersburg and went with a duchess satin fitted gown. She carried a white fur muff with white flowers attached. Her two bridesmaids also made our own gowns. It was an empire style long gown. Empire style is fitted just under the breast. The top was of red velveteen and the skirt white moire classic watermark cotton blend fabric. We each also carried a white muff with red flowers attached. She and Al were married in her family church and the reception was at her parents' home.

10

I Graduate College

I WOULD FINISH MY STUDIES at USF and graduate in the spring of 1971 with a degree in Elementary Education and a minor in Biology. As soon as I graduated, I signed up for junior college classes again because I would need them in the next five years to maintain my teaching certification. Doing so was my mother's idea, and I had the time to do it. As a college graduate my grades were better than other students. Not that I was any different, but I had to set an example to the undergraduates, so I worked harder. I was taking Chemistry, Chemistry Lab, and Earth Science.

In June 1971 I was the first in my family to walk across the stage and receive a college diploma. It was a big celebration, and my cousins from Ovida, Florida, would all come to the graduation ceremony at Curtis Hixon Hall in downtown Tampa. These were cousins from my mother's family that had moved to Florida from Philadelphia. I would graduate with a large group of students from the USF College of Education.

I applied for a job at the elementary school level with the Pinellas County School District. I would be a first-time teacher and take a job wherever one was available. In 1971, Disney World began mass hiring, as they were getting ready to open on October 1st of that year. It was quite the talk of the state of Florida. There was only Disneyland in California at the time, which I had a blast visiting in late 1959 with my family on our way to Stead AFB in Nevada. Walt Disney was creating something that had never been done before. Even though Walt died in 1966, his brother and the Disney Company continued with his plans, starting purchasing properties in Central Florida in 1964.

My father and I drove over to the Central Florida area to a building that was taking applications for jobs. I interviewed and the next day I was offered a job as a tour professional in the park. They were pleased that I spoke French, as they could use me for both English and French speaking tours. They were already expecting people from all over the world to come to the theme park. Then I found out I would only be making minimum wage, and they did not care about my having a degree in education. I didn't accept the job. I felt I had worked hard for my degree and wanted to use it!

I would soon hear from the Pinellas County School Board that I had secured a position in the pool. That meant I had not yet been assigned to a school, but I was one of a pool of new education graduates that would get the positions. I was invited to a meeting in a local school auditorium with other new hires in the pool of new teachers. It was there that I learned how fortunate I was to get a job. There had been forty other applications for the place I had gotten. I was happy and excited to be in the pool and securing a job using my degree.

I was still living at home. One day my mother and I went looking for condominiums. We were getting quotes for me to make plans for my future. This day would give me an idea of how much to save to get a place of my own. I also was looking at cars. I was still driving the 1960 red Ford Falcon, but I had my eye on a 240Z Datsun. I would save enough to pay cash for a car first, and then start saving for my condominium down payment. My parents were particularly good at thinking things through and always helping us kids find our way in the world.

In April of 1971, the Supreme Court of the United States ruling on

Swann v. Charlotte-Mecklenburg Board of Education unanimously upheld busing. The decision effectively sped up school integration, which had been slow to take root in some areas of the U.S. The policy of transporting children to schools outside their neighborhoods to achieve greater racial balance. The Supreme Court of the State of Florida also passed a ruling for what became known as "forced busing." This law required that each school to have 70% White students and 30% Black students. This ratio of 70% to 30% was the ratio of Blacks to Whites in Florida.

At the beginning of August, I found out I was assigned to Perkins Elementary School in St. Petersburg. Perkins was in the Black section of town. I had been there while at USF doing my teacher training. Neighborhoods were not integrated, so Whites lived in their areas and Blacks lived in theirs. Black culture was just as real as any culture I had experienced. The Black culture would refer to their neighborhood as just "The Hood."

Perkins Elementary opened in 1958 and was located at 2400 Queensboro Ave. South. It cost $240,442 to build and had twelve classrooms, ten teachers, and 256 students. The first principal was Fred Burney who was in that position until 1962. The formal dedication was on February 22, 1959. By 1964 the school had twenty-four classrooms, twenty-seven teachers and 851 students. George Wesley Perkins was born in Gainesville, Florida, and began teaching at the age of sixteen in a one-room schoolhouse in Archer, Florida. He moved to St. Petersburg in 1925 and became the principal of Jordan Elementary School and then Gibbs High School. When Gibbs opened during the depression, it was overcrowded and under-supplied. The county was unable to fund the school, so Perkins organized a program in which people bought a brick for ten dollars to build a combined gym, auditorium, and cafeteria for the school. Perkins died in 1955. He will be remembered as one of the early African American pioneer educators of St. Petersburg.

All the new hires and the rest of the faculty at Perkins showed up a full week before the kids would be coming. The new hires were sent to the teachers' lounge. There I was with several new teachers, many of us had been in the Block Program at USF. It was nice to see familiar faces. Principal Johnny Welch came into the room and welcomed us. In this school, White teachers were the minority. All my superiors and all the office staff were Black. Some of the retuning faculty were White women and men. Teachers had been integrated prior to the new busing laws. Pinellas County stuck by the law as written by the state of Florida Supreme Court. Some counties found loopholes in the law and integrated those schools in different ways.

During that first week of school, I spent a lot of alone time in my classroom doing bulletin boards and setting up the room to fit the way I wanted to teach. It was an interesting week. I picked up supplies for my bulletin boards in the office. Then I realized I had been assigned a grade but was given no further information. I went down to the office and spoke with the secretary and asked her for the Pinellas County minimum basic standards and books. I had not found any books in my room. The secretary referred me to the Principal. I walked into his office and asked for the standards and the books. He told me there were no minimum basic standards for Pinellas County schools and as for the books, "take a walk around the whole school and see what you can find." I did as he had suggested. There were no books to be found. Here I am with a job and apparently, I can do anything I want. I'm not sure what was going on, but a day later some old books showed up in my classroom. These books were about ten years old and in bad shape, but they were better than no books. From these books I put together a curriculum and started my lesson plans. About the third day into the week, I had finished for the day and went out to my car and started to drive home. As I got to the main street, I heard a loud pop hit my car. I didn't stop. I kept on driving.

When I finally reached a stop light a while later, I could see my side window had a hole in it. My car had been shot! I continued all the way home, parked my car in the driveway, and went to get my father. He came out and looked at the car and the hole in the window. Then he called the police. The officer came out and said it was a small-caliber bullet, possibly from a BB gun. He asked me where I was when my window shattered, I told him I was driving down the street. He told me to stay away from that neighborhood. I said nothing but thought to myself, *It will be impossible to stay out of that neighborhood, I work there.*

On the following Monday school started and thirteen kids showed up in my classroom. I taught these thirteen kids for two weeks and things went well. On Friday I heard that the system used for busing kids was not working and a new system was starting that following week. On Monday I had thirty-five students in my classroom and only the neighborhood kids were repeats. The county had redrawn the boundary lines and bused kids from disadvantaged neighborhoods into the Perkins School. Since these kids could not afford private school, they were forced to be in this school. That first year and for the five years I taught at Perkins, we never had a school Parent Teacher Association (PTA). Some of the local parents got involved from time to time. Parents showed up for conferences, but these conferences happened seldomly. Our school had no teachers' aides and little to no parent involvement. As teachers we were on our own. We did it all.

School busing had its positives points and its negative points. On the negative side, the high schools in Pinellas County were having protests from parents. My brother Mark started his freshmen year at Dixie Hollins High School in 1971. He had to endure the negative side. A sad fact was Dixie Hollins had always been integrated but now it had to have the 70% White to 30% ratio of Blacks. So, buses of Black students came into the school. Mark said it was hard to be at school during these years. He stayed focused on his goals and his jobs after school. He would end up graduating early.

There was a famous movie, starring Denzel Washington, that came out in 2000, *Remember the Titans*. It was based on a true story of those times and gave a glimpse of the era, especially for high schools in White neighborhoods.

On the positive side, kids were learning side-by-side and picking up good habits from one another. It was during this time that "high-fiving" started to become a part of the American culture. Before then it had only been a custom in "hood culture." The neighborhood kids taught me "up high, down low, take it slow," and even that varied from area to area. Some of my neighborhood Black boys walked into class from time to time with swagger. By Christmas, the whole class of boys, White and Black, walked with swagger. We were all learning about each other. The Black boys wore their hair in afros, and usually left a pick in it as a handy way to keep looking sharp for the day. One day before school started, I was in the classroom waiting for everyone to get organized. We were talking about hair and texture of hair. One Black boy said his hair was fine, and when I touched his hair it was so soft. I had fine hair too, and for years I had struggled with my hair getting tangled after washing it. I went out that day and bought myself a pick. It worked so well for me, my hair combed out faster with less pulling than before. I still use a pick for my hair today.

I have lived all over the world and learned a lot about different cultures. This was a mini culture right inside the U.S. and without the experience of busing I would not have learned any of it. It was working inside this neighborhood that gave me a sense of the Black culture in America. There were Blacks in the community that did not like that I was in their neighborhood. I was called a "cracker" by a few of my students. When I requested teacher conferences with some parents, they were not interested in talking to me. I worked with the assistant principal in these situations, and she would talk to those parents. A few times when I would be leaving school for the day, I would find the air was let out of my tires. The office staff was still on campus and would help me refill them. They knew the neighborhood and they also knew they had to protect the teachers coming into the hood.

I had lived during the time of segregation and the Civil Rights Movement in the U.S. I had been in Albany, GA, during the summer of 1962 when Martin Luther King, Jr. had peacefully marched there. I had experienced these things from my perspective. I had also lived in a military culture. I had always gone to school with Blacks, Hispanics, Asians, and others. My family experienced its own prejudicial cultures, my father because he was born out of wedlock. My mother was victim to it because her mother had multiple boyfriends, and because even though her parents lived apart, my grandmother was a married woman. Marie in Brussels was shunned by many people because she was a mistress. I was always the new kid, and some people didn't like kids they didn't know. Sadly, much of this prejudice is built on false information. People take a side and a hard stand without ever getting to know the people they take a stand against.

I really felt my years at Perkins gave me an insight into a wonderful neighborhood. We learned from each other. It was hard working at Perkins Elementary School. The school was not air conditioned, we had old warn textbooks, but as the Blacks and the Whites learned from each other we grew to understand a lot more. I was learning firsthand about racial inequality. I loved my job and all my students, and most of them felt the same way about me.

MY FATHER'S SECRETS

11

The Day My Life Changed

I STARTED TEACHING IN AUGUST of 1971. By October, it was time to crown the next Miss North Tampa. In mid-October of 1971, my mother, my friend Virginia, and I went to the preliminary for the third Miss North Tampa Pageant. The three of us walked into the room at TECO Hall (Tampa Electric Company). We took our seats and decided I would sit behind my mother and Virginia so we could talk better. I could lean forward and not over them. When I sat down there was a binder on the chair next to me. A few minutes later a very nice-looking young man dressed in a sport coat and slacks sat down next to the binder with a chair between us. I didn't say anything. My mother noticed him and decided to start up a conversation. She turned around to him and said, "Gee, you look familiar. Have we met?" He looked at her quizzically and said, "No, I don't think so." She came right back with, "Well, have you ever been in Okinawa?" This startled him and he answered, "Why, yes I have." This got his attention because he had stopped in Okinawa on his way to Vietnam in 1968. He had served in the Marine Corps and had done thirteen months of service.

He was at the pageant with the binder to take notes. He was a member of the Tampa Jaycees (United States Junior Chamber) and on the Miss Tampa Pageant committee. He had heard about the Miss

North Tampa Pageant and figured he'd come to take notes and learn more to help him with his responsibilities with the Miss Tampa Pageant. After we met that fateful day, he would contact the Miss North Tampa Pageant to get my phone number and ask me out for the following weekend. We started dating. At first it was just on the weekends, but then we spent more and more time together. It would be a whirlwind courtship. My mother had always told me not to elope but to give her at least three days' notice. She also told me not to marry before I graduated from college. Why she told me this I'll never know. She must have had some insight.

His name was William Martin Johansen, and he was twenty-six years old. He had his degree in business from Florida State University. He graduated college in three years to get a start at law school. He was in law school at Memphis State University when his draft notice arrived in the mail. He thought it was a mistake. He thought he had a four-year deferment. He was unaware it was four years or graduation from college. He decided if he had to go into the military and possibly be sent to Vietnam, he'd go into the Marine Corps. He was sent to MCB Quantico in Virginia. He would leave for Vietnam in March of 1968.

When we met, he was living with his brother and family in St. Petersburg and working in Tampa. He lived about thirty minutes from my parents' home. I was twenty-two years old and still living at home with my parents and my brothers. Bill's best friend, Larry, had married in September. He and Shirley were renting an apartment. We double dated a lot. I also spent a lot of time at Bill's brother's home. Bill's brother Wayne and his wife Sue had two young children, a toddler and an infant.

One of the things I admired most about Bill was that every Sunday he took his grandmother out to lunch. We never saw each other on Sunday because that was their day. Bill had a beautiful brand new two-tone Le Mans car. The body was a bright red with a white top. He was always the gentleman holding doors for me and making sure I was treated properly. His manners were very polished, and he dressed well. He had a job with the General Telephone and Electronics

(GTE) in Tampa. It was the largest independent telephone company in the U.S. during the days of the Bell System. He was in management, and wore a suit or sport coat to work each day.

Bill's service in Vietnam was still fresh and I understood military service and sacrifice. I admired him for his service. However, by 1971 the U.S. civilian population had turned against our country's involvement in Vietnam. A Vietnamese war campaign that had taken place during Bill's service was called the Tet Offensive.

The Tet Offensive

Vietnam is a long, skinny country on the map. It is part of a peninsula in the South China Sea. Other countries on that peninsula are Laos, Cambodia, and Thailand. Vietnam was divided into North Vietnam and South Vietnam by the Demilitarized Zone (DMZ). On January 30, 1968, Communist-affiliated troops from North Vietnam and the Viet Cong (a distinct political organization) launched what became known as the Tet Offensive against South Vietnam and its American allies. The Tet Offensive was one of the largest military operations of the Vietnam War and became a key turning point in the conflict.

The Tet Offensive was a surprise series of attacks launched during Tet, the Vietnamese New Year festival. Many South Vietnamese troops were on holiday when the attacks began, and the military was caught off guard. The campaign initially targeted more than 100 cities and towns, including the strategic southern capital of Saigon, now named Ho Chi Minh City. Bill had been with the second Battalion, Third Marine Division on the DMZ during the 1968 Tet Offensive. This military designation was about 800 marines. He had arrived in Vietnam in March of 1968. The Tet Offensive was strategized in three stages starting in January of 1968 with a second and third strategy lasting until the end of September 1968. He had arrived in time for the most horrific battles of Vietnam. He was part of the Headquarters and Service Company (H&S), a communications platoon. Like my father, he would send and receive secret information on the enemy and anything else the U.S. felt was important to the troops and troop morale.

The following is a letter he sent to his parents and siblings back home. Bill is from a family of six children:

April 1, 1968

Dear All,
Well, I'm in the rear alright-in the rear of a bamboo patch! I'm really roughing it now. We're living under poncho "tents". We're relatively secure as most of the action takes place up in the hills in the surrounding area.

The first night we got here, I had guard duty. That was cool- no holes dug, nothing. I was out in the middle of a field with two other guys with just tall grass to hide us. But nothing came of it.

Last night I had guard again. But I had no trouble staying awake as at midnight the operation started, and they were blowing the hell out of all the hills around us with artillery. Also, we can hear the B-52's dropping their loads over the Khe Sanh in the distance. All in all, though, we are pretty secure.

We did luck out and got near a small waterfall and pool and went down to bathe, wash our clothes and swim. It looks like a nudist colony when everyone is down there skinny dipping!

I thought the kids might be interested in the enclosed leaflets dropped before bombing to get the civilians out of here to safe passage to save lives.

Well, overall, I'm real lucky to be where I am. I'm as safe as you can be up here. I'm not exactly sure where we are but close to the DMZ and east of Khe Sanh.
They have an awful lot of men and artillery up here for this operation. So we should do OK.

Well, hope you get this as the incoming mail won't to incoming for another week or so. I think the mail is going out though. Will keep you posted!

—Love, Bill

Another letter read:

April 22, 1968

Dear All,

I know you are enjoying your apartment. It's just the right thing for you now with just four of you.

I'll bet Tommy likes it too- no grass to mow!

Well, I was beginning to think someone out there didn't like me. The other day a rocket hit so close to my bunker; I had a headache the whole day from the concussion. But lately, no close calls.

We got re-supplied for the first time in 3 days yesterday and got a lot of mail! We are involved in another operation now- searching for a platoon of men that got ambushed and annihilated outside Khe Sanh. We may be leaving after this operation.

I had a somewhat satisfying experience yesterday- helping refugees into a helicopter to take them to a secure area. There were about 50 old men and women and a few kids. It really takes something like this to counterbalance one loading dead marines onto the choppers the day before! I hope the good will outweigh the bad in the long run!

Well, another month is just about gone. Hope things have quieted down in Memphis. I'm thinking I might bring home my M-16 with me! (ha, ha)

Thanks for your letters, Dad, and Cathy. See if you can't get mom to write too!

I know you're concerned, but don't worry!

—Love, Bill

In early April, Bill would accept a dangerous mission. He was told to transport a secret document from one platoon to another. He would take a jeep along with another Marine, in the dark, not using headlights because that would make him an easy target for the enemy. When he arrived, he found out that the message he was transporting was that Martin Luther King, Jr. had been assassinated in Memphis, Tennessee. The Civil Rights leader that had created so much change through peaceful protests. The military was concerned that there may be problems between the White and Black marines. In war one of the most important problems is morale. Thankfully it did not cause problems with the troops.

1968

For those of us who lived during 1968, it was a defining time. It was one of the most tumultuous single years in modern history, marked by historic achievements, shocking assassinations, and the Vietnam War splayed out in ever home each night on the television screen. This was the dawn of the television age, the historic events of 1968 played out on TV screens across the country, bringing them home in a way that had never been possible before. It would be technology that changed the attitude toward the Vietnam War. In WWII the only way the civilian population got the war news was in the newspapers, radio, and news reels at the local movie theaters. The news reel footage in the movie theaters was edited film, cutting out the gory details so that the people did not have to see the horrors of war. TV became popular in homes in the early 1950s. The Korean Conflict was not televised much as the American people had just come out of WWII. Korea was a war, but it was called a "conflict," so it did not sound that catastrophic to the civilian population.

The television even changed the way we ate dinner. The 1950s even launched the TV dinner. A fast way to prepare dinner and eat it in front of the TV. Television stations broadcast programs for several hours a day. As technology and TV progressed in popularity, the stations stayed on longer and watching TV became an important American pastime. News reels in movie theaters became less important and eventually disappeared altogether.

There was a decision to not edit the battle footage shown on the TV of the Tet Offensive, thinking that the American people could see the cruelty of Communist North Vietnam. We were involved in Vietnam because of Communist aggression at the end of WWII. The Truman Doctrine and then the Eisenhower Doctrine had involved us in this fight to help countries not be taken by cruel Communist dictatorships.

The Tet Offensive was a catastrophic military failure for the Communists. Historians estimate as many as 50,000 Communist troops died in the effort to gain control of the southern part of the country. The South Vietnamese and American losses totaled a fraction of that number.

Although a military loss for North Vietnam, the Tet Offensive was a stunning propaganda victory for the Communists. In fact, it is often credited with turning the war in their favor. The South Vietnamese began to lose influence as Viet Cong guerrillas infiltrated rural areas formerly held by the South Vietnamese government. The offensive frayed the relationship between the South Vietnamese and the United States. The Tet Offensive had a devastating effect upon the American public. Many people at home watching nightly television news were appalled by the carnage they saw. The military draft and the American population did not live through the Communist aggression at the end of WWII. So, the Truman Doctrine and the Eisenhower Doctrine were forgotten. All this played into the American people turning against the Vietnam War. The U. S. would eventually pull out of Vietnam because you cannot fight a war the people don't support.

The National Museum of the U.S. Air Force at Wright Patterson Air Force Base outside of Cincinnati, Ohio, featured an installation with a sign that read

**Turning Point
South Vietnam:
Tet Offensive and Vietnamization**

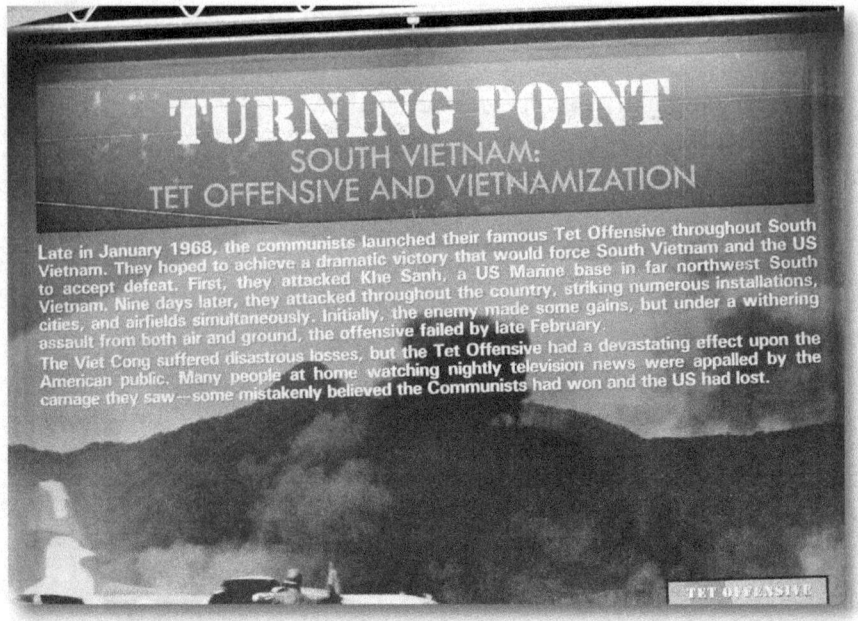

The installation plaque displayed at the National Museum of the U.S. Air Force at Wright Patterson AFB, located near Dayton, Ohio.

12

Wedding Bells

BILL AND I FELL IN love, and during the Christmas break we got married. This was not that unusual back in the early 1970s. Weddings back then in Florida were usually a ceremony at a church and a reception of cake and a fruit punch. He had proposed to me on December 22, and we were married on December 30, 1971. We thought about getting married on New Year's Eve but with little notice to our guests, thought it better to marry on the 30th. That Christmas my grandmother Nannie and my godmother were in Florida visiting us and our cousins, David, Nancy, and the girls. They could not afford to come back at Easter time for a wedding. The other advantage of getting married then was that friends were available during the Christmas break. We married in my parents' home, and all the neighbors brought a dish. It was a potluck wedding. We hired the pageant photographer, and all the neighbors, as well as pageant and high school friends, came to celebrate. Bill's oldest friend Larry and his wife Shirley stood for us as best man and matron-of-honor. Virginia made sure the bridal guestbook was signed so we had a list of all who attended. Both my brothers helped with parking cars and providing music for the reception. All the furniture in the living room was moved into the garage. Chairs were rented and the living room was set up like a church. All the furniture was taken out of the family room, and it was set up with massive tables for a buffet with a table for the three-layer cake with a working fountain on the bottom layer. My mother polished up the silver punch bowel that was purchased in Mexico when we lived in Laredo, TX. My parents masterminded the entire affair. It was perfect on so many levels!

Bill and I had rented an apartment near Larry and Shirley in St. Petersburg after he proposal. We rented furniture for the apartment. We got all this done the week before the wedding. After the reception I changed in my bedroom into a going-away outfit. My brothers and friends had sprayed shaving cream all over Bill's new car and then threw confetti inside. It was festive! All our friends got in their cars and as we pulled out of my parents' driveway, they followed us to the new apartment. A policeman stopped us just as we got to the apartment, but when he found out it was a wedding party, he told us, "Have a good evening."

I returned to Perkins in January of 1972 as Mrs. Johansen. Bill and I just had one weekend for our honeymoon. We would take a real honeymoon during the summer break of 1972. His plans to become a lawyer never came to fruition. The experience of the ravages of war in Vietnam in 1968-69 affected him deeply. He had been with the Second Battalion, Third Marine Division on the DMZ during the Tet Offensive and witnessed the loss of many friends.

Careers and Children

Bill and I would welcome our first son, William Martin Johansen Jr., eight pounds six ounces, on April 10, 1973, at St. Anthony's Hospital in St. Petersburg, FL. We would call him Billy. I took a leave of absence from Perkins Elementary School for the remainder of that school year and would start back for the next school year in August of 1973. Bill was not happy at the telephone company and would eventually find a career that was challenging and much more fulfilling for him. He became a stockbroker for Merrill Lynch in St. Petersburg. He loved the challenge of this job. It was hard, but slowly he grew a clientele and his career started to takeoff.

I would stay at Perkins until the end of 1976. I was pregnant again. During this pregnancy, Nannie came to live with my parents again. She was not doing well. She was seventy-eight years old, and it seemed like her mind was going. She called me the name of her sister sometimes, Joanna. My mother could no longer allow her to cook, as she would forget to turn off the stove or the oven. The doctor said she had carotid artery disease. He decided to scrape the plaque off the artery on one side of her neck. The procedure was successfully performed and when Nannie woke up, she was her old self again. The doctor decided to perform the operation on the other side as well. Sadly, she had a stroke during the second procedure and died on the table. I was teaching in my classroom at Perkins when the office called my class on the intercom to tell me the sad news of my grandmother. She had been such a vital part of my growing up, and now she was not going to be around for my children. Billy would remember her, but the next babies would not know her. Both my grandfathers had died before I was born and now both grandmothers were gone too. It was a sad time for me.

Things would turn to happier times when I gave birth to our second son, Randall (Randy) Thomas Johansen, on August 31, 1976, in St. Petersburg at St. Anthony's Hospital. Randy was eight pounds and ten ounces. Randy's baptism was scheduled for October 10, 1976, Bill's birthday. Bill's sister was going to be the godmother for our second son. She and her husband had flown in from Chicago for the event. That morning Bill's mother called us to tell us Bill's grandmother Frances had died in her sleep during the night. Bill's mother encouraged us to go ahead with the baptism. Randy's middle name of Thomas was for Bill's younger brother, Tommy, who had died too young the year before Randy was born.

After Randy's birth, I did not return to Perkins Elementary School. I had been teaching there five years. With two small children, I felt drained from teaching each day. Even though I loved what I did, it took its toll on me. I wanted to have meaningful times with my own children, to enjoy being with them and enjoy the day-to-day activities of being a mother. Bill's career was coming along, so I opted to substitute teach in the high schools in St. Petersburg. My college minor was biology, and I was certified for that subject at the high school level for substitute teaching. I soon realized that to get the kids' attention as a substitute teacher I had to have their respect. Teaching elementary school had given me a leg up on disciplining high school age students.

Several of the high school science teachers would take a two-week break from teaching to do their military reserve duty. I asked for those slots as a substitute teacher. I would ask the teacher for the chapter they wanted covered, and I made all my own lesson plans and tests. This way I got the kids' attention because I was giving them part of their grade for that period. They then had respect for me in the classroom. The regular teacher was thrilled as they did not have to leave anything for me. I was in demand in several of the high schools. I would drop off both boys at my parents' home in the morning and teach for the day. I made a little money and still got to do what I loved but only from time to time, which worked out well.

One of these substitute stints was for a history teacher. I will never forget the day I brought in my father as the guest speaker for the class. He spoke about being a WWII fighter pilot and being shot down, and finally his time as a POW in Stalag Luft III. All the students at that time knew of a TV series called *Hogan's Heroes*, loosely based on the POW camp, and of the movie *The Great Escape*—the movie about the POW camp Dad had been held in by the Germans and his time there during the escape. I had brought his book, *Clipped Wings*, that had been published by one of the POWs also at that camp, and allowed the kids to pass it around the room. This book was published in 1948. My mother had saved up to buy a copy for my father. When Dad got to the office of St. Petersburg High School there was quite a buzz about him. Several people that were not in my class came to hear him share his story. I still have fond memories of him sharing his story and those kids sitting on the edge of their seats listening and asking questions. I'm sure many of those kids still remember that day, when a man came to speak to them about a time in history they had only read about.

My parents had attended several Stalag Luft III reunions. These reunions started soon after the war. Many of the early reunions were held at Wright Patterson Airfield in Ohio. Father would attend these reunions from time to time. They were not held every year just when someone would volunteer to put the event together. At one reunion the event planners had even invited the former Stalag Luft III German Commandant. These reunions would bring in POWs from many countries. This camp had held allied prisoners, from all the countries that fought against the Axis Power of Germany, Italy, and Japan. The first reunions were large. As time went on, they got smaller.

By the end of 1979 I was no longer teaching, well maybe if you count Sunday school for my parish in St. Petersburg. I was active with my church and with a sewing store. I would be hired to make clothes and items for the window. I was not paid but got all the items to make the outfit and it would be for me to wear after the store had featured it in their windows. A new popular and expensive fabric was Ultrasuede. My skills with Ultrasuede were so popular that I was hired by many to make outfits for clients out of this fabric. Sewing lessons in Okinawa and my pattern making skills had come in handy. Interestingly, Ultrasuede was created by Toray, Japan, in the 1970s.

I was pregnant again and due in August of 1980. I had purchased a new crib for this baby. The crib had a canopy top. I would make all the sheets, bumper pads, blankets, and the canopy. The crib and all the handmade items were featured in the Sewing Circle Store windows in Tyrone Shopping Center strip mall in St. Petersburg.

On August 27, 1980, our third son was born, and we named him Lawrence Phillips Johansen. He was born at the same hospital as his brothers and weighed in at eight pounds and eight ounces. He and his brothers were all delivered by Dr. Peter B. Kersker. I had gone to Dr. Kersker because his daughter and I taught at Perkins Elementary School. He was a wonderful doctor. He never rushed through an appointment. When he took my blood pressure, he would put my arm around his waist. He was interesting and always shared new developments in the medical field. He would explain everything until I understood. He even encouraged me to make a list between appointments of questions I had. He had delivered much of the population of St. Petersburg, FL, including Bill's younger brother.

My Brother Lee Marries

Lee would meet the love of his life, Christina Dell, while he was living in Orlando, FL. Christina was working as a secretary for a national hotel chain. They would marry in 1982 at a Catholic church in Orlando. Mark was the best man, and I was in the wedding party. I made Christina's wedding gown and the gowns for all the bridesmaids. I even made a going-away outfit for her. It was a lovely July wedding. True to the story from Brussels of Lee being called Walt Disney for a week, they would have their reception at a Disney property hotel. Many of the theme park's characters would come through their reception. My parents, friends, and family attended this innovative and fun reception!

*　*　*

By 1983 Bill's career was taking off. He was hired by Bache Halsey Stuart and Shields, a Chicago-based investment bank founded in 1911. He was hired as a broker but soon got the offer of branch manager for the Fort Myers, FL office.

We packed up and moves our family to Fort Myers, FL. This was a wonderful area and we loved it. It was the first time I lived in a different city from my parents. Lee moved to Orlando after graduating from the University of South Florida in 1974 with an Engineering degree and the title Professional Engineer (P.E.) behind his name. In 1983 Mark was in medical school in Dublin, Ireland. Mark had gone to junior college as Lee and I had. He had transferred to Eckerd College and got his undergraduate degree. He had a difficult time getting into a medical school at that time with the influx of women and minorities applying and the new Affirmative Action Policy. Affirmative Action was a policy designed to bring more women, minorities, and lower socio-economic people to apply to medical school. It was a way to make things fair for all who aspire to the medical profession. Mark would finally apply to schools outside the U.S. and was accepted into Royal College of Surgeons in Dublin, Ireland. This college is one of the best in the world. He would graduate in 1986 with his medical degree.

In 1985, Bill was the manager of the Fort Myers office for Bache Halsey Stuart and Shields. He built one of the top offices in Florida. He was also turning forty years old. He had a talented group of stockbrokers. They were good at their jobs and had good comradery among themselves. I along with all the brokers decided to give Bill a surprise fortieth birthday party. Bill's parents and my parents were invited along with old and new friends. My parents had decided not to attend. We had a great crowd. The surprise started two days before the actual dinner party at our house. On Bill's birthday a funeral hearse showed up at our door to take him to work. They had signs all the way down the street to his office: "Mourning the death of your youth." The next day his office played in a softball game, and they threw out a black baseball when Bill was up to bat. Larry and Shirley had come down from St. Petersburg for the celebration. On the day of the surprise dinner, Larry kept Bill out until we were ready at the house. One big party and dinner, and then all the guys jumped in our pool.

That night as I was getting into bed, after cleaning up and settling several people sleeping over at our house, I had a strange feeling. My father had been on my mind all day getting ready for the party. I was sad my parents had decided not to come. I remember seeing an airplane in the sky as I was setting the tables around our pool. Why had it caught my attention? Was I sensitive to something coming?

The next morning everyone came into the kitchen area to have breakfast. I was taking care of Bill's parents and the kids as some guests were leaving. The phone rang. It was my mother telling me Dad had been in a terrible accident, and he was on his way to the hospital. Bill's mother saw my face turn white, she ran over and caught me as I was passing out.

Bill knew that we needed to get to St. Petersburg, about a three-hour drive from Fort Myers, soon. All the fun and happy times of the night before would change in an instant. We packed up the van with the boys and drove over to St. Petersburg. Our oldest son, Billy, gave me his rosary beads when we got in the car. He said, "Mom, pray with these on the way to the hospital." We would all meet up at the hospital where my father had been taken by ambulance. Lee came from Orlando. We would arrive at the hospital to find him unconscious, with a neck collar and incubated with an Ambu-Resuscitator. Shortly after we arrived, he was put on a ventilator. He would wake up the next day to a new life.

The next day would start a long period of time waiting in hospital rooms, waiting for good news. But good news never came. Father had been helping a friend cut down a tree in his back yard. He had rented a tackle and pulley used to wrap the branches of the tree to keep them from falling on the house. Dad was up in the tree wrapping the limbs when his friend pulled the rope and my father landed on his head. He had broken his neck and spinal cord. It would take my family weeks before we could use the word *quadriplegic.* My mother was afraid to call Mark in Ireland. Mark had mid-term exams coming up and she was afraid it would affect his tests. Lee and I encouraged her to call him anyway. It would be worse to let him think all was fine when it was far from fine. She agreed. The college gave Mark some time off and allowed him to come back home to see our father. Mark was in shock and beyond upset about what had happened when he arrived at Tampa Airport, we all were in shock. My mother most of all.

Mark would eventually go back to Ireland to finish his studies. Lee and I were there for our mother at the drop of a hat. My parents' life had changed in an instant. It was hard for all of us to adjust to the new reality.

When Lee was a child, he had dreams that woke him up, and as a small child he said they seemed so real. When he would share these back then it just seemed like nightmares to my parents and me. Lee's dreams when he was a kid kicked in one day when Lee was watching me look through the window into my father's hospital room. He had seen that scene in one of his dreams. Lee's boyhood dreams had been a peak into the future. No one really knows how deja vu or vivid dreams occur, but for Lee it was seeing his future.

The reality would become harder and harder for my mother when my father was asked to leave the hospital. She had no experience with this new reality. Dad would go to Bay Pines Veterans' Hospital for a while, then to another veterans hospital in Tampa. Eventually, going to hospitals, sitting, and visiting became too much for Mom. She requested that my father be allowed to live at their home in St. Petersburg. She would study all the procedures to care for him and take all the classes needed. She would learn how to suction his lungs and clean the ventilator that helped him breathe. She took classes to give him sponge baths and other procedures needed to care for a quadriplegic on a ventilator.

I would never hear my father talk again. He could talk, but the ventilator kept that from happening. The only time one of us would hear his words following that accident was during a short weekend when the hospital put him in an Iron Lung. The Iron Lung was a machine used during the polio epidemic in the late 1930s-1950s. However, only my mother was there, and they never put him into one again. The doctors tried to get Dad a ventilator that would allow him to talk, but for some reason that never worked for him.

Communication with my father was hard after the accident. We tried many things, but nothing worked very well. Finally, the electrolarynx hand-held device worked from time to time. This is a device that people who have lost their larynx can use to talk. It is small and you hold it up to your neck. There would have to be someone to hold it up to my father's neck because he had no movement in his arms. My mother got him a very expensive wheelchair giving him control over going forward and backward and slow or fast by blowing and sipping through a pipe

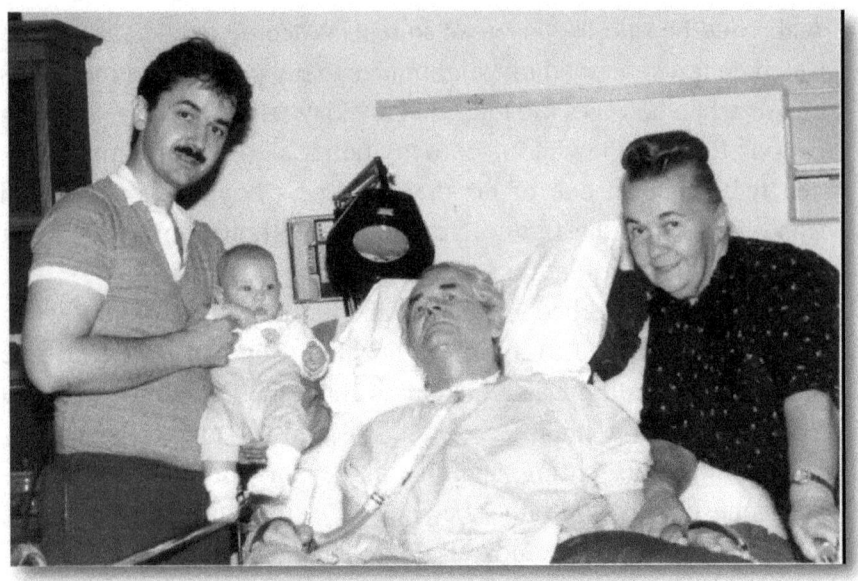

L-R: Lee, his son Matthew, my father and mother.

near his mouth. He could move his head and his neck, though limited. My father could work that wheelchair very well. The fancy wheelchair was not used much. Getting him up and into the chair became a problem. My mother was good with ideas to help Dad and get what he needed but, in the end, she was worn out. It was the day-to-day routines that finally got her down. She started suffering from depression. Thank goodness for my brother Lee. He and Christina were getting ready to start having children, but they had more free time than I with our three boys. Lee came almost every weekend to be with my mother.

My Father's Personal Secret.

It was during this time in my life that I figured out my dad's birth story. He had many military secrets, but this was by far the biggest. Suddenly the story that I had heard all my life, "Your father was named after his mother's two boyfriends," didn't make sense anymore. If she had fallen in love with Ed and married him, why would she name their first son after two old boyfriends? Why had I not questioned it earlier? I asked my mother about it; she told me to write to my father's Aunt Marie. I learned the truth in a letter from my Great Aunt Marie.

Her letter told the story of my grandmother. She had worked in a bakery in her last year of high school. She was smitten with a young man that also worked at the bakery. All her sisters had a crush on him. He was quite good looking. He was of German descent. When he found out she was pregnant he left because he already had a family. I questioned her answer. Years later, Ancestry DNA testing came out and my Great Aunt Marie's story was correct. Elizabeth got pregnant, dropped out of school, and was sent to live in an unwed mother's home in Cleveland, Ohio. Her sister Marie was the only family member to visit her while she was there. She would stay there until my father was adopted.

This is the story that my mother had learned about at the family reunion all those years ago when I heard my parents' raised voices in the room next to mine at my grandmother's home. My father's biggest secret was now out for all three of his children to know. Back in 1921 attitudes were harsh. He was ashamed of where he had come from all his life because those were the attitudes from that time in history. By 1985 all that was changing. The harsh attitudes of the past that shamed people were just that, a thing of the past.

The miracle of my grandmother's story was that she would meet her husband through the birth of my father. She would get to raise her son because Edward Phillips adopted him and married her. Edward was thirty years old, and Elizabeth was nineteen at the time of their wedding. After my grandmother married, her parents warmed up to her again and all was forgotten. The harsh judgments against her were dropped. Edward loved my dad, his oldest son by adoption. They had a special bond. Ed had volunteered to go to Europe to fight in WWI. He found Elizabeth the match for him. It was a strange love story that produced six children. My father and almost all his brothers would also join the military. A family of service to their country.

Now I knew why my father was so protective of me. Why he waited up for me to come home from a date. He had been called names by some in his small town of Plymouth. His concern was that I may end up in the same predicament as his mother. Before I knew his whole story, I understood his actions to protect me as his way of taking care of me. I was right, he just wanted the best for me.

The Anniversary Party for My Parents

In January of 1987, my brothers and I would host an anniversary party for my parents. Mark had graduated from The Royal College of Surgeons in Dublin, Ireland in 1986. He was home and working toward his five-year residency in pathology. My mother, who had grown up with only one parent, admired a family in her neighborhood that had a big anniversary party. She had waited her whole life for a big anniversary celebration. It just never seemed to happen before for one reason or another. We would finally have the anniversary party my mother had wanted. It was my parents' fortieth wedding anniversary. The young people that had met in 1945 in Atlantic City, NJ, were still very much in love and together. They had been true to their vows, and they would be together to renew those vows at a very trying time.

My father's condition was not getting better or worse, yet the daily concerns of it were hard for my mother. My parents' anniversary party would be talked about for years. It was held in their home where Bill and I had married. We placed Dad's hospital bed where we had stood and recited our wedding vows. My mother had dressed him in a t-shirt that looked like a tuxedo. A tent was set up in the backyard along with tables and chairs. We hired a one-man-band to entertain. A caterer was hired to provide a buffet luncheon. I had invitations printed with return RSVPs. The day of the celebration we had a full house. As everyone entered the front door, they went over to my father's bed to say hello. He couldn't talk, so most people would raise their voice to talk to him. It made no sense, but it was what happened. At the end of the festivities my parents would renew their wedding vows. As my mother stood next to Dad's bed, a Catholic priest performed the ceremony. There wasn't a dry eye in the crowd as the priest recited the vows, "For richer or poorer, in sickness and in health, until death do you part."

My father would go from my parents' home to ventilator hospitals. The needs of the quadriplegic state varied for my dad. It took its toll on my mother as well. Before my dad's accident my mother was working at a children's dress store as the manager. She liked working. She certainly kept us kids busy with jobs when we lived at home. Because of the accident, my mother had to leave her job. She was faithful to her husband at all costs to herself. She learned all the nursing skills to care for him and she taught them to all of us. Even my boys helped when we came to visit.

Mark Gets Married

In December of 1988 Mark would marry Brenda Sheehan. They had known each other growing up. The wedding was held in Orlando, FL. My father was unable to attend, but my mother did. It was a happy reprise during a challenging time for all of us—especially for my mother.

MY FATHER'S SECRETS

13

My Father Passes Away

IN JANUARY 1990 MY FATHER passed away. The cause of death would be the fall from the tree. My father qualified to be buried at Arlington National Cemetery in Washington, D.C., with all his military service. My brothers and I thought he should be buried there. But my mother wanted him close so she could visit him. She had him buried at Bay Pines National Cemetery in St. Petersburg, FL. Bay Pines is a beautiful cemetery with many oak trees, and near my father's grave is a bell tower, the bells ring at a specific time daily. At Christmas time wreaths are laid at each gravesite and in July, small American flags are set at each. My father's friend from the POW camp at Stalag Luft III, Carl Hager, would be moved from his grave to be next to my dad. They had saved each other in the prison camp and now they rested together for eternity. Later, Carl's wife would join him at Bay Pines, and twenty-five years later, my mother would join them as well. My father was right the night I won the Miss Bay Pines Pageant in 1968: Bay Pines was always going to be a special place for my military family.

My father's funeral was so special to our family and extended family. It was a cold and overcast day and we were under a canopy. My mother had my father cremated, and the small box lay on a base large enough for a full body coffin. The DoD is responsible for providing military funeral honors to veterans who have defended our nation. A special unit of military came out and laid the American flag over the box of ashes. A Catholic priest spoke, and then I and both my brothers spoke. Lee's wife, Christina, wrote a very memorable tribute which Lee read. *Taps* were played on a single bugle.

The soldiers folded the flag that had been over Father's ashes into a triangle and handed it to my mother, with the words, "On behalf of the President of the United States, the USAF, and a grateful nation, please accept this flag as a symbol of our appreciation for your loved one's honorable and faithful service."

There was a twenty-one-gun salute. The strange thing was, I kept seeing my father out of the corner of my eye, dressed in civilian clothes, a short sleeve shirt and slacks, leaning against a pole that held up the canopy. It was reassuring to see this apparition, because he was released from the body of the quadriplegic he had been at the end. My mother hired a videographer to record the funeral, she sent each of her children a copy of the edited video.

Awareness That Comes from War

After the Vietnam War there were many POWs and Missing-in-Action (MIA) soldiers. There were many who saw the need to take care of our military families. The Vietnam War and all the protests with all the carnage displayed on the TVs in living rooms made the public aware of war. No other war had been brought into people's living rooms with such graphic detail. The good thing that came from this was a new law. Since World War I, more than 142,000 Americans, including eighty-five women, have been captured and interned as POWs. Not included in this figure are nearly 93,000 Americans who were lost or never recovered. In 1981, Congress passed Public Law 97-37 entitled "Former Prisoners-of-War Benefit Act." This law accomplished several things. It established an Advisory Committee on Former Prisoners of War and mandated medical and dental care. It also identified certain diagnoses as presumptive service-connected conditions for former POWs. The U.S. government started a pension for widows of POWs. After Dad passed my mother received this pension money. Because of the paperwork she would have to fill out to receive this money, she reconnected with some of the pilots my father had been with in Tunisia and the POW camp. Friendships were re-established. We would also learn more about his time in the POW camp from these reconnections. It was so interesting to get other's views of his life during that time.

MY FATHER'S SECRETS

14

Stalag Luft III Reunions

MY MOTHER WOULD MISS ALL the Stalag Luft III reunions after losing Dad. In 2011 we cleaned out my parents' home, my mother was not physically able to live alone any longer, nor was she able to travel. Lee encouraged Bill and I to attend the reunions, so we did in 2012 and 2013. By this time most of the people attending the reunions were not the POWs themselves but the family members. There was a name for the family members at the reunions, we were referred to as the "Kriege Kids." The Germans had called the captured Allied airean the German word for prisoner, *Kriege*.

    Bill and I would make so many new acquaintances. Many of the kriegs in attendance had written books of their experiences in the camps and how they were shot down. They all would tell the length of time in the camps. All my life I remembered my father commemorating the day he was shot down, the day he was liberated, and the time of the march to Moosburg. Growing up I didn't know anyone whose father did that, but at the reunion, they all talked about doing it in their own way. I gained a new perspective of their trauma from attending that first reunion. For these brave men, this was the norm of their life. This is how they all survived that period of their life. They had made a lifelong bond in that camp. Somehow their bond had extended to their families. After I left that first reunion, I stayed in contact with the organizer. What surprised me was that I realized these people and I had a bond through our parents. We were an extended family; we were there for each other. We had to continue to share these stories. I bought every book that the kriegs at the reunion had written. I had found a wealth of interesting history and felt privileged to have access to such a pivotal part of history.

The reunions were organized by several families, children of the POWs. Their fathers' time in the camps had so influenced them. They knew the importance of saving history. Some of them would write their own books about the camp and continue to share the information with the rest of the families. Our addresses and emails were collected. I was told that after the fall of the Iron Curtain in 1990 the site of the Stalag Luft III camp was identified. The Polish people started a museum to honor this camp and all the POWs that had been interned there. At the reunions many of the men would tell their stories. These stories were taped for the purpose of an oral history. I would learn so much, so many pieces of his life made more sense to me now. I had never realized how this time in father's life would affect my life. When Bill and I left that first reunion I knew I had to help share these stories too.

The first reunion Bill and I attended was in Dayton, Ohio, in late April. We had a busy agenda that had been sent to us before we got there. We all stayed at a local hotel where the meeting room was decorated with photos and documents of the camp. I would learn that the camp was destroyed after the men were marched out in January of 1945. The Russians would take that land as part of Poland. It was under Communist control until 1990 when the Iron Curtain came down. A new documentary film, *The Lost Airmen of Buchenwald*, was shown. It was made by a grandson of one of the POWs. Later that year the film won many awards at various film festivals. This story was about 166 airmen that had been sent to a concentration camp, Buchenwald, before being sent to Stalag Luft III. Some of the men attending this reunion were part of this group. One spoke out about how he was told not to tell this story of being in the concentration camp by the U.S. Army. For years he kept this story to himself. The U.S. helped countries like Germany and Italy get back on their feet after they lost everything. The civilian population in these countries was trying to survive and rebuild. The U.S. felt it was not helpful to keep telling stories of horror when countries needed to heal.

The first reunion had a special event. The U.S. Air Force was honoring the Doolittle Raiders. We all took buses to Wright Patterson Airfield. We toured the National Museum of the USAF. This museum had a special display of POWs in the European Theater. It also featured a special exhibit of the Doolittle Raiders, a group of eighty pilots lead by Lt. Colonel Jimmy Doolittle in a joint Army Air Corps and Navy bombing project after the attack on Pearl Harbor in December of 1941. Sixteen B-25 bombers and eighty airmen flew off the U.S. naval aircraft carrier *Hornet.* This attack would cost the lives of three airmen. All sixteen planes had no landing plan. The crews were to bail out with parachutes or crash. In 2012 there were only four Raiders still alive. All four were honored and sixteen restored B-25 airplanes flew over the celebration ceremony. These airmen that took on this dangerous mission would boost the morale of Allies and therefore became a symbol of promise to win a war that seemed overwhelming. Those who lived during the early years of WWII knew about this mission of hope, known as the Dolittle Raid. After the Doolittle Raid, Lt. Colonel Jimmy Dolittle was sent to Tunisia, Africa, to oversee the 15th Army Air Corps; my father was in his unit.

One of those Doolittle Raiders was also a Stalag Luft III POW. He spoke at our reunion the next day. He came with his children, grandchildren, and great-grandchildren.

Interestingly, my father's Purple Heart medal for being shot down during WWII was not received until after he retired in 1966 and had the time to file the paperwork. I found out at these reunions that all those who were captured had to apply for these prestigious medals because during their time in the POW camp the paperwork was never filed.

One of the attendees at this reunion was a Tuskegee Airman, Alexander Jefferson. He came decked out in his Tuskegee brown leather jacket and a cap with the Tuskegee Airmen logo on it too. He had an impressive personality. He spoke about his training in Tuskegee, Alabama. He would tell stories about Stalag Luft III and the other twelve Tuskegee Airmen in the camp. He had been born in Detroit, Michigan, and received his college degree from Clark College (now Clark Atlanta University). He spoke about his commanding officer during his training. This officer had been a West Point graduate in the early 1900s. Because he was a Black man, no one would talk to him or have anything to do with him while he was at West Point. That brave Black West Pointer would survive the other West Pointer's attitudes to go on and make history. In my research, West Point was open to Black men after the Civil War. West Point Academy and all other military academies would not open to women until 1976.

As an artist I wanted to tell these stories and share what could not be shared earlier. Before the reunion I had done a painting to honor my husband's service in Vietnam. When we returned home, I started a painting of the "Lost Airmen of Buchenwald." I had taken a photo of the old men watching the documentary of their story for the first time. I used that photo to paint their story. Over time I would add more paintings and family related stories to my series of paintings that later became known as "Soldier Stories." Included in these paintings would be one of Alexander Jefferson, the Tuskegee Airman.

Some of the local galleries asked for these paintings for various exhibition themes. I kept adding more paintings. Traveling to Ohio to meet and talk with my father's family, I learned that my dad had shared stories of his military service with his brothers, and these stories had been passed on to their children and grandchildren. Some of the stories I didn't even know. I also learned that many members of his family were also serving in today's military. I wanted to share all these stories. Whenever I install "Soldier Stories," I also speak at the venue and do a question-and-answer session. Then more paintings would come from those questions.

The second Stalag Luft III reunion was held in Washington, D.C. We had another super busy schedule. When Bill and I arrived, it was like old home week, getting to see old friends again. We started the reunion the same as the others, in a room welcoming various talks and guest speakers, and many were taped for posterity. Washington would provide different events to visit. Among these would be a visit to the Holocaust Museum. As we toured the halls, there were groups of school children touring with museum docents. Several of the prisoners from the Buchenwald camp were in the halls with these children. The teacher in me went up to one of the docents and I said to her, "These men were in Buchenwald Concentration Camp. Would you like them to talk to the children?" She was in shock and quickly agreed. The concentration camp survivors shared their stories with the docents and the children, and questions and answers ensued.

The next day we went to the WWII Memorial to honor those who died in that war. During this visit there was a group of Air Force Combat Controllers staying at the same hotel. Combat Controllers are specially trained operations forces and certified FAA air traffic controllers. They deploy undetected into hostile environments to establish assault zones or airfields. This group was in D.C. to bury the remains of one of their comrades at Arlington Cemetery. We had signage on our buses saying "Stalag Luft III POWs." This elite force of specially trained airmen came over and talked to us. The first time we met them they were in civilian clothing. I heard one say, "Do you think this will be us in the future, having reunions and sharing our stories?" These airmen had fought in Afghanistan.

These airmen, in full uniform, would meet up with our reunion group at the WWII Memorial. They participated in a special ceremony for all the POW at Stalag Luft III. Most of those soldiers and many who fought in WWII would never live to see this memorial the construction of which was started in 2001 and completed in 2004. My father died in January 1990. Why had it taken so long?

The Vietnam War Memorial was dedicated on Veteran's Day 1982. The Vietnam veterans came home to criticism and harsh words. The memorial to those who died in Vietnam was another turning point. Many powerful politicians and Washington elite were against it being built. The fact that it got built was a miracle. Today it is the most visited memorial in D.C. It was built without government funds, and a college student won the memorial design contest. After 1982 other memorials to those who died in war were built. People's attitude toward our military would change. Soldiers were thanked for their service.

My husband had returned home from Vietnam to the put-downs and criticism. For many years he would not participate in any veterans' events. After the September11, 2001 (better known as 9/11) attack at the World Trade Center, Bill and I flew to New York to see Ground Zero. My husband's career in the finance and brokerage business had taken us to the Big Apple many times. As we were at the airport going through security, there was an exchange of conversation between the National Guardsman and Bill. I heard him say to Bill, "Thank you for your service." This was the first time Bill would hear those words. He had returned to the U.S. from Vietnam in 1969, this "thank you" came in 2002. I teared up when I heard the Guardsman say it to my husband. Out of the horror of 9/11 people would start to appreciate the military and first responders.

15

Appreciation of the U.S. Military

MANY CIVILIANS DO NOT UNDERSTAND that the military is on a constant vigil to protect them. Our country is part of North America, we have some geographic protection.

The military is made up of six branches, each with their own active duty and part-time components. Each varies in service commitment, location and how its members contribute to the overall mission of protecting our country.

Army
As the oldest branch of the U.S. Military, the Army protects the security of the United States and its resources.

Marines
The Marine Corps is often first on the ground in combat situations.

Navy
The Navy delivers combat-ready naval forces while maintaining security in the air and at sea.

Air Force
The Air Force protects American interests at home and abroad with a focus on air power.

Space Force

The Space Force defends U.S. interests on land, in the air, and from orbit with a range of advanced training and technology. This is the newest branch of the military. It has no part-time component.

Coast Guard

The Coast Guard is a maritime force offering military, law enforcement, humanitarian, regulatory and diplomatic capabilities.

Reserve and National Guards are Part-time Components of the Military.

Part-time service members include the Reserve and National Guard, and train one weekend per month and two weeks per year.

Army National Guard

Army National Guard (ANG) members deploy with the Army on a part-time basis. Their service focus is on the state level, but they may also serve nationally. The ANG trains part-time to assist, first on the state level, but they may also serve nationally.

Advances That Arise from the Ashes of War

War is terrible and some of the experiences that some endure in a time of war are horrendous and awful. There are advances in our world that come from war too.

The Geneva Convention consists of a set of four treaties, and three additional protocols, that establish international legal standards for humanitarian treatment in war. The rules apply only in times of armed conflict and seek to protect people who are not or are no longer taking part in hostilities; these include the sick and wounded of Armed Forces in the field and shipwrecked members of Armed Forces at sea, prisoners-of-war, and civilians. I had described the experience I had as a young girl visiting the battlefield of Waterloo, which took place in 1815.

The history of the Geneva Convention goes back to a Swiss businessman, Henry Dunant, who went to visit wounded soldiers' posterior to the Battle of Solferino in 1859. He was shocked by the lack of facilities, personnel, and medical aid available to help these soldiers. After that visit he published a book, A Memory of Solferino, in 1862, on the horrors of war. His war time experience inspired him to propose: A permanent relief agency for humanitarian aid in times of war and a government treaty recognizing the neutrality of the agency and allowing it to provide aid in a war zone. These proposals would lead to the establishment of the Red Cross and the 1864 Geneva Convention. For his work, Henry Dunant would become co-recipient of the first Nobel Peace Prize in 1901. The Geneva Convention would continue to see many more world gatherings and changes as wars and technologies changed. The need for what Dunant saw still exists.

My father would experience the rules of war and the aid of the Red Cross as a POW during WWII. He would also see the rules broken. They were broken and ignored in WWII in the European Theater of Operation (ETO) and the Pacific Theater of Operation (PTO). Wars put an enormous demand upon a nation's resources. Those resources include everything from materials to military personnel. It's expensive to wage war and war places a burden upon a nation's citizens. As soldiers march off to battle, the people left behind must work even harder to keep the nation's infrastructure from collapsing.

But wars can also have beneficial effects on economic and technological development. In general, wars tend to accelerate technological development to adapt tools for the purpose of solving specific military needs. Later, these military tools may evolve into non-military devices.

A relatively recent example of this is radar. While scientists around the world worked on using radio antennae to detect distant objects during the early part of the 20th century, we credit Sir Robert Watson-Watt with building the first practical radar set in 1935. The British Air Ministry adopted his design and used it to detect aggressors during the early days of World War II.

Radar became a crucial tool with many militaries around the world. In turn, radar's adoption required countries to adapt to new warfare strategies. It also prompted the United States to invest in research and development for new ways to confound radar. The result was stealth aircraft technology.

On the civilian front, radar played a different role. A scientist by the name of Percy L. Spencer made an interesting discovery while standing near a magnetron—a device that powers radar sets. Spencer had a chocolate bar in his pocket. The bar began to melt when Spencer stood near the magnetron. This piqued Spencer's curiosity, and he began to examine what was going on. This led to the invention of the microwave oven.

During WWII Alan Turing invented computer science. He was hired by the British government to break the German codes including the Enigma codes. He along with a team of mathematicians and researchers would have their story immortalized in a movie titled *The Imitation Game* in 2014.

The U.S. Interstate Highways:

On June 29, 1956, President Dwight D. Eisenhower signed legislation funding the construction of the U.S. Interstate Highway System (IHS)—something Americans had dreamed of since Detroit starting building cars.

President Eisenhower is widely regarded as the catalyst for the IHS. His motivations for a highway network stemmed from three events: his assignment as a military observer to the First Transcontinental Motor Convoy, his experience in World War II where he observed the efficiencies of the German autobahn, and the Soviet Union's 1953 detonation of the hydrogen bomb, which instigated a fear that insufficient roads would keep Americans from being able to escape a nuclear disaster.

The Internet

In a way, the Internet itself began as a military project. Beginning in the 1960s, the U.S. Department of Defense funded a project called Advanced Research Projects Agency Network (ARPANET). The purpose of the project was to develop the technologies and protocols necessary to allow multiple computers to connect directly to one another. This would allow people to share information with each other at unprecedented speeds.

A computer network could also have another benefit: national security. By creating a robust and flexible network, the United States could ensure that in the event of catastrophe, access to the nation's supercomputers could remain intact. ARPANET's protocols allowed information to travel across different routes. If something happened to a computer node along one route, the information could take another path to get to the right destination.

The foundation for the Internet is in the protocols and designs built by the ARPANET team. And while no war directly played into its development, the threat of future conflicts did. Today, the United States Department of Defense funds research and development projects across multiple disciplines.

Another example of how the possibility of war affected technological development is the Space Race between the United States and what was then known as the Soviet Union. On October 4, 1957, the Soviet Union succeeded in launching the first man-made satellite into the Earth's orbit. Its name was Sputnik, and it spurred an intense, focused era of innovation. Part of that research went into projects like ARPANET. Much of it focused on getting the United States' space technology ahead of the Soviets'.

Innovations of the Cold War Space Race

Here are thirty innovations from the Cold War space race. The orange juice-flavored mix TANG, freeze-dried ice cream, and Teflon are not included in this list.

Artificial limbs

Innovations originally designed for space vehicles, including artificial muscle systems, robotic sensors, diamond-joint coatings, and temper foam, make artificial human limbs more functional, durable, comfortable, and life-like.

Scratch-resistant lenses

After NASA developed scratch-resistant astronaut helmets, the agency gave a license to Foster-Grant Corporation to continue experimenting with scratch-resistant plastics, which now comprise most sunglasses and prescription lenses.

Insulin pump

Needing to monitor astronauts' vital signs in space, the Goddard Space Flight Center created monitoring systems that have been adapted to regulate blood sugar levels and release insulin as needed.

Firefighting equipment

The polymers created for use in spacesuits have been valuable in creating flame-retardant, heat-resistant suits for firefighters. Newer suits also feature circulating coolant to keep firefighters from succumbing to heat and advanced breathing systems modeled after astronaut life support systems.

Dust Busters

During the Apollo moon landings, NASA partnered with Black & Decker to invent various battery-powered tools for drilling and taking rock samples in space. This led to the creation of the ultra-light, compact, cordless Dust Buster.

LASIK

Technology used to track astronauts' eyes during periods in space to assess how humans' frames of reference are affected by weightlessness has become essential for use during LASIK surgery. The device tracks a patient's eye positions for the surgeon.

Shock absorbers for buildings

Shock absorbers designed to protect equipment during space shuttle launches are now used to protect bridges and buildings in areas prone to earthquakes.

Solar cells

Out of a need to power space missions, NASA has invented, and consistently improved, photovoltaic cells, sharing the advancements with other companies to accelerate the technology.

Water filtration

In the 1970s, NASA developed filtration systems that utilized iodine and cartridge filters to ensure that astronauts had access to safe, tasteless water. This filtering technology is now standard.

Better tires

After the Goodyear Tire and Rubber Company invented the material used in NASA's Viking Lander parachute shrouds, the company began using it in its everyday radial tires. The material is stronger than steel and adds thousands of miles of life to the tires.

Wireless headsets

Along with two airline pilots who'd invented a prototype of a wireless headset, NASA built a light, hands-free communication system that would allow astronauts to communicate with teams on Earth. The technology was utilized in the Mercury and Apollo missions.

Adjustable smoke detector

In partnership with the Honeywell Corporation, NASA improved smoke detector technology in the 1970s, creating a unit with adjustable sensitivity to avoid constant false alarms.

Invisible braces

After NASA and Ceradyne invented a clear material that could protect radar equipment without blocking the radar's signal, Unitek Corporation/3M teamed up with Ceradyne, using the material to invent invisible braces.

Freeze-dried foods

During long space missions where every ounce of weight and inch of space aboard a shuttle must be maximized, freeze-dried foods have become a staple. Freeze-dried foods are incredibly light, and they retain their nutritional value. Once reconstituted, they are also easier and more pleasant to eat than former meal sources that were packed into squeeze tubes.

Camera phones

In the 1990s, NASA's Jet Propulsion Laboratory invented a light, miniature imaging system that required little energy to take high quality photographs from space. This technology has become standard in cell phones and computer cameras.

CAT scans

NASA's digital signal technology, originally used to recreate images of the moon during the Apollo missions, is the underlying technology that makes CAT scans and MRIs possible.

Baby formula

A nutritious, algae-based vegetable oil invented by NASA scientists who were searching for a recycling agent to use during long space missions is now an additive in many infant formulas. It contains two essential fatty acids that cannot be synthesized by the human body.

Lifeshears

The pyrotechnic mechanism used to detach a space shuttle from its rocket boosters after launch is the same used in Lifeshears, but on a smaller scale. Lifeshears are a tool that can be used in emergency situations to cut into cars or collapsed buildings to rescue people trapped inside.

Grooved pavement

The requirements for landing space shuttles led NASA scientists to do extensive research on minimizing hydroplaning – when vehicles slide uncontrollably on a wet surface – on runways. They discovered that cutting grooves into runways helps channel water away from the runway and significantly reduces accidents. Many highways and airports now have grooved pavement.

Air purifier

In the sealed, artificial environment of a spacecraft, attempts to grow plants have led to ethylene buildup. NASA invented an air purifier for the International Space Station that is now used widely on Earth— everywhere from restaurants, to hospitals, to refrigerators – to remove ethylene, which hastens decay, as well as other particulates and pathogens.

Memory foam

Memory foam was originally invented as a pad for astronaut seats that would mold to their bodies during the high forces of takeoff and landing, then return to a neutral state. This eliminated the need to customize seats to individual astronauts' body sizes.

Workout machines

Because prolonged exposure to zero-gravity leads to bone loss and muscle atrophy, NASA created workout machines to enable astronauts to maintain physical fitness while in space.

Home insulation

NASA began experimenting with insulation technology for the Apollo spacecrafts and suits, leading to the invention of common construction insulation.

Infrared ear thermometers

Infrared ear thermometers, which allow for instant temperature capture without the risk of picking up pathogens and causing cross-infection, utilize the same technology developed for assessing the temperature of distant planets.

Ice-resistant airplanes

Ice is a real threat for shuttles in space, and NASA has devised multiple electronic solutions to prevent ice formation on spacecrafts, some of which are now used on commercial aircraft.

Portable computer

The first portable computer, the Grid Compass, was used on multiple shuttle missions in the 1980s. Then there was the Shuttle Portable Onboard Computer (nicknamed SPOC), which could communicate with onboard devices and was used to launch satellites off space shuttles.

LEDs

Intended for use to help in growing plants aboard space shuttles, NASA's LED technology has been utilized in the development of LED medical devices that relax muscles and relieve pain in soldiers, cancer patients, and those with Parkinson's disease.

3D food printing

The ability to cook food on long space missions is no longer impossible with the invention of 3D food printers. This technology is now being refined for commercial use to produce chocolates and other confections as well as to create nutritious foods for diabetics and others with specific dietary needs.

Computer mouse

While searching for a way to increase interaction with onboard computers and allow users to perform tasks like manipulating data, NASA and Stanford researchers developed the first mouse.

Athletic shoes

A shock-absorbent rubber molding designed for astronauts' helmets inspired what is now a common feature in the soles of modern athletic shoes.

Several factors fueled the space race. One was fear that if the Soviets could launch a rocket with a payload the size of Sputnik into orbit, it was feasible the country could launch a missile attack on the United States from across the globe. Even though there were plenty of scientific reasons to pursue the space race, on one level it boiled down to saber-rattling between the two nations.

While the motives behind the Space Race may not have been purely founded upon a desire to extend our scientific knowledge, that in no way diminishes the accomplishments made by both countries. The Space Race was a symbolic conflict between both countries and put pressure on the scientists and engineers developing the systems and vehicles necessary to put men and women into space. Some of this technology later evolved into other forms and was eventually adapted to serve civilian purposes. You can thank the Cold War for your GPS systems. Sputnik is related to your GPS ability.

Advances in Medicine

Besides the well-known technical advances that have occurred during major wars of the past 150 years, each one has also produced significant advances in medicine. Some of these advances were completely innovative because of circumstances that occurred primarily during wartime.

The American Civil War brought about the significant use of anesthesia which had only been discovered in 1846. Despite the rather gruesome scenes of piles of bloody limbs often shown on television, the patients who underwent the procedures did it with complete insensibility of the previous ghastly pain of all surgeries. Prior to anesthesia, the key hallmark of surgical excellence was how quickly the procedure could be completed. The use of anesthesia enabled significant advances in surgical capabilities that continue to the modern day.

In World War I, Hydrogen Peroxide was developed to clean wounds. The regular use of blood transfusions up to then was quite rare. Battlefield aid stations were set up very close to the battle areas, saving many lives.

Another important advance during WWI was the use of volunteer ambulance drivers who went out into the battlefield during the fighting to pick up the wounded. The less time spent after wounding and transport to receiving medical care significantly improved survival rates. The volunteers were primarily conscientious objectors (American Quakers) who provided these dangerous services rather than use weapons.

A little-known outcome from WWI was the development of chemotherapy for cancer treatment. The use of poison gases demonstrated that synthetic molecules killed normal cells. It took some time, but eventually molecules were produced that could kill cancer cells more than normal cells to the benefit of patients with cancer.

World War II would see the expanded use of antibiotics as a very significant advance. Sulfa drugs, discovered in 1935, and penicillin, developed in 1939, have led the way to the obvious worldwide benefit we have today from any number of effective antibiotics. Prior to antibiotics, infectious disease was the leading cause of death worldwide.

Another significant advance during WWII was the use of metal plates to help heal fractures. This technic was developed by the German military medical services and discovered by allies when examining captured German prisoners who had needed x-rays. To the surprise of the medical staff, the German troops were back on duty in half the time compared to normal healing. The widespread use of metal plates and joints is now common.

The Korean War- This war led to even greater savings of lives using helicopters for battlefield evacuations and much quicker removal to more capable medical facilities, such as the Mobile Army Surgical Hospital (MASH).

The Vietnam War produced several important advances in medical practice. Among them was the use of frozen blood products. Fresh blood can only be used for twenty-one-thirty days before deteriorating. Frozen blood can be used for up to a year. The normal blood volume in a young adult is approximately eight-ten pints. In catastrophic injuries that occur in war, it is not uncommon to transfuse ten, twenty, or even more pints of blood and have the patient survive. Obtaining and storing massive amounts of fresh blood in wartime conditions is impossible. The military has been a leader in developing frozen blood products that have been lifesaving in many instances.

Advances in burn care also occurred during the Vietnam War. The use of antiseptic and antibiotic impregnated dressings helped reduce dangerous infections. Also, excessive loss of body fluids is a major problem with widespread loss of protective skin cover. Better fluid management of these patients added to survival and recovery.

In the extremely hot and humid climate of Vietnam, body fluid loss was a major problem, especially for newly arrived troops transported to country aboard comfortable airconditioned ships. By acclimating the troops to the new conditions through exercise programs in hot and stuffy holds of ships with no air conditioning and the liberal use of balanced salt solutions (Gatorade), troops landed ready to go without required acclimatization over three to seven days.

An especially important advance, for civilians as well as military personnel, was the post-war recognition of Post-Traumatic Stress Disorder or more commonly known as PTSD. This was carefully described for the first time as a recognized diagnosis by a Veterans Affairs psychiatrist treating many Vietnam veterans. Of course, it has been present in every war. In the Civil War, it was called "Lost Heart"; in WWI, it was "Shell Shock"; in WWII, it was "Battle Fatigue." These individuals were often regarded as cowards and ordered to court-martial. Now, it is officially recognized and treated.

Another new discovery during the war was the experience of cardiac arrest in patients with spinal cord injuries caused using a routine drug while undergoing anesthesia. The drug, succinylcholine, has been used for decades entirely safely during general anesthesia to facilitate muscle relaxation enabling necessary procedures. But with injuries to the spinal cord, a sensitivity to the drug occurs not previously recognized. This sensitivity releases extraordinary amounts of potassium into the blood that is carried to the heart causing cardiac arrest. It is now recognized throughout the field, and another safe drug is used in these situations.

The knowledge gained from war has improved the civilian populations quality of life. We now have Emergency Medical Service (EMS) programs. These programs respond to accidents in the community with Emergency Medical Technicians (EMTs) or paramedics.

MY FATHER'S SECRETS

16

My Mother Passes Away and I Reflect on My Life

MY MOTHER'S HEALTH BEGAN TO slowly deteriorate. The spunky Philadelphia girl that had survived growing up during the depression as the daughter of a single immigrant mother to become a wonderful military wife and mother, was finally worn out. She passed away in 2015, on my birthday, at ninety years of age. I had her remains cremated. She was interred with my father's remains and a new stone with her name added was put in place. There was Gene and Helen's headstone next to Carl and June Hager, Dad's friend from the POW camp. My dad and Carl had rekindled their relationship in St. Petersburg after retirement from the military. They were now keeping each other company in a beautiful national cemetery.

My father would live through many wars, and he would see the end of most of them during his lifetime. However, he would not see the end of the Cold War. He died before that happened. During 1989 and 1990, the Berlin Wall came down, borders opened, and free elections ousted Communist regimes everywhere in Eastern Europe. In late 1991, the Soviet Union itself dissolved into its component republics. The Iron Curtain was lifted, and the Cold War ended.

World problems continue and our young men and women today help to protect the civilian population just as my family had. Today extended members of my family are serving in the military. They will have their own stories to share. Historians emphasize the value of primary sources, that is, those sources dating from a particular time. These sources include diaries, letters, interviews, oral histories, photographs, newspaper articles, government documents, poems, novels, plays, and music.

My family and I were part of a top-secret operation that the American people were not to know about when Dad was tasked with becoming a missile site commander for the 498th Tactical Mace Nuclear missiles sites going up on the Pacific Island of Okinawa. My father grew up during the golden age of flight when everything was new and so much was being developed for the first time. He also started writing philosophical articles about war and where the world stood during his time fighting for freedom. Perhaps he wanted to make sense of his life and its meaning.

I grew up on the front row of history as a military dependent child. My life was influenced by the era and norms of my time. I served my country too as a child in a military family. Looked at by civilians as an outsider. I would eventually become a civilian myself. However, my many years as a military dependent child have stayed with me. I wrote this story so others could learn more about our military from the prospective of a child raised in the military culture. The military has been a vital part of this country from its inception. I hope you have a better understanding of this history. Conflicts are a part of humankind. It's fascinating to me how one war often weaves into the next.

Where Am I From? What Happened to My Military Homes?

I have no traditional hometown. Home and who I am were intimately tied to assignments and the cultures of a place.

Turner AFB in Albany, GA, is gone. The land is now Molson Coors Albany Brewery. This plant makes craft beers. When Miller

Brewing Company first bought the property, they had a website that honored Turner AFB and even listed all the pilots of Fox Peter One, the in-air refueling mission my father flew. Due to changes in company ownership and the streamlining of websites, that history is no longer there. However, there is a separate website, Turnerfield-Miller.com. This website does pay tribute to the military accomplishments at Turner Field Military Base.

* * *

When military personnel live outside the U.S. and do not live on a military base it is called "living on the economy." In Belgium we lived on the economy. The embassy in Brussels, Belgium, is still there and so is the apartment building we lived in, even the elementary school, Bois de la Cambre, remains. NATO was established in Brussels just as my family moved back to the U.S. Today there are several military bases in Brussels.

-Laredo AFB is now Laredo International Airport. There are many military bases in the state of Texas.

-Stead AFB near Reno, Nevada, is gone, and our base housing was sold to private individuals. The once remote AFB is now a suburb of Reno, and the airfield is Reno Stead Airport.

-Lowry AFB near Denver, CO, is also closed. Some of the large hangers remain and serve as an Air and Space Museum along with restaurants and retail stores.

-Orlando, AFB is also now closed. Orlando Executive Airport was once Orlando Air Force Base.

-Kadena, AB is a major hub of airpower, in fact it is the largest AB in the Pacific. It is still known as the "Keystone to the Pacific." In addition to Kubasaki High School there are several other high schools now on the island.

-MacDill AFB in Tampa is now U.S. Central Command. One of the largest military coalitions in U.S. History. After 9/11 terrorist attacks in 2001, the coalition began to form with a common purpose to fight terrorism.

I am a little of all these places. I'm a little of Philadelphia, PA; a little of Albany, GA,; a little Belgian; a little Laredo, TX; a little Sierra, NV; and a bit of Colorado, Orlando, Okinawa, and Florida. I'm a northerner, a southerner, a westerner with skills in French, American history, military and military weaponry history, European history, and Asian culture. I was raised in the Christian faith but appreciate all religions. I am a flexible thinker because of living in so many places. I had to move and adjust quickly. I'm unique in my own way. Even my brothers had a different take on all the moving around. Each military kid has a completely different development. We are a special class of individuals. Some things made us stronger, and some did not. We do have a larger picture of the world than most. Our experience depends on the job the military person holds and the years our life relates to the military.

I was born a "baby boomer." We were the children of those who had lived through the Great Depression and WWII. We would be such a large group of children that many new schools were built to accommodate us. We are called boomers because of the boom in births after the return of soldiers from WWII. The history I lived through growing up would include the Korean War Era, Cold War era, and Vietnam. This time would also include dealing with racial discrimination, the space race, and amazing advances in technology. I still remember the first dishwasher my parents bought. We would be the generation to see the TV come into every home. TV would go from being on for a few hours a day to around-the-clock in my lifetime. Ahh, the age of information.

By the time I was sixteen years old I had been around the world. Not on vacations but living in many places and different cultures. When I started teaching school at Perkins Elementary in St. Petersburg,

FL, I learned that subcultures exist within countries. These subcultures have their own dialects and traditions. The world is a complex place. Much of our world is filtered through a civilian perspective. This book offers a military perspective. Military life and military family life is a culture that exists in our country and around the world. All wars are horrible, there are no contests for the worst war. Some say, "War is Hell!"—and it is. No one knows this better than a soldier and that soldier's family.

Epilogue

IT WOULD TAKE ME A lifetime to understand and appreciate growing up in a military family. When my father retired, my experience as a military kid abruptly ended. I had never known any other way of life. I had to pay attention and figure it out slowly. I wanted to write this book so others could understand what military children endure. Like all things in life there are positives and negatives. Military families like mine are pretty much invisible to the civilian population. We are less than one percent of the population. Many news outlets tell the story of a mom or dad coming home after being away for months or years and there is the surprise reunion. This is just a small part of the military family story. I hope this book with some sad and funny adventures expands understanding.

As I wrote and researched, I found many buried memories. Some of them were wonderful surprises and others were healing. Just like the Stalag Luft III reunions gave me a perspective on my father's experience, writing this book gave me perspective on myself. I was so influenced by events that happened to my parents before my birth because their experiences made them who they were, and they raised me. My older brother Roger Bruce Phillips lived four hours and forty-two minutes after birth; he never had a life. The hours he did live he was in excruciating pain. He was always a part of our family. After my father and my grandmother Nannie buried him, my brother Lee and I would visit his grave site in Philadelphia many years later. When our youngest brother Mark was born, his French godmother, Marie, told us it was European custom to include him in the birth announcement. She said it should read "Roger, our angel in heaven, Marilyn and Lee announces the birth of their brother Mark Gerard

Phillips." It actually read "Marilyn and Lee announce the birth of their brother Mark Gerard Phillips." Many family members did not know about Roger's birth and death. My parents had not shared it with family in Ohio and younger family members in Philadelphia.

Even though my mother never visited his grave she never forgot him. We talked about him as a family from time to time. He was part of us. I was the oldest sibling of the family and when that responsibility got too much for me, I would talk to him and complain to him about the burden of being the oldest. He was always there for me. Mother told me every Christmas Eve was hard for her. She kept it to herself. After my first son Billy was born in April of 1973, she told me that was when she finally made peace with Roger's death.

After both my parents passed away, my Aunt Mary Ellen on my father's side of the family encouraged me to reacquaint myself with family in Ohio and all my cousins. On my first visit my Uncle Henry and Aunt Shirley hosted a big family party at St. Joseph's Catholic Church Hall. It was overwhelming and wonderful. What I learned from the two trips I took to visit was that my father had shared his story on his trips home to Ohio that he had not shared with us. My cousins shared things about my father that helped me put so much together. After I started this book, I also visited Philadelphia again, but those relatives were all in cemeteries. Somehow visiting the city where my mother grew up and visiting the grave sites of the immigrant family I had known was also healing.

All my life I have tried to fit in, to become a part of the place I was living, because I didn't come from anywhere. When my father retired, I tried to fit in then. I got busy with teaching, married my husband and started our family. Bill and I have a great life! The Stalag Luft III reunions changed something in both of us. It changed our perspective. I painted compositions in watercolor of military stories. The art exhibits were accompanied by talks on Stalag Luft III documentary films made by children and grandchildren of the POW's. I did paintings from some of the books written by many of the POW's. The history of our time builds on the history of the past and possibilities for the future. In 2024 a TV miniseries, *Masters of the Air*, featured Stalag Luft III and the January 1945 forced march and train ride to Bavaria. The historian of the Stalag Luft III reunion committee provided much information to the film writers. The Air Force Academy Library has the best collection of books on Stalag Luft III. The National Museum of the U.S. Air Force near Dayton, Ohio has an interesting display of the Stalag Luft III story.

After my paintings were in many exhibits, and especially two exhibits at the Fort Lauderdale/Hollywood International Airport, one of the women from the airport suggested I investigate an Honor Flight for my husband. He had returned from Vietnam to such disgust of the war by so many Americans, but also the disgust of those fighting the war. He just wanted to forget it! I knew I had to help him to see it was a good thing. I rallied our sons, and with some coaxing, he did finally agree. Our middle son, Randy, was going as his guardian that day. It was a full day of appreciation for the veterans on the flight. They left Fort Lauderdale/ Hollywood Airport with a water cannon salute and arrived in Washington, D.C., with another water cannon salute. There were crowds everywhere at each memorial they visited that day to cheer his group of about seventy-five veterans plus their guardians. Our whole family greeted him when he and our son arrived at the airport that evening, with more appreciation, a disc jockey playing patriotic songs, many singing along, and lots of kids waving American flags as the vets deplaned. He had finally gotten his thank you and appreciation for his service to his country.

The next day he volunteered to bring this appreciation to other veterans. This included giving talks to organizations on Memorial Day, Veterans Day, and going to the Veterans Administration to talk to veterans about signing up for an Honor Flight.

Reflections

My husband would look around our house and wonder why I decorated it with items from all the places I had lived. All these were possessions my family had collected during our many assignments. I have no hometown, but I have a home full of items from all the places I lived, my mother's silver coffee and tea service she purchased in Brussel: the table she won at the Bingo games at the American Embassy, the silver punch bowl from Laredo, the shoji screen form Okinawa, and so many more pieces of the times and places I experienced growing up in military life. These are items that make me feel at home, my home. But the thing that really moves me is when I hear the thunder of the jets flying overhead. Then I'm home.

Acknowledgments

I WANT TO THANK MY FAMILY for encouraging me to write this memoir. To my husband for helping me get started, to our boys especially our youngest son who set up my website and helped me with ideas and marketing. My brothers gave me continued information on dates, events and timelines. My Uncle Henry and cousins who filled in the gaps to so much I didn't know during my trips to Ohio. To the organizers of the Stalag Luft III reunions for giving me a perspective that was priceless. My editors, Claudette Freeman and Mark Antony Rossi, for helping me organize my thoughts and advise on publishing. Thank you to my Book Club who welcomed me and made reading one of my favorite passtimes that so enriches my life.

Finally, to my mother and father who gave me a wonderful and exciting life.

Resources

Books

Bender, Edward M. *Lest They Forget Freedom's Price.* Author House, 2008.

Bird, Sarah. *The Yokota Officers Club.* Ballantine Books, 2001.

Chiesl, O.M. *Clipped Wings.* R.W. Kimball, 1948.

Clark, Albert P. *33 Months as a POW in Stalag Luft III.* Fulcrum Publishing, 2004.

Durand, Arthur. *Stalag Luft III: The Secret Story.* Louisiana State University Press, 1988.

Jefferson, Alexander. *Red Tail Captured, Red Tail Free.* Fordham University Press, 2005.

Miller, Carolyn Clark. *We Also Served.* Book Baby, 2017.

Mindling, George and Bolton, Robert. *U.S. Air Force Tactical Missiles 1949-1969.* Lulu.com Publishing, 2008, 2011.

Samuel, Wolfgang W.E. *German Boy.* University Press of Mississippi, 2000.

Spivey, Delmar. *POW Odyssey.* Colonial Lithograph Inc., 1984.

Wright, Arnold. *Behind the Wire: Stalag Luft III South Compound.* Benton Printing & Composition, 1993.

Newspapers

Stars and Stripes, Various articles, 1956.

Saint Petersburg Times, "Miss Bay Pines," 1968.

Tampa Tribune, "Miss North Tampa," 1970.

Plymouth Ohio Advertiser, "Eugene F. Phillips War II Updates," 1941-1943.

Presidential Libraries

Dwight D. Eisenhower. Abilene, Kansas.

Franklin Delano Roosevelt. Hyde Park, New York.

Harry S. Truman. Independence, Missouri.

Documentary Films
Dorsey, Mike. *Lost Airmen of Buchenwald* (United States), 2012.
Wilson, Lindy. *For Which I Am Prepared to Die* (South Africa), 2009.

Online Sources
Bouregeois, Lane. "Operation Fox Peter One," https://globalsecurity.org, 7/6/12.

Greyson, Howard. "Trukee fire, Aug. 1961, Sierra Nevada," https://sierrasun.com, 8/20/10.

Spadoni, Aldo. "How Technology from the Space Race changed the world," https://now.northropgrumman.com, 4/9/20.

Tobey, Raymond E. "Advances in medicine during wars," https://fpri.org, 2/23/18.

Vanderbey, General Hoyt S., "teacher-resource-korean-war.pdf," https://nationalmuseum.af.mil, 1950-1953.

Records
Air Force Flight Log Book, 1948-1966.
Military Records of Eugene Francis Phillips, 1941-1966.
WWII Flight Information Documents, 1948-1966.

www.hellgatepress.com

www.ingramcontent.com/pod-product-compliance
Lightning Source LLC
LaVergne TN
LVHW051823080426
835512LV00018B/2698